Past and Future

Elective Courses in English
for Level II

Von

Horst Bodden, Herbert Kaußen, Rudi Renné

D1670803

Langenscheidt-Longman

Past and Future

Elective Courses in English for Level II (GK, LK)

Students' Textbook

Erarbeitet von
OStR Dr. Horst Bodden, Valls/Niederlande
StD Herbert Kaußen, Aachen
StD Dr. Rudi Renné, Kerpen

Verlagsredaktion Langenscheidt-Longman
Anne Moss M.A.

Auflage:	5.	4.	3.	2.	1.	Letzte Zahlen
Jahr:	1983	82	81	80	79	maßgeblich

© 1979 Langenscheidt-Longman GmbH, München
Druck: Kösel, Kempten
Printed in Germany · ISBN 3-526-50310-9

Contents

I. FICTION

VERSE

DRAMA

II. NON-FICTION

Fiction

Wystan Hugh Auden

1 The Unknown Citizen

(To JS/07/M/378
This Marble Monument
Is Erected by the State)

He was found by the Bureau of Statistics to be
One against whom there was no official complaint,
And all the reports on his conduct agree
That, in the modern sense of an old-fashioned word, he was a saint,
5 For in everything he did he served the Greater Community.
Except for the War till the day he retired
He worked in a factory and never got fired,
But satisfied his employers, Fudge Motors Inc.
Yet he wasn't a scab or odd in his views,
10 For his Union reports that he paid his dues,
(Our report on his Union shows it was sound)
And our Social Psychology workers found
That he was popular with his mates and liked a drink.
The Press are convinced that he bought a paper every day
15 And that his reactions to advertisements were normal in every way.
Policies taken out in his name prove that he was fully insured,
And his Health-card shows he was once in hospital but left it cured.
Both Producers Research and High-Grade Living declare
He was fully sensible to the advantages of the Instalment Plan
20 And had everything necessary to the Modern Man,
A phonograph, a radio, a car and a frigidaire.
Our researchers into Public Opinion are content
That he held the proper opinions for the time of year;
When there was peace, he was for peace; when there was war, he went.
25 He was married and added five children to the population,
Which our Eugenist says was the right number for a parent of his generation,
And our teachers report that he never interfered with their education.
Was he free? Was he happy? The question is absurd:
Had anything been wrong, we should certainly have heard.

From *Collected Shorter Poems* by W.H. Auden. (1939)

John Betjeman

2 Devonshire Street W. 1

The heavy mahogany door with its wrought-iron screen
   Shuts. And the sound is rich, sympathetic, discreet.
The sun still shines on this eighteenth-century scene
   With Edwardian faience adornments—Devonshire Street

5 No hope. And the X-ray photographs under his arm
   Confirm the message. His wife stands timidly by.
The opposite brick-built house looks lofty and calm
   Its chimneys steady against a mackerel sky.

No hope. And the iron knob of this palisade
10   So cold to the touch, is luckier now than he
"Oh merciless, hurrying Londoners! Why was I made
   For the long and the painful deathbed coming to me?"

She puts her fingers in his as, loving and silly,
   At long-past Kensington dances she used to do
15 "It's cheaper to take the tube to Piccadilly
   And then we can catch a nineteen or a twenty-two."

From *Collected Poems* by John Betjeman. (1954)

John Betjeman

3 Sun and Fun

Song of a Night-Club Proprietress

I walked into the night-club in the morning;
    There was kummel on the handle of the door.
The ashtrays were unemptied,
The cleaning unattempted,
5   And a squashed tomato sandwich on the floor.

I pulled aside the thick magenta curtains
    —So Regency, so Regency, my dear—
And a host of little spiders
Ran a race across the ciders
10   To a box of baby 'pollies by the beer.

Oh sun upon the summer-going by-pass
    Where ev'rything is speeding to the sea,
And wonder beyond wonder
That here where lorries thunder
15   The sun should ever percolate to me.

When Boris used to call in his Sedánca,
    When Teddy took me down to his estate
When my nose excited passion,
When my clothes were in the fashion,
20   When my beaux were never cross if I was late.

There was sun enough for lazing upon beaches,
    There was fun enough for far into the night.
But I'm dying now and done for,
What on earth was all the fun for?
25   For I'm old and ill and terrified and tight.

ibid.

John Betjeman

4 The Licorice Fields at Pontefract

In the licorice fields at Pontefract
   My love and I did meet
And many a burdened licorice bush
   Was blooming round our feet;
5 Red hair she had and golden skin,
Her sulky lips were shaped for sin,
Her sturdy legs were flannel-slack'd,
The strongest legs in Pontefract.

The light and dangling licorice flowers
10   Gave off the sweetest smells;
From various black Victorian towers
   The Sunday evening bells
Came pealing over dales and hills
And tanneries and silent mills
15 And lowly streets where country stops
And little shuttered corner shops.

She cast her blazing eyes on me
   And plucked a licorice leaf;
I was her captive slave and she
20   My red-haired robber chief.
Oh love! for love I could not speak,
It left me winded, wilting, weak
And held in brown arms strong and bare
And wound with flaming ropes of hair.

ibid.

William Blake

5 London

I wander thro' each charter'd street,
Near where the charter'd Thames does flow,
And mark in every face I meet
Marks of weakness, marks of woe.

5 In every cry of every Man,
In every Infant's cry of fear,
In every voice, in every ban,
The mind-forg'd manacles I hear.

How the Chimney-sweeper's cry
10 Every black'ning Church appalls;
And the hapless Soldier's sigh
Runs in blood down Palace walls.

But most thro' midnight streets I hear
How the youthful Harlot's curse
15 Blasts the new born Infant's tear,
And blights with plagues the Marriage hearse.

(1794)

6 *e. e. cummings*

"l (a"

l (a
le
af
fa

ll

s)
one
l
iness

From *Complete Poems* by e. e. cummings. (1958)

e. e. cummings

7 "of all the blessings which to man"

of all the blessings which to man
kind progress doth impart
one stands supreme i mean the an
imal without a heart.

5 Huge this collective pseudobeast
(sans either pain or joy)
does nothing except preexist
its hoi in its polloi

and if sometimes he's prodded forth
10 to exercise her vote
(or made by threats of something worth
than death to change their coat

— which something as you'll never guess
in fifty thousand years
15 equals the quote and unquote loss
of liberty my dears —

or even is compelled to fight
itself from tame to teem)
still doth our hero contemplate
20 in raptures of undream

that strictly (and how) scienti
fic land of supernod
where freedom is compulsory
and only man is god.

25 Without a heart the animal
is very very kind
so kind it wouldn't like a soul
and couldn't use a mind

(1944)

Thomas Stearns Eliot

8 The Cultivation of Christmas Trees

There are several attitudes towards Christmas,
Some of which we may disregard:
The social, the torpid, the patently commercial,
The rowdy (the pubs being open till midnight),
5 And the childish—which is not that of the child
For whom the candle is a star, and the gilded angel
Spreading its wings at the summit of the tree
Is not only a decoration, but an angel.
The child wonders at the Christmas Tree:
10 Let him continue in the spirit of wonder
At the Feast as an event not accepted as a pretext,
So that the glittering rapture, the amazement
Of the first-remembered Christmas Tree,
So that the surprises, delight in new possessions
15 (Each one with its peculiar and exciting smell),
The expectation of the goose or turkey
And the expected awe on its appearance,
So that the reverence and the gaiety
May not be forgotten in later experience,
20 In the bored habituation, the fatigue, the tedium,
The awareness of death, the consciousness of failure,
Or in the piety of the convert
Which may be tainted with a self-conceit
Displeasing to God and disrespectful to the children
25 (And here I remember also with gratitude
St. Lucy, her carol, and her crown of fire):
So that before the end, the eightieth Christmas
(By 'eightieth' meaning whichever is the last)
The accumulated memories of annual emotion
30 May be concentrated into a great joy
Which shall be also a great fear, as on the occasion
When fear came upon every soul:
Because the beginning shall remind us of the end
And the first coming of the second coming.

From *Collected Poems 1909–1962* by T.S. Eliot. (1927)

Robert Herrick

9 To Daffodils

Fair daffodils, we weep to see
    You haste away so soon;
As yet the early-rising sun
    Has not attain'd his noon.
5   Stay, stay
      Until the hasting day
        Has run
      But to the evensong;
And, having pray'd together, we
10   Will go with you along.

We have short time to stay, as you,
    We have as short a spring;
As quick a growth to meet decay,
    As you, or anything.
15   We die,
      As your hours do, and dry
        Away
      Like to the summer's rain;
Or as the pearls of morning's dew
20   Ne'er to be found again.

(1648)

Gerard Manley Hopkins

10 'The Child is Father to the Man'

(Wordsworth)

'The child is father to the man.'
How can he be? The words are wild.
Suck any sense from that who can:
'The child is father to the man.'
5 No; what the poet did write ran,
'The man is father to the child.'
'The child is father to the man!'
How *can* he be? The words are wild.

(1879)

Ted Hughes

11 The Thought-Fox

I imagine this midnight moment's forest:
Something else is alive
Beside the clock's loneliness
And this blank page where my fingers move.

5 Through the window I see no star:
Something more near
Though deeper within darkness
Is entering the loneliness:

Cold, delicately as the dark snow,
10 A fox's nose touches twig, leaf;
Two eyes serve a movement, that now
And again now, and now, and now

Sets neat prints into the snow
Between trees, and warily a lame
15 Shadow lags by stump and in hollow
Of a body that is bold to come

Across clearings, an eye,
A widening deepening greenness,
Brilliantly, concentratedly,
20 Coming about its own business

Till, with a sudden sharp hot stink of fox
It enters the dark hole of the head.
The window is starless still; the clock ticks,
The page is printed.

From *The Hawk In The Rain* by Ted Hughes. (1957)

Edwin Morgan

12 Chicago May 1971

The elegant vice-presidential office of U.S. Steel
is the scene of a small ceremony.
A man has placed a miniature coffin
on the vice-president's couch, and in the coffin
5 you can see frog, perch, crawfish, dead.
They have swallowed the laborious effluent
of U.S. Steel in Lake Michigan.
The man is poised ready to run,
wrinkling his nose as he pours from a held-out bottle
10 a dark brown viscous Michigan sludge
over the vice-president's white rug. This is
the eco-man. On the table his card,
The Fox.

From *Instamatic Poems* by Edwin Morgan. (1972)

Edwin Morgan

13 London June 1970

It is opening night at Paolozzi's
crashed car exhibition.
Crowds drift and mill, drinking hard
around the hot gallery, maul
5 a dismal concertina'd Mini,
paw and punch a tottering A40, but
thick as flies on carrion they've clustered
about the stove-in grin
of a king-sized flare-finned 'fifties Pontiac
10 that squats on its own wreckage like its name.
One guest has thrown his glass at it,
smiles muzzily at the effect. Another
has crawled on the roof with a bottle,
crisscrosses claret down the shivered windscreen
15 with weaving hands. A third
intensely between hiccups, wrenches
a door off, you can see the sweat
spreading through his mohair.
And in the front left corner
20 a noted art critic nailed down
by a topless girl is slowly being
interviewed.
The interview is being viewed
in the back right corner slowly
25 on live closed-circuit TV.
The art of dying
is in the cars.

ibid.

Brian Patten

14 Little Johnny's Final Letter

Mother,
      I won't be home this evening, so
      don't worry; don't hurry to report me missing.
      Don't drain the canals to find me,
5   I've decided to stay alive, don't
      search the woods, I'm not hiding,
      simply gone to get myself classified.
      Don't leave my shreddies out,
      I've done with security.
10   Don't circulate my photograph to society
      I have disguised myself as a man
      and am giving priority to obscurity.
      It suits me fine;
      I have taken off my short trousers
15   and put on long ones, and
      now am going out into the city, so
      don't worry; don't hurry to report me missing.

      I've rented a room without any curtains
      and sit behind the windows growing cold,
20   heard your plea on the radio this morning,
      you sounded sad and strangely old. . .

From *Little Johnny's Confession* by Brian Patten. (1967)

Brian Patten

15 Somewhere Between Heaven and Woolworth's

A Song

She keeps kingfishers in their cages
And goldfish in their bowls,
She is lovely and is afraid
Of such things as growing cold.

5 She's had enough men to please her
Though they were more cruel than kind
And their love an act in isolation,
A form of pantomime.

She says she has forgotten
10 The feelings that she shared
At various all-night parties
Among the couples on the stairs,

For among the songs and dancing
She was once open wide,
15 A girl dressed in denim
With boys dressed in lies.

She's eating roses on toast with tulip butter,
Praying for her mirror to stay young;
On its no longer gilted surface
20 This message she has scrawled:

'O somewhere between Heaven and Woolworth's
I live I love I scold,
I keep kingfishers in their cages
And goldfish in their bowls.'

ibid.

Barry Sadler

16 The Ballad of the Green Berets

Fighting soldiers from the sky,
Fearless men who jump and die,
Men who mean just what they say,
The brave men of The Green Beret.

5 Silver wings upon their chests,
These are men, America's best.
One hundred men we'll test today
But only three win The Green Beret.

Trained to live off nature's land,
10 Trained to combat, hand to hand.
Men who fight by night and day,
Courage take from The Green Beret.

Silver wings upon their chests,
These are men, America's best.
15 One hundred men we'll test today
But only three win The Green Beret.

Back at home a young wife waits,
Her Green Beret has met his fate.
He has died for those oppressed,
20 Leaving her this last request.

Put silver wings on my son's chest,
Make him one of America's best.
He'll be a man they'll test one day,
Have him win The Green Beret.

Song '*The Ballad of the Green Berets*' by Barry Sadler and
Robin Moore. (1963)

Carl Sandburg

17 Chicago

    Hog Butcher for the World,
    Tool Maker, Stacker of Wheat,
    Player with Railroads and the Nation's Freight Handler;
    Stormy, husky, brawling,
5   City of the Big Shoulders:

They tell me you are wicked and I believe them, for I have seen your painted women under the gas lamps luring the farm boys.
And they tell me you are crooked and I answer: Yes, it is true I have seen the gunman kill and go free to kill again.
10 And they tell me you are brutal and my reply is: On the faces of women and children I have seen the marks of wanton hunger.
And having answered so I turn once more to those who sneer at this my city, and I give them back the sneer and say to them:
Come and show me another city with lifted head singing so proud to be alive and
15   coarse and strong and cunning.
Flinging magnetic curses amid the toil of piling job on job, here is a tall bold slugger set vivid against the little soft cities;
Fierce as a dog with tongue lapping for action, cunning as a savage pitted against the wilderness,
20   Bareheaded,
    Shoveling,
    Wrecking,
    Planning,
    Building, breaking, rebuilding,
25 Under the smoke, dust all over his mouth, laughing with white teeth,
Under the terrible burden of destiny laughing as a young man laughs,
Laughing even as an ignorant fighter laughs who has never lost a battle,
Bragging and laughing that under his wrist is the pulse, and under his ribs the heart of the people,
30   Laughing!
Laughing the stormy, husky, brawling laughter of Youth, half-naked, sweating, proud to be Hog Butcher, Tool Maker, Stacker of Wheat,
    Player with Railroads and Freight Handler to the Nation.

From *Chicago Poems* by Carl Sandburg. (1914)

Siegfried Sassoon

18 Dreamers

Soldiers are citizens of death's grey land,
   Drawing no dividend from time's to-morrows.
In the great hour of destiny they stand,
   Each with his feuds, and jealousies, and sorrows.
5 Soldiers are sworn to action; they must win
   Some flaming, fatal climax with their lives.
Soldiers are dreamers; when the guns begin
   They think of firelit homes, clean beds and wives.

I see them in foul dug-outs, gnawed by rats,
10   And in the ruined trenches, lashed with rain,
Dreaming of things they did with balls and bats,
   And mocked by hopeless longing to regain
Bank-holidays, and picture shows, and spats,
   And going to the office in the train.

From *Selected Poems* by Siegfried Sassoon. (1917)

Siegfried Sassoon

19 Does It Matter?

Does it matter?—losing your legs? . . .
For people will always be kind,
And you need not show that you mind
When the others come in after hunting
5 To gobble their muffins and eggs.

Does it matter?—losing your sight? . . .
There's such splendid work for the blind;
And people will always be kind,
As you sit on the terrace remembering
10 And turning your face to the light.

Do they matter?—those dreams from the pit? . . .
You can drink and forget and be glad,
And people won't say that you're mad;
For they'll know you've fought for your country
15 And no one will worry a bit.

ibid.

Siegfried Sassoon

20 Progessions

A lovely child alone, singing to himself serenely,—
Playing with pebbles in an unfrequented garden
Through drowse of summer afternoon where time drifts greenly

A youth, impassioned by he knows not what, exploring
5 Delusive labyrinths in errors age will pardon,—
A youth, all ignorance, all grace, his dreams adoring.

A man, confounded by the facts of life that bind him
Prometheus-like to rocks where vulture doubts assail him,—
A man, with blank discarded youthfulness behind him.

10 A mind, matured in wearying bones, returning slowly
Toward years revisioned richly while fruitions fail him,—
A mind, renouncing hopes and finding lost loves holy.

(1940)

Siegfried Sassoon

21 'They'

The Bishop tells us: 'When the boys come back
'They will not be the same; for they'll have fought
'In a just cause: they lead the last attack
'On Anti-Christ; their comrades' blood has bought
5 'New right to breed an honourable race,
'They have challenged Death and dared him face to face.'

'We're none of us the same!' the boys reply.
'For George lost both his legs; and Bill's stone blind;
'Poor Jim's shot through the lungs and like to die;
10 'And Bert's gone syphilitic: you'll not find
'A chap who's served that hasn't found *some* change.'
And the Bishop said: 'The ways of God are strange!'

(1917)

William Shakespeare

22 Sonnet 73

That time of year thou may'st in me behold
When yellow leaves, or none, or few, do hang
Upon those boughs which shake against the cold,
Bare ruined choirs, where late the sweet birds sang.
5 In me thou see'st the twilight of such day
As after sunset fadeth in the west,
Which by and by black night doth take away,
Death's second self, that seals up all in rest.
In me thou see'st the glowing of such fire
10 That on the ashes of his youth doth lie,
As the death-bed whereon it must expire,
Consumed with that which it was nourished by.
   This thou perceiv'st, which makes thy love more strong,
   To love that well which thou must leave ere long.

(1609)

Raymond Souster

23 The Twenty-Fifth of December

Pile the windows high
till they almost crack,
heap the monumental
junkpile of Christmas,
5 forty-nine price tags
and a picture of Santa Claus,
fifty-nine price tags.
and a barber-pole-candy-cane,
hark the herald angels
10 sing all sales final,
peace on earth and mercy
to all cash customers,
O little town of Bethlehem
ONLY TWO SHOPPING DAYS
15 Noel, Noel,
Scotch pines $2.50
sixty-nine price tags
and a tinsel-coloured sky,
Good King Wenceslas
20 in the bargain basement—

Merry Christmas
suckers

From *The Colour of the Times/Ten Elephants on Yonge Street*
by Raymond Souster. (1964)

John Updike

24 Superman

I drive my car to supermarket,
The way I take is superhigh,
A superlot is where I park it,
And Super Suds are what I buy.

5 Supersalesmen sell me tonic—
Super-Tone-O, for Relief,
The Planes I ride are supersonic.
In trains, I like the Super Chief.

Supercilious men and women
10 Call me superficial — me
Who so superbly learned to swim in
Supercolossality.

Superphosphate-fed foods feed me;
Superservice keeps me new.
15 Who would dare to supersede me,
Super-super-superwho?

From *Hoping For A Hoopoe* by John Updike. (1959)

William Wordsworth

25 Composed Upon Westminster Bridge

September 3, 1802

Earth has not anything to show more fair:
Dull would he be of soul who could pass by
A sight so touching in its majesty:
This City now doth, like a garment, wear
5 The beauty of the morning; silent, bare,
Ships, towers, domes, theatres, and temples lie
Open unto the fields, and to the sky;
All bright and glittering in the smokeless air.
Never did sun more beautifully steep
10 In his first splendour, valley, rock, or hill;
Ne'er saw I, never felt, a calm so deep!
The river glideth at his own sweet will:
Dear God! the very houses seem asleep;
And all that mighty heart is lying still!

(1807)

William Wordsworth

26 The Daffodils

I wandered lonely as a cloud
That floats on high o'er vales and hills,
When all at once I saw a crowd,
A host of golden daffodils,
5 Beside the lake, beneath the trees,
Fluttering and dancing in the breeze.

Continuous as the stars that shine
And twinkle on the milky way,
They stretched in never-ending line
10 Along the margin of a bay:
Ten thousand saw I at a glance,
Tossing their heads in sprightly dance.

The waves beside them danced, but they
Out-did the sparkling waves in glee:
15 A poet could not but be gay
In such a jocund company!
I gazed—and gazed—but little thought
What wealth the show to me had brought.

For oft, when on my couch I lie
20 In vacant or in pensive mood,
They flash upon that inward eye
Which is the bliss of solitude;
And then my heart with pleasure fills,
And dances with the daffodils.

(1807)

William Wordsworth

27 "My Heart Leaps Up When I Behold"

My heart leaps up when I behold
    A rainbow in the sky:
So was it when my life began;
So it is now I am a man;
5 So be it when I shall grow old,
    Or let me die!
The Child is father of the Man;
And I could wish my days to be
Bound each to each by natural piety.

(1807)

William Butler Yeats

28 Down by the Salley Gardens

Down by the salley gardens my love and I did meet;
She passed the salley gardens with little snow-white feet.
She bid me take love easy, as the leaves grow on the tree;
But I, being young and foolish, with her would not agree.

5 In a field by the river my love and I did stand,
And on my leaning shoulder she laid her snow-white hand.
She bid me take life easy, as the grass grows on the weirs;
But I was young and foolish, and now am full of tears.

From *The Collected Poems of W.B. Yeats* by William Butler Yeats. (1889)

29 Humorous Verse

Anonymous Limericks

There was an old party of Lyme
Who married three wives at one time.
    When asked: 'Why the third?'
    He replied, 'One's absurd,
And bigamy, sir, is a crime.'

There was a young girl, a sweet lamb,
Who smiled as she entered a tram.
    After she had embarked
    The conductor remarked,
'Your fare!' And she said, 'Yes, I am.'

There was a young man of Japan
Whose limericks never would scan;
    When they said it was so,
    He replied, 'Yes, I know,
But I always try to get as many words into the
        last line as ever I possibly can.'

A diner while dining at Crewe
Found a rather large mouse in his stew.
    Said the waiter, 'Don't shout
    And wave it about,
Or the rest will be wanting one, too.'

A wonderful bird is the pelican,
His mouth can hold more than his belican,
    He can take in his beak
    Enough food for a week—
I'm damned if I know how the helican.

There was a young lady of Riga
Who smiled as she rode on a tiger:
    They returned from the ride
    With the lady inside
And the smile on the face of the tiger.

Uncle

Uncle, whose inventive brains
Kept evolving aeroplanes,
Fell from an enormous height
On my garden lawn, last night.
   Flying is a fatal sport,
   Uncle wrecked the tennis-court.

Harry Graham

The Termite

Some primal termite knocked on wood
And tasted it, and found it good;
And that is why your Cousin May
Fell through the parlour floor today.

Ogden Nash

The Rain

The rain it raineth every day,
   Upon the just and unjust fellow,
But more upon the just, because
   The unjust hath the just's umbrella.

Anon

The Giraffe

The Giraffe is tall,
Looks down on us all,

Lofty, stiff-necked,
Lip curled, erect,

5 With humourless eye
Looks down from on high,

Gives a curt little nod,
Says, 'I'm nearer to God.'

He's his own High Horse,
10 Can't get down, of course.

Michael Flanders

Routine

No matter what we are and who,
Some duties everyone must do:

A Poet puts aside his wreath
To wash his face and brush his teeth,

5 And even Earls
Must comb their curls,

And even Kings
Have underthings.

Arthur Guiterman

The Pessimist

Nothing to do but work,
   Nothing to eat but food,
Nothing to wear but clothes,
   To keep one from going nude.

5 Nothing to breathe but air,
   Quick as a flash 'tis gone;
Nowhere to fall but off,
   Nowhere to stand but on.

Nothing to comb but hair,
10   Nowhere to sleep but in bed,
Nothing to weep but tears,
   Nothing to bury but dead.

Nothing to sing but songs,
   Ah, well, alas! alack!
15 Nowhere to go but out,
   Nowhere to come but back.

Nothing to see but sights,
   Nothing to quench but thirst,
Nothing to have but what we've got,
20   Thus through life we are cursed.

Nothing to strike but a gait;
   Everything moves that goes.
Nothing at all but common sense
   Can ever withstand these woes.

Ben King

Ray Bradbury

30 Marionettes, Inc.

They walked slowly down the street at about ten in the evening, talking, calmly. They were both about thirty-five, both eminently sober.

"But why so early?" said Smith.

"Because," said Braling.

5   "Your first night out in years and you go home at ten o'clock."

"Nerves, I suppose."

"What I wonder is how you ever managed it. I've been trying to get you out for ten years for a quiet drink. And now, on the one night, you insist on turning in early."

10   "Mustn't crowd my luck," said Braling.

"What did you do, put sleeping powder in your wife's coffee?"

"No, that would be unethical. You'll see soon enough."

They turned a corner. "Honestly, Braling, I hate to say this, but you *have* been patient with her. You may not admit it to me, but marriage has been awful for 15 you, hasn't it?"

"I wouldn't say that."

"It's got around, anyway, here and there, how she got you to marry her. That time back in 1979 when you were going to Rio—"

"Dear Rio. I never *did* see it after all my plans."

20   "And how she tore her clothes and rumpled her hair and threatened to call the police unless you married her."

"She always was nervous, Smith, understand."

"It was more than unfair. You didn't love her. You told her as much, didn't you?"

25   "I recall that I was quite firm on the subject."

"But you married her anyhow."

"I had my business to think of, as well as my mother and father. A thing like that would have killed them."

"And it's been ten years."

30   "Yes," said Braling, his gray eyes steady. "But I think perhaps it might change now. I think what I've waited for has come about. Look here."

He drew forth a long blue ticket.

"Why, it's a ticket for Rio on the Thursday rocket!"

"Yes, I'm finally going to make it."

35   "But how wonderful! You *do* deserve it! But won't *she* object? Cause trouble?"

Braling smiled nervously. "She won't know I'm gone. I'll be back in a month and no one the wiser, except you."

Smith sighed. "I wish I were going with you."

"Poor Smith, your marriage hasn't exactly been roses, has it?"

40   "Not exactly, married to a woman who overdoes it. I mean, after all, when you've been married ten years, you don't expect a woman to sit on your lap for

two hours every evening, call you at work twelve times a day and talk baby talk. And it seems to me that in the last month she's gotten worse. I wonder if perhaps she isn't a little simple-minded?"

45   "Ah, Smith, always the conservative. Well, here's my house. Now, would you like to know my secret? How I made it out this evening?"

"Will you really tell?"

"Look up, there!" said Braling.

They both stared up through the dark air.

50   In the window above them, on the second floor, a shade was raised. A man about thirty-five years old, with a touch of gray at either temple, sad gray eyes, and a small thin mustache looked down at them.

"Why, that's *you*!" cried Smith.

"Sh-h-h, not so loud!" Braling waved upward. The man in the window

55 gestured significantly and vanished.

"I must be insane," said Smith.

"Hold on a moment."

They waited.

The street door of the apartment opened and the tall spare gentleman with the

60 the mustache and the grieved eyes came out to meet them.

"Hello, Braling," he said.

"Hello, Braling," said Braling.

They were identical.

Smith stared. "Is this your twin brother? I never knew—"

65   "No, no," said Braling quietly. "Bend close. Put your ear to Braling Two's chest."

Smith hesitated and then leaned forward to place his head against the uncomplaining ribs.

Tick-tick-tick-tick-tick-tick-tick-tick.

70   "Oh no! It *can't* be!"

"It is."

"Let me listen again."

Tick-tick-tick-tick-tick-tick-tick-tick.

Smith staggered back and fluttered his eyelids, apalled. He reached out and

75 touched the warm hands and the cheeks of the thing.

"Where'd you get him?"

"Isn't he excellently fashioned?"

"Incredible. Where?"

"Give the man your card, Braling Two."

80   Braling Two did a magic trick and produced a white card:

MARIONETTES, INC.

Duplicate self or friends; new humanoid plastic 1990 models, guaranteed against all physical wear. From $7,600 to our $15,00 de luxe model.

"No," said Smith.

85   "Yes," said Braling.

"Naturally," said Braling Two.

"How long has this gone on?"

"I've had him for a month. I keep him in the cellar in a toolbox. My wife never goes downstairs, and I have the only lock and key to that box. Tonight I said I
90 wished to take a walk to buy a cigar. I went down to the cellar and took Braling Two out of his box and sent him back up to sit with my wife while I came on out to see you, Smith."

"Wonderful! He even *smells* like you: Bond Street and Melachrinos!"

"It may be splitting hairs, but I think it highly ethical. After all, what my wife
95 wants most of all is *me*. This marionette *is* me to the hairiest detail. I've been home all evening. I shall be home with her for the next month. In the meantime another gentleman will be in Rio after ten years of waiting. When I return from Rio, Braling Two here will go back in his box."

Smith thought that over a minute or two. "Will he walk around without
100 sustenance for a month?" he finally asked.

"For six months if necessary. And he's built to do everything—eat, sleep, perspire—everything, natural as natural is. You'll take good care of my wife, won't you, Braling Two?"

"Your wife is rather nice," said Braling Two. "I've grown rather fond of her."
105 Smith was beginning to tremble. "How long has Marionettes, Inc., been in business?"

"Secretly, for two years."

"Could I—I mean, is there a possibility—." Smith took his friend's elbow earnestly. "Can you tell me where I can get one, a robot, a marionette, for myself?
110 You *will* give me the address, won't you?"

"Here you are."

Smith took the card and turned it round and round. "Thank you," he said. "You don't know what this means. Just a little respite. A night or so, once a month even. My wife loves me so much she can't bear to have me gone an hour.
115 I love her dearly, you know, but remember the old poem: 'Love will fly if held too lightly, love will die if held too tightly.' I just want her to relax her grip a little bit."

"You're lucky, at least, that your wife loves you. Hate's my problem. Not so easy."
120 "Oh, Nettie loves me madly. It will be my task to make her love me comfortably."

"Good luck to you, Smith. Do drop around while I'm in Rio. It will seem strange, if you sudenly stop calling by, to my wife. You're to treat Braling Two, here, just like me."
125 "Right! Good-by. And thank you."

Smith went smiling down the street. Braling and Braling Two turned and walked into the apartment hall.

On the crosstown bus Smith whistled softly, turning the white card in his fingers:

130   Clients must be pledged to secrecy, for while an act is pending in Congress
to legalize Marionettes, Inc., it is still a felony, if caught, to use one.

"Well," said Smith.

Clients must have a mold made of their body and a color index check of
their eyes, lips, hair, skin, etc. Clients must expect to wait for two months
135   until their model is finished.

Not so long, thought Smith. Two months from now my ribs will have a chance
to mend from the crushing they've taken. Two months from now my hand will
heal from being so constantly held. Two months from now my bruised underlip
will begin to reshape itself. I don't mean to sound *ungrateful* . . . He flipped the
140 card over.

Marionettes, Inc., is two years old and has a fine record of satisfied customers
behind it. Our motto is "No Strings Attached." Address: 43 South Wesley
Drive.

The bus pulled to his stop; he alighted, and while humming up the stairs he
145 thought, Nettie and I have fifteen thousand in our joint bank account. I'll just
slip eight thousand out as a business venture, you might say. The marionette will
probably pay back my money, with interest, in many ways. Nettie needn't know.
He unlocked the door and in a minute was in the bedroom. There lay Nettie, pale,
huge, and piously asleep.
150   "Dear Nettie." He was almost overwhelmed with remorse at her innocent face
there in the semidarkness. "If you were awake you would smother me with kisses
and coo in my ear. Really, you make me feel like a criminal. You have been such
a good, loving wife. Sometimes it is impossible for me to believe you married me
instead of that Bud Chapman you once liked. It seems that in the last month you
155 have loved me more wildly than *ever* before."
Tears came to his eyes. Suddenly he wished to kiss her, confess his love, tear up
the card, forget the whole business. But as he moved to do this, his hand ached
and his ribs cracked and groaned. He stopped, with a pained look in his eyes, and
turned away. He moved out into the hall and through the dark rooms. Humming,
160 he opened the kidney desk in the library and filched the bankbook. "Just take
eight thousand dollars is all," he said. "No more than that." He stopped. "Wait
a minute."
He rechecked the bankbook frantically. "Hold on here!" he cried. "Ten thousand dollars is missing!" He leaped up. "There's only five thousand left! What's
165 she done? What's Nettie done with it? More hats, more clothes, more perfume!
Or, wait—I know! She bought that little house on the Hudson she's been talking
about for months, without so much as a by your leave!"
He stormed into the bedroom, righteous and indignant. What did she mean,
taking their money like this? He bent over her. "Nettie!" he shouted. "Nettie,
170 wake up!"
She did not stir "What've you done with my money!" he bellowed.
She stirred fitfully. The light from the street flushed over her beautiful cheeks.

There was something about her. His heart throbbed violently. His tongue dried. He shivered. His knees suddenly turned to water. He collapsed. "Nettie,
175 Nettie!" he cried. "What've you done with my money!"

And then, the horrid thought. And then the terror and the loneliness engulfed him. And then the fever and disillusionment. For, without desiring to do so, he bent forward and yet forward again until his fevered ear was resting firmly and irrevocably upon her round pink bosom. "Nettie!" he cried.
180 *Tick-tick-tick-tick-tick-tick-tick-tick-tick-tick-tick.*

As Smith walked away down the avenue in the night, Braling and Braling Two turned in at the door to the apartment. "I'm glad he'll be happy too," said Braling.

"Yes," said Braling Two abstracted.

"Well, it's the cellar box for you, B-Two." Braling guided the other creature's
185 elbow down the stairs to the cellar.

"That's what I want to talk to you about," said Braling Two, as they reached the concrete floor and walked across it. "The cellar. I don't like it. I don't like that toolbox."

"I'll try and fix up something more comfortable."
190 "Marionettes are made to move, not lie still. How would you like to lie in a box most of the time?"

"Well—"

"You wouldn't like it at all. I keep running. There's no way to shut me off. I'm perfectly alive and I have feelings."
195 "It'll only be a few days now. I'll be off to Rio and you won't have to stay in the box. You can live upstairs."

Braling Two gestured irritably. "And when you come back from having a good time, back in the box I go."

Braling said, "They didn't tell me at the marionette shop that I'd get a difficult
200 specimen."

"There's a lot they don't know about us," said Braling Two. "We're pretty new. And we're sensitive. I hate the idea of you going off and laughing and lying in the sun in Rio while we're stuck here in the cold."

"But I've wanted that trip all my life," said Braling quietly.
205 He squinted his eyes and could see the sea and the mountains and the yellow sand. The sound of the waves was good to his inward mind. The sun was fine on his bared shoulders. The wine was most excellent.

"*I'll* never get to go to Rio," said the other man. "Have you thought of that?"

"No, I—"
210 "And another thing. Your wife."

"What about her?" asked Braling, beginning to edge toward the door.

"I've grown quite fond of her."

"I'm glad you're enjoying your employment." Braling licked his lips nervously.
215 "I'm afraid you don't understand. I think—I'm in love with her."

Braling took another step and froze. "You're *what?*"

"And I've been thinking," said Braling Two, "how nice it is in Rio and how

40

I'll never get there, and I've thought about your wife and—I think we could be very happy."

220   "Th-that's nice." Braling strolled as casually as he could to the cellar door. "You won't mind waiting a moment, will you? I have to make a phone call."

"To whom?" Braling Two frowned.

"No one important."

"To Marionettes, Incorporated? To tell them to come get me?"

225   "No, no—nothing like that!" He tried to rush out the door.

A metal-firm grip seized his wrists. "Don't run!"

"Take your hands off!"

"No."

"Did my wife put you up to this?"

230   "No."

"Did she guess? Did she talk to you? Does she know? Is *that* it?" He screamed. A hand clapped over his mouth.

"You'll never know, will you?" Braling Two smiled delicately. "You'll never know."

235   Braling struggled. "She *must* have guessed; she *must* have affected you!"

Braling Two said, "I'm going to put you in the box, lock it, and lose the key. Then I'll buy another Rio ticket for your wife."

"Now, now, wait a minute. Hold on. Don't be rash. Let's talk this over!"

"Good-by, Braling."

240   Braling stiffened. "What do you mean, 'good-by'?"

Ten minutes later Mrs. Braling awoke. She put her hand to her cheek. Someone had just kissed it. She shivered and looked up. "Why—you haven't done that in years," she murmured.

"We'll see what we can do about that," someone said.

From *The Illustrated Man* by Ray Bradbury. (1949)

Ray Bradbury

31 The Pedestrian

To enter out into that silence that was the city at eight o'clock of a misty evening in November, to put your feet upon that buckling concrete walk, to step over grassy seams and make your way, hands in pockets, through the silences, that was what Mr. Leonard Mead most dearly loved to do. He would stand upon the
5 corner of an intersection and peer down long moonlit avenues of sidewalk in four directions, deciding which way to go, but it really made no difference; he was alone in this world of 2053 A.D., or as good as alone, and with a final decision made, a path selected, he would stride off, sending patterns of frosty air before him like the smoke of a cigar.
10 Sometimes he would walk for hours and miles and return only at midnight to his house. And on his way he would see the cottages and homes with their dark windows, and it was not unequal to walking through a graveyard where only the faintest glimmers of firefly light appeared in flickers behind the windows. Sudden gray phantoms seemed to manifest upon inner room walls where a curtain was
15 still undrawn against the night, or there were whisperings and murmurs where a window in a tomb-like building was still open.

Mr. Leonard Mead would pause, cock his head, listen, look, and march on, his feet making no noise on the lumpy walk. For long ago he had wisely changed to sneakers when strolling at night, because the dogs in intermittent squads would
20 parallel his journey with barkings if he wore hard heels, and lights might click on and faces appear and an entire street be startled by the passing of a lone figure, himself, in the early November evening.

On this particular evening he began his journey in a westerly direction, toward the hidden sea. There was a good crystal frost in the air; it cut the nose and made
25 the lungs blaze like a Christmas tree inside; you could feel the cold light going on and off, all the branches filled with invisible snow. He listened to the faint push of his soft shoes through autumn leaves with satisfaction, and whistled a cold quiet whistle between his teeth, occasionally picking up a leaf as he passed, examining its skeletal pattern in the infrequent lamplights as he went on, smelling
30 its rusty smell.

"Hello, in there," he whispered to every house on every side as he moved. "What's up tonight on Channel 4, Channel 7, Channel 9? Where are the cowboys rushing, and do I see the United States Cavalry over the next hill to the rescue?"

The street was silent and long and empty, with only his shadow moving like
35 the shadow of a hawk in mid-country. If he closed his eyes and stood very still, frozen, he could imagine himself upon the center of a plain, a wintry, windless Arizona desert with no house in a thousand miles, and only dry river beds, the streets, for company.

"What is it now?" he asked the houses, noticing his wrist watch. "Eight-thirty
40 P.M.? Time for a dozen assorted murders? A quiz? A revue? A comedian falling off the stage?"

Was that a murmur of laughter from within a moon-white house? He hesitated, but went on when nothing more happened. He stumbled over a particularly uneven section of sidewalk. The cement was vanishing under flowers and grass. In ten years of walking by night or day, for thousands of miles, he had never met another person walking, not one in all that time.

He came to a cloverleaf intersection which stood silent where two main highways crossed the town. During the day it was a thunderous surge of cars, the gas stations open, a great insect rustling and a ceaseless jockeying for position as the scarab-beetles, a faint incense puttering from their exhausts, skimmed homeward to the far directions. But now these highways, too, were like streams in a dry season, all stone and bed and moon radiance.

He turned back on a side street, circling around toward his home. He was within a block of his destination when the lone car turned a corner quite suddenly and flashed a fierce white cone of light upon him. He stood entranced, not unlike a night moth, stunned by the illumination, and then drawn toward it.

A metallic voice called to him:

"Stand still. Stay where you are! Don't move!"

He halted.

"Put up your hands!"

"But——" he said.

"Your hands up! Or we'll shoot!"

The police, of course, but what a rare, incredible thing; in a city of three million, there was only *one* police car left, wasn't that correct? Ever since a year ago, 2052, the election year, the force had been cut down from three cars to one. Crime was ebbing; there was no need now for the police, save for this one lone car wandering and wandering the empty streets.

"Your name?" said the police car in a metallic whisper. He couldn't see the men in it for the bright light in his eyes.

"Leonard Mead," he said.

"Speak up!"

"Leonard Mead!"

"Business or profession?"

"I guess you'd call me a writer."

"No profession," said the police car, as if talking to itself. The light held him fixed, like a museum specimen, needle thrust through chest.

"You might say that," said Mr. Mead. He hadn't written in years. Magazines and books didn't sell any more. Everything went on in the tomb-like houses at night now, he thought, continuing his fancy. The tombs, ill-lit by television light, where the people sat like the dead, the gray or multi-colored lights touching their faces, but never really touching them.

"No profession," said the phonograph voice, hissing. "What are you doing out?"

"Walking," said Leonard Mead.

"Walking!"

"Just walking," he said simply, but his face felt cold.

"Walking, just walking, walking?"

"Yes, sir."

"Walking where? For what?"

90 "Walking for air. Walking to *see*."

"Your address!"

"Eleven South Saint James Street."

"And there is air *in* your house, you have an air *conditioner*, Mr. Mead?"

"Yes."

95 "And you have a viewing screen in your house to see with?"

"No."

"No?" There was a crackling quiet that in itself was an accusation.

"Are you married, Mr. Mead?"

"No."

100 "Not married," said the police voice behind the fiery beam. The moon was high and clear among the stars and the houses were gray and silent.

"Nobody wanted me," said Leonard Mead with a smile.

"Don't speak unless you're spoken to!"

Leonard Mead waited in the cold night.

105 "Just *walking*, Mr. Mead?"

"Yes."

"But you haven't explained for what purpose."

"I explained; for air, and to see, and just to walk."

"Have you done this often?"

110 "Every night for years."

The police car sat in the center of the street with its radio throat faintly humming.

"Well, Mr. Mead," it said.

"Is that all?" he asked politely.

115 "Yes," said the voice. "Here." There was a sigh, a pop. The back door of the police car sprang wide. "Get in."

"Wait a minute, I haven't done anything!"

"Get in."

"I protest!"

120 "Mr. Mead."

He walked like a man suddenly drunk. As he passed the front window of the car he looked in. As he had expected, there was no one in the front seat, no one in the car at all.

"Get in."

125 He put his hand to the door and peered into the back seat, which was a little cell, a little black jail with bars. It smelled of riveted steel. It smelled of harsh antiseptic; it smelled too clean and hard and metallic. There was nothing soft there.

"Now if you had a wife to give you an alibi," said the iron voice. "But—"

130 "Where are you taking me?"

The car hesitated, or rather gave a faint whirring click, as if information, somewhere, was dropping card by punch-slotted card under electric eyes. "To the Psychiatric Center for Research on Regressive Tendencies."

44

He got in. The door shut with a soft thud. The police car rolled through the
135 night avenues, flashing its dim lights ahead.

They passed one house on one street a moment later, one house in an entire
city of houses that were dark, but this one particular house had all of its electric
lights brightly lit, every window a loud yellow illumination, square and warm
in the cool darkness.

140 "That's *my* house," said Leonard Mead.

No one answered him.

The car moved down the empty river-bed streets and off away, leaving the
empty streets with the empty sidewalks, and no sound and no motion all the rest
of the chill November night.

From *Golden Apples Of The Sun* by Ray Bradbury. (1951)

Mel Calman

32 The Artist

An allegory? I think not.
Something universal but not commercial.
Personal but
not too private..

1

4

A fresh canvas...
All I need is a
subject
worthy of it...

2

One mustn't rush these things...
The mood must be right..
The ambience.. etc..
Great art takes
time to mature..

5

Something epic, of course—
But with truth, humanity,
compassion, irony,
wit, passion,
insight..

3

Perhaps I'm not quite ready to begin.
I ought to suffer more, meditate more,
live more
before I start.

6

I feel a seed germinating inside me..
If I stay very still perhaps it will grow
& grow into something
beautiful...

Was it not Jung who said:
The artist is the mythmaker
of the tribe...

No!
It seems to have
aborted itself...

I'm ready to begin now..

At last I think I see it... The creative
process is truly absorbing... the way
the unconscious sifts one's experience
and renders it into the true concepts
of art...

Ah....

From *Penguin Modern Stories 9* by Mel Calman. (1971)

Roald Dahl

33 Yesterday Was Beautiful

He bent down and rubbed his ankle where it had been sprained with the walking so that he could see the ankle bone. Then he straightened up and looked around him. He felt in his pocket for a packet of cigarettes, took one out and lit it. He wiped the sweat from his forehead with the back of his hand and he stood in the
5 middle of the street looking around him.

'Dammit, there must be someone here,' he said aloud, and he felt better when he heard the sound of his voice.

He walked on, limping, walking on the toe of his injured foot, and when he turned the next corner he saw the sea and the way the road curved around be-
10 tween the ruined houses and went on down the hill to the edge of the water. The sea was calm and black. He could clearly make out the line of hills on the mainland in the distance and he estimated that it was about eight miles away. He bent down again to rub his ankle. 'God dammit,' he said. 'There must be some of them still alive.' But there was no noise anywhere, and there was a stillness about the
15 buildings and about the whole village which made it seem as though the place had been dead for a thousand years.

Suddenly he heard a little noise as though someone had moved his feet on the gravel and when he looked around he saw the old man. He was sitting in the shade on a stone beside a water trough, and it seemed strange that he hadn't
20 seen him before.

'Health to you,' said the pilot. 'Ghia sou.'

He had learned Greek from the people up around Larissa and Yanina.

The old man looked up slowly, turning his head but not moving his shoulders. He had a greyish-white beard. He had a cloth cap on his head and he wore a shirt
25 which had no collar. It was a grey shirt with thin black stripes. He looked at the pilot and he was like a blind man who looks towards something but does not see.

'Old man, I am glad to see you. Are there no other people in the village?'

There was no answer.

The pilot sat down on the edge of the water trough to rest his ankle.
30 'I am Inglese,' he said. 'I am an aviator who has been shot down and jumped out by the parachute. I am Inglese.'

The old man moved his head slowly up and down. 'Inglesus,' he said quietly. 'You are Inglesus.'

'Yes, I am looking for someone who has a boat. I wish to go back to the
35 mainland.

There was a pause, and when he spoke, the old man seemed to be talking in his sleep. 'They come over all the time,' he said. 'The Germanoi they come over all the time.' The voice had no expression. He looked up into the sky, then he turned and looked behind him in the sky. 'They will come again today, Inglese. They
40 will come again soon.' There was no anxiety in his voice. There was no expression whatsoever. 'I do not understand why they come to us,' he added.

The pilot said, 'Perhaps not today. It is late now. I think they have finished for today.'

'I do not understand why they come to us, Inglese. There is no one here.'

45 The pilot said, 'I am looking for a man who has a boat who can take me across to the mainland. Is there a boat owner now in the village?'

'A boat?'

'Yes.' There was a pause while the question was considered.

'There is such a man.'

50 'Could I find him? Where does he live?'

'There is a man in the village who owns a boat.'

'Please tell me what is his name?'

The old man looked up again at the sky. 'Joannis is the one here who has a boat.'

55 'Joannis who?'

'Joannis Spirakis,' and he smiled. The name seemed to have a significance for the old man and he smiled.

'Where does he live?' the pilot said. 'I am sorry to be giving you this trouble.'

'Where he lives?'

60 'Yes.'

The old man considered this too. Then he turned and looked down the street towards the sea. 'Joannis was living in the house nearest to the water. But his house isn't any more. The Germanoi hit it this morning. It was early and it was still dark. You can see the house isn't any more. It isn't any more.'

65 'Where is he now?'

'He is living in the house of Antonina Angelou. That house there with the red colour on the window.' He pointed down the street.

'Thank you very much. I will go and call on the boat owner.'

'Ever since he was a boy,' the old man went on, 'Joannis has had a boat. His
70 boat is white with a blue line around the top,' and he smiled again. 'But at the moment I do not think he will be in the house. His wife will be there. Anna will be there, with Antonina Angelou. They will be home.'

'Thank you again. I will go and speak to his wife.'

The pilot got up and started to go down the street, but almost at once the man
75 called after him, 'Inglese.'

The pilot turned.

'When you speak to the wife of Joannis—when you speak to Anna . . . you should remember something.' He paused, searching for words. His voice wasn't expressionless any longer and he was looking up at the pilot.

80 'Her daughter was in the house when the Germanoi came. It is just something that you should remember.'

The pilot stood on the road waiting.

'Maria. Her name was Maria.'

'I will remember,' answered the pilot. 'I am sorry.'

85 He turned away and walked down the hill to the house with the red windows. He knocked and waited. He knocked again louder and waited. There was the noise of footsteps and the door opened.

It was dark in the house and all he could see was that the woman had black hair and that her eyes were black like her hair. She looked at the pilot who was standing
90 out in the sunshine.

'Health to you,' he said. 'I am Inglese.'

She did not move.

'I am looking for Joannis Spirakis. They say that he owns a boat.'

Still she did not move.

95 'Is he in the house?'

'No.'

'Perhaps his wife is here. She could know where he is.'

At first there was no answer. Then the woman stepped back and held open the door. 'Come in, Inglesus,' she said.

100 He followed her down the passage and into a back room. The room was dark because there was no glass in the windows—only patches of cardboard. But he could see the old woman who was sitting on the bench with her arms resting on the table. She was tiny. She was small like a child and her face was like a little screwed-up ball of brown paper.

105 'Who is it?' she said in a high voice.

The first woman said, 'This is an Inglesus. He is looking for your husband because he requires a boat.'

'Health to you, Inglesus,' the old woman said.

The pilot stood by the door, just inside the room. The first woman stood by
110 the window and her arms hung down by her sides.

The old woman said, 'Where are the Germanoi?' Her voice seemed bigger than her body.

'Now they are around Lamia.'

'Lamia.' She nodded. 'Soon they will be here. Perhaps tomorrow they will be
115 here. But I do not care. Do you hear me, Inglesus, I do not care.' She was leaning forward a little in her chair and the pitch of her voice was becoming higher. 'When they come it will be nothing new. They have already been here. Every day they have been here. Every day they come over and they bom bom bom and you shut your eyes and you open them again and you get up and you go outside and
120 the houses are just dust—and the people.' Her voice rose and fell.

She paused, breathing quickly, then she spoke more quietly. 'How many have you killed, Inglesus?'

The pilot put out a hand and leaned against the door to rest his ankle.

'I have killed some,' he said quietly.

125 'How many?'

'As many as I could, old woman. We cannot count the number of men.'

'Kill them all,' she said softly. 'Go and kill every man and every woman and every baby. Do you hear me, Inglesus? You must kill them all.' The little brown ball of paper became smaller and more screwed up. 'The first one I see I shall
130 kill.' She paused. 'And then, Inglesus, and then later, his family will hear that he is dead.'

The pilot did not say anything. She looked up at him and her voice was different. 'What is it you want Inglesus?'

He said, 'About the Germanoi, I am sorry. But there is not much we can do.'

135 'No,' she answered, 'there is nothing. And you?'

'I am looking for Joannis. I wish to use his boat.'

'Joannis,' she said quietly, 'he is not here. He is out.'

Suddenly she pushed·back the bench, got to her feet and went out of the room. 'Come,' she said. He followed her down the passage towards the front door.

140 She looked even smaller when she was standing than when she was sitting down and she walked quickly down the passage towards the door and opened it. She stepped out into the sunshine and for the first time he saw how very old she was.

She had no lips. Her mouth was just wrinkled skin like the rest of her face and she screwed up her eyes at the sun and looked up the road.

145 'There he is,' she said. 'That's him.' She pointed at the old man who was sitting beside the drinking trough.

The pilot looked at the man. Then he turned to speak to the old woman, but she had disappeared into the house.

From *Over To You* by Roald Dahl. (1945)

Graham Greene

34 The Destructors

It was on the eve of August Bank Holiday that the latest recruit became the leader of the Wormsley Common Gang. No one was surprised except Mike, but Mike at the age of nine was surprised by everything. "If you don't shut your mouth," somebody once said to him, "you'll get a frog down it." After that
5 Mike had kept his teeth tightly clamped except when the surprise was too great.

The new recruit had been with the gang since the beginning of the summer holidays, and there were possibilities about his brooding silence that all recognised. He never wasted a word even to tell his name until that was required of him by the rules. When he said "Trevor" it was a statement of fact, not as it
10 would have been with the others a statement of shame or defiance. Nor did anyone · laugh except Mike, who finding himself without support and meeting the dark gaze of the newcomer opened his mouth and was quiet again. There was every reason why T., as he was afterwards referred to, should have been an object of mockery—there was his name (and they substituted the initial because otherwise
15 they had no excuse not to laugh at it), the fact that his father, a former architect and present clerk, had "come down in the world" and that his mother considered herself better than the neighbours. What but an odd quality of danger, of the unpredictable, established him in the gang without any ignoble ceremony of initiation?
20 The gang met every morning in an impromptu car-park, the site of the last bomb of the first blitz. The leader, who was known as Blackie, claimed to have heard it fall, and no one was precise enough in his dates to point out that he would have been one year old and fast asleep on the down platform of Wormsley Common Underground Station. On one side of the car-park leant the first
25 occupied house, No. 3, of the shattered Northwood Terrace—literally leant, for it had suffered from the blast of the bomb and the side walls were supported on wooden struts. A smaller bomb and some incendiaries had fallen beyond, so that the house stuck up like a jagged tooth and carried on the further wall relics of its neighbour, a dado, the remains of a fireplace. T., whose words were almost
30 confined to voting "Yes" or "No" to the plan of operations proposed each day by Blackie, once startled the whole gang by saying broodingly, "Wren built that house, father says."

"Who's Wren?"

"The man who built St. Paul's."

35 "Who cares?" Blackie said. "It's only Old Misery's."

Old Misery—whose real name was Thomas—had once been a builder and decorator. He lived alone in the crippled house, doing for himself: once a week you could see him coming back across the common with bread and vegetables, and once as the boys played in the car-park he put his head over the smashed wall
40 of his garden and looked at them.

"Been to the loo," one of the boys said, for it was common knowledge that since the bombs fell something had gone wrong with the pipes of the house and Old Misery was too mean to spend money on the property. He could do the redecorating himself at cost price, but he had never learnt plumbing. The loo
45 was a wooden shed at the bottom of the narrow garden with a star-shaped hole in the door: it had escaped the blast which had smashed the house next door and sucked out the window-frames of No. 3.

The next time the gang became aware of Mr. Thomas was more surprising. Blackie, Mike and a thin yellow boy, who for some reason was called by his
50 surname Summers, met him on the common coming back from the market. Mr. Thomas stopped them. He said glumly, "You belong to the lot that play in the car-park?"

Mike was about to answer when Blackie stopped him. As the leader he had responsibilities. "Suppose we are?" he said ambiguously.

55 "I got some chocolates," Mr. Thomas said. "Don't like 'em myself. Here you are. Not enough to go round, I don't suppose. There never is," he added with sombre conviction. He handed over three packets of Smarties.

The gang were puzzled and perturbed by this action and tried to explain it away. "Bet someone dropped them and he picked 'em up," somebody suggested.
60 "Pinched 'em and then got in a bleeding funk," another thought aloud.

"It's a bribe," Summers said. "He wants us to stop bouncing balls on his wall."

"We'll show him we don't take bribes," Blackie said, and they sacrificed the whole morning to the game of bouncing that only Mike was young enough to
65 enjoy. There was no sign from Mr. Thomas.

Next day T. astonished them all. He was late at the rendezvous, and the voting for that day's exploit took place without him. At Blackie's suggestion the gang was to disperse in pairs, take buses at random and see how many free rides could be snatched from unwary conductors (the operation was to be carried out in
70 pairs to avoid cheating.) They were drawing lots for their companions when T. arrived.

"Where you been, T.?" Blackie asked. "You can't vote now. You know the rules."

"I've been *there*," T. said. He looked at the ground, as though he had thoughts
75 to hide.

"Where?"

"At Old Misery's." Mike's mouth opened and then hurriedly closed again with a click. He had remembered the frog.

"At Old Misery's?" Blackie said. There was nothing in the rules against it,
80 but he had a sensation that T. was treading on dangerous ground. He asked hopefully, "Did you break in?"

"No. I rang the bell."

"And what did you say?"

"I said I wanted to see his house."
85 "What did he do?"

"He showed it me."

54

"Pinch anything?"

"No."

"What did you do it for then?"

90 The gang had gathered round: it was as though an impromptu court were about to form and to try some case of deviation. T. said, "It's a beautiful house," and still watching the ground, meeting no one's eyes, he licked his lips first one way, then the other.

"What do you mean, a beautiful house?" Blackie asked with scorn.

95 "It's got a staircase two hundred years old like a corkscrew. Nothing holds it up."

"What do you mean, nothing holds it up. Does it float?"

"It's to do with opposite forces, Old Misery said."

"What else?"

100 "There's panelling."

"Like in the Blue Boar?"

"Two hundred years old."

"Is Old Misery two hundred years old?"

Mike laughed suddenly and then was quiet again. The meeting was in a serious 105 mood. For the first time since T. had strolled into the car-park on the first day of the holidays his position was in danger. It only needed a single use of his real name and the gang would be at his heels.

"What did you do it for?" Blackie asked. He was just, he had no jealousy, he was anxious to retain T. in the gang if he could. It was the word "beautiful" 110 that worried him—that belonged to a class world that you could still see parodied at the Wormsley Common Empire by a man wearing a top hat and a monocle, with a haw-haw accent. He was tempted to say, "My dear Trevor, old chap," and unleash his hell hounds. "If you'd broken in," he said sadly—that indeed would have been an exploit worthy of the gang.

115 "This was better," T. said. "I found out things." He continued to stare at his feet, not meeting anybody's eye, as though he were absorbed in some dream he was unwilling—or ashamed—to share.

"What things?"

"Old Misery's going to be away all tomorrow and Bank Holiday."

120 Blackie said with relief, "You mean we could break in?"

"And pinch things?" somebody asked.

Blackie said, "Nobody's going to pinch things. Breaking in—that's good enough, isn't it? We don't want any court stuff."

"I don't want to pinch anything," T. said. "I've got a better idea."

125 "What is it?"

T. raised eyes, as grey and disturbed as the drab August day. "We'll pull it down," he said. "We'll destroy it."

Blackie gave a single hoot of laughter and then, like Mike, fell quiet, daunted by the serious implacable gaze. "What'd the police be doing all the time?" he 130 said.

"They'd never know. We'd do it from inside. I've found a way in." He said with a sort of intensity, "We'd be like worms, don't you see, in an apple. When we came out again there'd be nothing there, no staircase, no panels, nothing but just walls, and then we'd make the walls fall down—somehow."

135 "We'd go to jug," Blackie said.

"Who's to prove? and anyway we wouldn't have pinched anything." He added without the smallest flicker of glee, "There wouldn't be anything to pinch after we'd finished."

"I've never heard of going to prison for breaking things," Summers said.

140 "There wouldn't be time," Blackie said. "I've seen housebreakers at work."

"There are twelve of us," T. said. "We'd organise."

"None of us know how . . ."

"I know," T. said. He looked across at Blackie, "Have you got a better plan?"

"Today," Mike said tactlessly, "we're pinching free rides . . ."

145 "Free rides," T. said. "You can stand down, Blackie, if you'd rather . . ."

"The gang's got to vote."

"Put it up then."

Blackie said uneasily, "It's proposed that tomorrow and Monday we destroy Old Misery's house."

150 "Here, here," said a fat boy called Joe.

"Who's in favour?"

T. said, "It's carried."

"How do we start?" Summers asked.

"He'll tell you," Blackie said. It was the end of his leadership. He went away
155 to the back of the car-park and began to·kick a stone, dribbling it this way and that. There was only one old Morris in the park, for few cars were left there except lorries: without an attendant there was no safety. He took a flying kick at the car and scraped a little paint off the rear mudguard. Beyond, paying no more attention to him than to a stranger, the gang had gathered round T.; Blackie was
160 dimly aware of the fickleness of favour. He thought of going home, of never returning, of letting them all discover the hollowness of T.'s leadership, but suppose after all what T. proposed was possible—nothing like it had ever been done before. The fame of the Wormsley Common car-park gang would surely reach around London. There would be headlines in the papers. Even the grown-
165 up gangs who ran the betting at the all-in wrestling and the barrow-boys would hear with respect of how Old Misery's house had been destroyed. Driven by the pure, simple and altruistic ambition of fame for the gang, Blackie came back to where T. stood in the shadow of Misery's wall.

T. was giving his orders with decision: it was as though this plan had been
170 with him all his life, pondered through the seasons, now in his fifteenth year crystallised with the pain of puberty. "You," he said to Mike, "bring some big nails, the biggest you can find, and a hammer. Anyone else who can better bring a hammer and a screwdriver. We'll need plenty of them. Chisels too. We can't have too many chisels. Can anybody bring a saw?"

175 "I can," Mike said.

"Not a child's saw," T. said. "A real saw."

Blackie realised he had raised his hand like any ordinary member of the gang.

56

"Right, you bring one, Blackie. But now there's a difficulty. We want a hack-saw."

180 "What's a hacksaw?" someone asked.

"You can get 'em at Woolworth's," Summers said.

The fat boy called Joe said gloomily, "I knew it would end in a collection."

"I'll get one myself," T. said. "I don't want your money. But I can't buy a sledge-hammer."

185 Blackie said, "They are working on No. 15. I know where they'll leave their stuff for Bank Holiday."

"Then that's all," T. said. "We meet here at nine sharp."

"I've got to go to church," Mike said.

"Come over the wall and whistle. We'll let you in."

2

190 On Sunday morning all were punctual except Blackie, even Mike. Mike had had a stroke of luck. His mother felt ill, his father was tired after Saturday night, and he was told to go to church alone with many warnings of what would happen if he strayed. Blackie had had difficulty in smuggling out the saw, and then in finding the sledge-hammer at the back of No. 15. He approached the house from a lane at
195 the rear of the garden, for fear of the policeman's beat along the main road. The tired evergreens kept off a stormy sun: another wet Bank Holiday was being prepared over the Atlantic, beginning in swirls of dust under the trees. Blackie climbed the wall into Misery's garden.

There was no sign of anybody anywhere. The loo stood like a tomb in a neglect-
200 ed graveyard. The curtains were drawn. The house slept. Blackie lumbered nearer with the saw and the sledge-hammer. Perhaps after all nobody had turned up: the plan had been a wild invention: they had woken wiser. But when he came close to the back door he could hear a confusion of sound, hardly louder than a hive in swarm: a clickety-clack, a bang bang bang, a scraping, a creaking, a sudden
205 painful crack. He thought: it's true, and whistled.

They opened the back door to him and he came in. He had at once the impres-sion of organisation, very different from the old happy-go-lucky ways under his leadership. For a while he wandered up and down stairs looking for T. Nobody addressed him: he had a sense of great urgency, and already he could begin to see
210 the plan. The interior of the house was being carefully demolished without touching the outer walls. Summers with hammer and chisel was ripping out the skirting-boards in the ground floor dining-room: he had already smashed the panels of the door. In the same room Joe was heaving up the parquet blocks, exposing the soft wood floor-boards over the cellar. Coils of wire came out of
215 the damaged skirting and Mike sat happily on the floor, clipping the wires.

On the curved stairs two of the gang were working hard with an inadequate child's saw on the banisters—when they saw Blackie's big saw they signalled for it wordlessly. When he next saw them a quarter of the banisters had been dropped into the hall. He found T. at last in the bathroom—he sat moodily in the least
220 cared-for room in the house, listening to the sounds coming up from below.

"You've really done it," Blackie, said with awe. "What's going to happen?"

"We've only just begun," T. said. He looked at the sledge-hammer and gave his instructions. "You stay here and break the bath and the wash-basin. Don't bother about the pipes. They come later."

225 Mike appeared at the door. "I've finished the wire, T.," he said.

"Good. You've just got to go wandering round now. The kitchen's in the basement. Smash all the china and glass and bottles you can lay hold of. Don't turn on the taps — we don't want a flood — yet. Then go into all the rooms and turn out drawers. If they are locked get one of the others to break them open.
230 Tear up any papers you find and smash all the ornaments. Better take a carving-knife with you from the kitchen. The bedroom's opposite here. Open the pillows and tear up the sheets. That's enough for the moment. And you, Blackie, when you've finished in here crack the plaster in the passage up with your sledge-hammer."

235 "What are you going to do?" Blackie asked.

"I'm looking for something special," T. said.

It was nearly lunch-time before Blackie had finished and went in search of T. Chaos had advanced. The kitchen was a shambles of broken glass and china. The dining-room was stripped of parquet, the skirting was up, the door had been
240 taken off its hinges, and the destroyers had moved up a floor. Streaks of light came in through the closed shutters where they worked with the seriousness of creators—and destruction after all is a form of creation. A kind of imagination had seen this house as it had now become.

Mike said, "I've got to go home for dinner."

245 "Who else?" T. asked, but all the others on one excuse or another had brought provisions with them.

They squatted in the ruins of the room and swapped unwanted sandwiches. Half an hour for lunch and they were at work again. By the time Mike returned, they were on the top floor, and by six the superficial damage was completed.
250 The doors were all off, all the skirtings raised, the furniture pillaged and ripped and smashed—no one could have slept in the house except on a bed of broken plaster. T. gave his orders—eight o'clock next morning, and to escape notice they climbed singly over the garden wall, into the car-park. Only Blackie and T. were left: the light had nearly gone, and when they touched a switch, nothing worked—
255 Mike had done his job thoroughly.

"Did you find anything special?" Blackie asked.

T. nodded. "Come over here," he said, "and look." Out of both pockets he drew bundles of pound notes. "Old Misery's savings," he said. "Mike ripped out the mattress, but he missed them."

260 "What are you going to do? Share them?"

"We aren't thieves," T. said. "Nobody's going to steal anything from this house. I kept these for you and me—a celebration." He knelt down on the floor and counted them out—there were seventy in all. "We'll burn them," he said, "one by one," and taking it in turns they held a note upwards and lit the top
265 corner, so that the flame burnt slowly towards their fingers. The grey ash floated

above them and fell on their heads like age. "I'd like to see Old Misery's face when we are through," T. said.

"You hate him a lot?" Blackie asked.

"Of course I don't hate him," T. said. "There'd be no fun if I hated him."
270 The last burning note illuminated his brooding face. "All this hate and love," he said, "it's soft, it's hooey. There's only things, Blackie," and he looked round the room crowded with the unfamiliar shadows of half things, broken things, former things. "I'll race you home, Blackie," he said.

3

Next morning the serious destruction started. Two were missing—Mike and
275 another boy whose parents were off to Southend and Brighton in spite of the slow warm drops that had begun to fall and the rumble of thunder in the estuary like the first guns of the old blitz. "We've got to hurry," T. said.

Summers was restive. "Haven't we done enough?" he said. "I've been given a bob for slot machines. This is like work."

280 "We've hardly started," T. said. "Why, there's all the floors left, and the stairs. We haven't taken out a single window. You voted like the others. We are going to *destroy* this house. There won't be anything left when we've finished."

They began again on the first floor picking up the top floor-boards next to the outer wall, leaving the joists exposed. Then they sawed through the joists and
285 retreated into the hall, as what was left of the floor heeled and sank. They had learnt with practice, and the second floor collapsed more easily. By the evening an odd exhilaration seized them as they looked down the great hollow of the house. They ran risks and made mistakes: when they thought of the windows it was too late to reach them. "Cor," Joe said, and dropped a penny down into the
290 dry rubble-filled well. It cracked and span among the broken glass.

"Why did we start this?" Summers asked with astonishment; T. was already on the ground, digging at the rubble, clearing a space along the outer wall. "Turn on the taps," he said. "It's too dark for anyone to see now, and in the morning it won't matter." The water overtook them on the stairs and fell through the
295 floorless rooms.

It was then they heard Mike's whistle at the back. "Something's wrong," Blackie said. They could hear his urgent breathing as they unlocked the door.

"The bogies?" Summers asked.

"Old Misery," Mike said. "He's on his way." He put his head between his
300 knees and retched. "Ran all the way," he said with pride.

"But why?" T. said. "He told me . . ." He protested with the fury of the child he had never been, "It isn't fair."

"He was down at Southend," Mike said, "and he was on the train coming back. Said it was too cold and wet." He paused and gazed at the water. "My, you've
305 had a storm here. Is the roof leaking?"

"How long will he be?"

"Five minutes. I gave Ma the slip and ran."

"We better clear," Summers said. "We've done enough, anyway."

"Oh no, we haven't. Anybody could do this—" "this" was the shattered
310 hollowed house with nothing left but the walls. Yet walls could be preserved.
Facades were valuable. They could build inside again more beautifully than before.
This could again be a home. He said angrily, "We've got to finish. Don't move.
Let me think."

"There's no time," a boy said.

315 "There's got to be a way," T. said. "We couldn't have got this far . . ."

"We've done a lot," Blackie said.

"No. No, we haven't. Somebody watch the front."

"We can't do any more."

"He may come in at the back."

320 "Watch the back too." T. began to plead. "Just give me a minute and I'll fix it.
I swear I'll fix it." But his authority had gone with his ambiguity. He was only
one of the gang.

"Please," he said.

"Please," Summers mimicked him, and then suddenly struck home with the
325 fatal name. "Run along home, Trevor."

T. stood with his back to the rubble like a boxer knocked groggy against the
ropes. He had no words as his dreams shook and slid. Then Blackie acted before
the gang had time to laugh, pushing Summers backward. "I'll watch the front,
T.," he said, and cautiously he opened the shutters of the hall. The grey wet
330 common stretched ahead, and the lamps gleamed in the puddles. "Someone's
coming, T. No, it's not him. What's your plan, T.?"

"Tell Mike to go out to the loo and hide close beside it. When he hears me
whistle he's got to count ten and start to shout."

"Shout what?"

335 "Oh, 'Help', anything."

"You hear, Mike," Blackie said. He was the leader again. He took a quick look
between the shutters. "He's coming, T."

"Quick, Mike. The loo. Stay here, Blackie, all of you till I yell."

"Where are you going, T.?"

340 "Don't worry. I'll see to this. I said I would, didn't I?"

Old Misery came limping off the common. He had mud on his shoes and he
stopped to scrape them on the pavement's edge. He didn't want to soil his house,
which stood jagged and dark between the bomb-sites, saved so narrowly, as he
believed, from destruction. Even the fan-light had been left unbroken by the
345 bomb's blast. Somewhere somebody whistled. Old Misery looked sharply round.
He didn't trust whistles. A child was shouting: it seemed to come from his own
garden. Then a boy ran into the road from the car-park. "Mr. Thomas," he called,
"Mr. Thomas."

"What is it?"

350 "I'm terribly sorry, Mr. Thomas. One of us got taken short, and we thought
you wouldn't mind, and now he can't get out."

"What do you mean, boy?"

"He's got stuck in your loo."

"He'd no business . . . Haven't I seen you before?"

60

355   "You showed me your house."

"So I did. So I did. That doesn't give you the right to . . ."

"Do hurry, Mr. Thomas. He'll suffocate."

"Nonsense. He can't suffocate. Wait till I put my bag in."

"I'll carry your bag."

360   "Oh no, you don't. I carry my own."

"This way, Mr. Thomas."

"I can't get in the garden that way. I've got to go through the house."

"But you *can* get in the garden this way, Mr. Thomas. We often do."

"You often do?" He followed the boy with a scandalised fascination. "When?
365 What right? . . ."

"Do you see . . .? the wall's low."

"I'm not going to climb walls into my own garden. It's absurd."

"This is how we do it. One foot here, one foot there, and over." The boy's
face peered down, an arm shot out, and Mr. Thomas found his bag taken and
370 deposited on the other side of the wall.

"Give me back my bag," Mr. Thomas said. From the loo a boy yelled and
yelled. "I'll call the police."

"Your bag's all right, Mr. Thomas. Look. One foot there. On your right. Now
just above. To your left." Mr. Thomas climbed over his own garden wall.
375 "Here's your bag, Mr. Thomas."

"I'll have the wall built up," Mr. Thomas said, "I'll not have you boys coming
over here, using my loo." He stumbled on the path, but the boy caught his elbow
and supported him. "Thank you, thank you, my boy," he murmured automatically. Somebody shouted again through the dark. "I'm coming, I'm coming,"
380 Mr. Thomas called. He said to the boy beside him, "I'm not unreasonable. Been
a boy myself. As long as things are done regular. I don't mind you playing round
the place Saturday mornings. Sometimes I like company. Only it's got to be regular. One of you asks leave and I say Yes. Sometimes I'll say No. Won't feel like it.
And you come in at the front door and out at the back. No garden walls."

385   "Do get him out, Mr. Thomas."

"He won't come to any harm in my loo," Mr. Thomas said, stumbling slowly
down the garden. "Oh, my rheumatics," he said. "Always get 'em on Bank
Holiday. I've got to go careful. There's loose stones here. Give me your hand.
Do you know what my horoscope said yesterday? 'Abstain from any dealings in
390 first half of week. Danger of serious crash.' That might be on this path," Mr.
Thomas said. "They speak in parables and double meanings." He paused at the
door of the loo. "What's the matter in there?" he called. There was no reply.

"Perhaps he's fainted," the boy said.

"Not in my loo. Here, you, come out," Mr. Thomas said, and giving a great
395 jerk at the door he nearly fell on his back when it swung easily open. A hand first
supported him and then pushed him hard. His head hit the opposite wall and he
sat heavily down. His bag hit his feet. A hand whipped the key out of the lock
and the door slammed. "Let me out," he called, and heard the key turn in the
lock. "A serious crash," he thought, and felt dithery and confused and old.

400 A voice spoke to him softly through the star-shaped hole in the door. "Don't worry, Mr. Thomas," it said, "we won't hurt you, not if you stay quiet."

Mr. Thomas put his head between his hands and pondered. He had noticed that there was only one lorry in the car-park, and he felt certain that the driver would not come for it before the morning. Nobody could hear him from the
405 road in front, and the lane at the back was seldom used. Anyone who passed there would be hurrying home and would not pause for what they would certainly take to be drunken cries. And if he did call "Help", who, on a lonely Bank Holiday evening, would have the courage to investigate? Mr. Thomas sat on the loo and pondered with the wisdom of age.

410 After a while it seemed to him that there were sounds in the silence—they were faint and came from the direction of his house. He stood up and peered through the ventilation-hole—between the cracks in one of the shutters he saw a light, not the light of a lamp, but the wavering light that a candle might give. Then he thought he heard the sound of hammering and scraping and chipping. He thought
415 of burglars—perhaps they had employed the boy as a scout, but why should burglars engage in what sounded more and more like a stealthy form of carpentry? Mr. Thomas let out an experimental yell, but nobody answered. The noise could not even have reached his enemies.

4

Mike had gone home to bed, but the rest stayed. The question of leadership no
420 longer concerned the gang. With nails, chisels, screwdrivers, anything that was sharp and penetrating they moved around the inner walls worrying at the mortar between the bricks. They started too high, and it was Blackie who hit on the damp course and realised the work could be halved if they weakened the joints immediately above. It was a long, tiring, unamusing job, but at last it was fin-
425 ished. The gutted house stood there balanced on a few inches of mortar between the damp course and the bricks.

There remained the most dangerous task of all, out in the open at the edge of the bomb-site. Summers was sent to watch the road for passers-by, and Mr. Thomas, sitting on the loo, heard clearly now the sound of sawing. It no longer came
430 from his house, and that a little reassured him. He felt less concerned. Perhaps the other noises too had no significance.

A voice spoke to him through the hole. "Mr. Thomas."

"Let me out," Mr. Thomas said sternly.

"Here's a blanket," the voice said, and a long grey sausage was worked through
435 the hole and fell in swathes over Mr. Thomas's head.

"There's nothing personal," the voice said. "We want you to be comfortable to-night."

"To-night," Mr. Thomas repeated incredulously.

"Catch," the voice said. "Penny buns—we've buttered them, and sausage-rolls.
440 We don't want you to starve, Mr. Thomas."

Mr. Thomas pleaded desperately, "A joke's a joke, boy. Let me out and I won't say a thing. I've got rheumatics. I got to sleep comfortable."

"You wouldn't be comfortable, not in your house, you wouldn't. Not now."

"What do you mean, boy?" but the footsteps receded. There was only the
silence of night: no sound of sawing. Mr. Thomas tried one more yell, but he
was daunted and rebuked by the silence—a long way off an owl hooted and made
away again on its muffled flight through the soundless world.

At seven next morning the driver came to fetch his lorry. He climbed into the
seat and tried to start the engine. He was vaguely aware of a voice shouting, but it
didn't concern him. At last the engine responded and he backed the lorry until it
touched the great wooden shore that supported Mr. Thomas's house. That way
he could drive right out and down the street without reversing. The lorry moved
forward, was momentarily checked as though something were pulling it from
behind, and then went on to the sound of a long rumbling crash. The driver was
astonished to see bricks bouncing ahead of him, while stones hit the roof of his
cab. He put on his brakes. When he climbed out the whole landscape had suddenly
altered. There was no house beside the car-park, only a hill of rubble. He went
round and examined the back of his car for damage, and found a rope tied there
that was still twisted at the other end round part of a wooden strut.

The driver again became aware of somebody shouting. It came from the wood-
en erection which was the nearest thing to a house in that desolation of broken
brick. The driver climbed the smashed wall and unlocked the door. Mr. Thomas
came out of the loo. He was wearing a grey blanket to which flakes of pastry
adhered. He gave a sobbing cry. "My house," he said, "Where's my house?"

"Search me," the driver said. His eye lit on the remains of a bath and what had
once been a dresser and he began to laugh. There wasn't anything left anywhere.

"How dare you laugh," Mr. Thomas said. "It was my house. My house."

"I'm sorry," the driver said, making heroic efforts, but when he remembered
the sudden check to his lorry, the crash of bricks falling, he became convulsed
again. One moment the house had stood there with such dignity between the
bomb-sites like a man in a top hat, and then, bang, crash, there wasn't anything
left—not anything. He said, "I'm sorry. I can't help it, Mr. Thomas. There's
nothing personal, but you got to admit it's funny."

From *Collected Stories* by Graham Greene. (1954)

Ernest Hemingway

35 Old Man at the Bridge

An old man with steel rimmed spectacles and very dusty clothes sat by the side of the road. There was a pontoon bridge across the river and carts, trucks, and men, women and children were crossing it. The mule-drawn carts staggered up the steep bank from the bridge with soldiers helping push against the spokes of
5 the wheels. The trucks ground up and away heading out of it all and the peasants plodded along in the ankle deep dust. But the old man sat there without moving. He was too tired to go any farther.

It was my business to cross the bridge, explore the bridgehead beyond and find out to what point the enemy had advanced. I did this and returned over the bridge.
10 There were not so many carts now and very few people on foot, but the old man was still there.

"Where do you come from?" I asked him.

"From San Carlos," he said, and smiled.

That was his native town and so it gave him pleasure to mention it and he
15 smiled.

"I was taking care of animals," he explained.

"Oh," I said, not quite understanding.

"Yes," he said, "I stayed, you see, taking care of animals. I was the last one to leave the town of San Carlos."

20 He did not look like a shepherd nor a herdsman and I looked at his black dusty clothes and his gray dusty face and his steel rimmed spectacles and said, "What animals were they?"

"Various animals," he said, and shook his head. "I had to leave them."

I was watching the bridge and the African looking country of the Ebro Delta
25 and wondering how long now it would be before we would see the enemy, and listening all the while for the first noises that would signal that ever mysterious event called contact, and the old man still sat there.

"What animals were they?" I asked.

"There were three animals altogether," he explained. "There were two goats
30 and a cat and then there were four pairs of pigeons."

"And you had to leave them?" I asked.

"Yes. Because of the artillery. The captain told me to go because of the artillery."

"And you have no family?" I asked, watching the far end of the bridge where
35 a few last carts were hurrying down the slope of the bank.

"No," he said, "only the animals I stated. The cat, of course, will be all right. A cat can look out for itself, but I cannot think what will become of the others."

"What politics have you?" I asked.

"I am without politics," he said. "I am seventy-six years old. I have come
40 twelve kilometers now and I think now I can go no further."

"This is not a good place to stop," I said. "If you can make it, there are trucks up the road where it forks for Tortosa."

"I will wait a while," he said, "and then I will go. Where do the trucks go?"

"Towards Barcelona," I told him.

45 "I know no one in that direction," he said, "but thank you very much. Thank you again very muc ."

He looked at me very blankly and tiredly, then said, having to share his worry with someone, "The cat will be all right, I am sure. There is no need to be unquiet about the cat. But the others. Now what do you think about the others?"

50 "Why they'll probably come through it all right."

"You think so?"

"Why not," I said, watching the far bank where now there were no carts.

"But what will they do under the artillery when I was told to leave because of the artillery?"

55 "Did you leave the dove cage unlocked?" I asked.

"Yes."

"Then they'll fly."

"Yes, certainly they'll fly. But the others. It's better not to think about the others," he said.

60 "If you are rested I would go," I urged. "Get up and try to walk now."

"Thank you," he said and got to his feet, swayed from side to side and then sat down backwards in the dust.

"I was taking care of animals," he said dully, but no longer to me. "I was only taking care of animals."

65 There was nothing to do about him. It was Easter Sunday and the Fascists were advancing toward the Ebro. It was a gray overcast day with a low ceiling so their planes were not up. That and the fact that cats know how to look after themselves was all the good luck that old man would ever have.

From *The Short Stories of Ernest Hemingway* by Ernest Hemingway. (1938)

George Orwell

36 Animal Farm: Old Major's Speech

All the animals were now present except Moses, the tame raven, who slept on a perch behind the back door. When Major saw that they had all made themselves comfortable and were waiting attentively, he cleared his throat and began:

"Comrades, you have heard already about the strange dream that I had last
5 night. But I will come to the dream later. I have something else to say first. I do not think, comrades, that I shall be with you for many months longer, and before I die, I feel it my duty to pass on to you such wisdom as I have acquired. I have had a long life, I have had much time for thought as I lay alone in my stall, and I think I may say that I understand the nature of life on this earth as well as any
10 animal now living. It is about this that I wish to speak to you.

"Now, comrades, what is the nature of this life of ours? Let us face it: our lives are miserable, laborious, and short. We are born, we are given just so much food as will keep the breath in our bodies, and those of us who are capable of it are forced to work to the last atom of our strength; and the very instant that our
15 usefulness has come to an end we are slaughtered with hideous cruelty. No animal in England knows the meaning of happiness or leisure after he is a year old. No animal in England is free. The life of an animal is misery and slavery: that is the plain truth.

"But is this simply part of the order of nature? Is it because this land of ours is
20 so poor that it cannot afford a decent life to those who dwell upon it? No, comrades, a thousand times no! The soil of England is fertile, its climate is good, it is capable of affording food in abundance to an enormously greater number of animals than now inhabit it. This single farm of ours would support a dozen horses, twenty cows, hundreds of sheep—and all of them living in a comfort and
25 a dignity that are now almost beyond our imagining. Why then do we continue in this miserable condition? Because nearly the whole of the produce of our labour is stolen from us by human beings. There, comrades, is the answer to all our problems. It is summed up in a single word—Man. Man is the only real enemy we have. Remove Man from the scene, and the root cause of hunger and over-
30 work is abolished forever.

"Man is the only creature that consumes without producing. He does not give milk, he does not lay eggs, he is too weak to pull the plough, he cannot run fast enough to catch rabbits. Yet he is lord of all the animals. He sets them to work, he gives back to them the bare minimum that will prevent them from starving,
35 and the rest he keeps for himself. Our labour tills the soil, our dung fertilizes it, and yet there is not one of us that owns more than his bare skin. You cows that I see before me, how many thousands of gallons of milk have you given during this last year? And what has happened to that milk which should have been breeding up sturdy calves? Every drop of it has gone down the throats of our enemies.
40 And you hens, how many eggs have you laid in this last year, and how many of those eggs ever hatched into chickens? The rest have all gone to market to bring

in money for Jones and his men. And you, Clover, where are those four foals you bore, who should have been the support and pleasure of your old age? Each was sold at a year old—you will never see one of them again. In return for your four
45 confinements and all your labour in the fields, what have you ever had except your bare rations and a stall?

"And even the miserable lives we lead are not allowed to reach their natural span. For myself I do not grumble, for I am one of the lucky ones. I am twelve years old and have had over four hundred children. Such is the natural life of a pig.
50 But no animal escapes the cruel knife in the end. You young porkers who are sitting in front of me, every one of you will scream your lives out at the block within a year. To that horror we all must come—cows, pigs, hens, sheep, everyone. Even the horses and the dogs have no better fate. You, Boxer, the very day that those great muscles of yours lose their power, Jones will sell you to the
55 knacker, who will cut your throat and boil you down for the foxhounds. As for the dogs, when they grow old and toothless, Jones ties a brick round their necks and drowns them in the nearest pond.

"Is it not crystal clear, then, comrades, that all the evils of this life of ours spring from the tyranny of human beings? Only get rid of Man, and the produce of our
60 labour would be our own. Almost overnight we could become rich and free. What then must we do? Why, work night and day, body and soul, for the overthrow of the human race! That is my message to you, comrades: Rebellion! I do not know when that Rebellion will come, it might be in a week or in a hundred years, but I know, as surely as I see this straw beneath my feet, that sooner or later
65 justice will be done. Fix your eyes on that, comrades, throughout the short remainder of your lives! And above all, pass on this message of mine to those who come after you, so that future generations shall carry on the struggle until it is victorious.

"And remember, comrades, your resolution must never falter. No argument
70 must lead you astray. Never listen when they tell you that Man and the animals have a common interest, that the prosperity of the one is the prosperity of the others. It is all lies. Man serves the interests of no creature except himself. And among us animals let there be perfect unity, perfect comradeship in the struggle. All men are enemies. All animals are comrades."

75 [At this moment there was a tremendous uproar. While Major was speaking four large rats had crept out of their holes and were sitting on their hindquarters, listening to him. The dogs had suddenly caught sight of them, and it was only by a swift dash for their holes that the rats saved their lives. Major raised his trotter for silence.

80 "Comrades," he said, "here is a point that must be settled. The wild creatures, such as rats and rabbits—are they our friends or our enemies? Let us put it to the vote. I propose this question to the meeting: Are rats comrades?"

The vote was taken at once, and it was agreed by an overwhelming majority that rats were comrades. There were only four dissentients, the three dogs and the
85 cat, who was afterwards discovered to have voted on both sides. Major continued:]

"I have little more to say. I merely repeat, remember always your duty of en-
mity towards Man and all his ways. Whatever goes upon two legs is an enemy.
Whatever goes upon four legs, or has wings, is a friend. And remember also that,
90 in fighting against Man, we must not come to resemble him. Even when you have
conquered him, do not adopt his vices. No animal must ever live in a house, or
sleep in a bed, or wear clothes, or drink alcohol, or smoke tobacco, or touch
money, or engage in trade. All the habits of Man are evil. And, above all, no
animal must ever tyrannize over his own kind. Weak or strong, clever or simple,
95 we are all brothers. No animal must ever kill any other animal. All animals are
equal.

"And now, comrades, I will tell you about my dream of last night. I cannot
describe that dream to you. It was a dream of the earth as it will be when Man has
vanished. But it reminded me of something that I had long forgotten. Many years
100 ago, when I was a little pig, my mother and the other sows used to sing an old
song of which they knew only the tune and the first three words. I had known that
tune in my infancy, but it had long since passed out of my mind. Last night,
however, it came back to me in my dream. And what is more, the words of the
song also came back—words, I am certain, which were sung by the animals of
105 long ago and have been lost to memory for generations. I will sing you that song
now, comrades. I am old and my voice is hoarse, but, when I have taught you the
tune, you can sing it better for yourselves. It is called 'Beasts of England'."

Old Major cleared his throat and began to sing. As he had said, his voice was
hoarse, but he sang well enough, and it was a stirring tune, something between
110 "Clementine" and "La Cucaracha". The words ran:

Beasts of England, beasts of Ireland,
Beasts of every land and clime,
Hearken to my joyful tidings
Of the golden future time.

115 *Soon or late the day is coming,*
Tyrant Man shall be o'erthrown,
And the fruitful fields of England
Shall be trod by beasts alone.

Rings shall vanish from our noses,
120 *And the harness from our back,*
Bit and spur shall rust forever,
Cruel whips no more shall crack.

Riches more than mind can picture,
Wheat and barley, oats and hay,
125 *Clover, beans, and mangel-wurzels*
Shall be ours upon that day.

Bright will shine the fields of England,
Purer shall its waters be,
Sweeter yet shall blow its breezes
130 *On the day that sets us free.*

For that day we all must labour,
Though we die before it break;
Cows and horses, geese and turkeys,
All must toil for freedom's sake.

135 *Beasts of England, beasts of Ireland,*
Beasts of every land and clime,
Hearken well and spread my tidings
Of the golden future time.

From *Animal Farm* by George Orwell. (1945)

Edgar Allan Poe

37 The Black Cat

For the most wild, yet most homely narrative which I am about to pen, I neither
expect nor solicit belief. Mad indeed would I be to expect it, in a case where my
very senses reject their own evidence. Yet, mad am I not—and very surely do I
not dream. But to-morrow I die, and to-day I would unburden my soul. My
5 immediate purpose is to place before the world, plainly, succinctly, and without
comment, a series of mere household events. In their consequences, these events
have terrified—have tortured—have destroyed me. Yet I will not attempt to
expound them. To me, they have presented little but horror—to many they will
seem less terrible than *baroques*. Hereafter, perhaps, some intellect may be found
10 which will reduce my phantasm to the commonplace—some intellect more calm,
more logical, and far less excitable than my own, which will perceive, in the
circumstances I detail with awe, nothing more than an ordinary succession of
very natural causes and effects.

From my infancy I was noted for the docility and humanity of my disposition.
15 My tenderness of heart was even so conspicuous as to make me the jest of my
companions. I was especially fond of animals, and was indulged by my parents
with a great variety of pets. With these I spent most of my time, and never was so
happy as when feeding and caressing them. This peculiarity of character grew
with my growth, and, in my manhood, I derived from it one of my principal
20 sources of pleasure. To those who have cherished an affection for a faithful and
sagacious dog, I need hardly be at the trouble of explaining the nature or the
intensity of the gratification thus derivable. There is something in the unselfish
and self-sacrificing love of a brute, which goes directly to the heart of him who
has had frequent occasion to test the paltry friendship and gossamer fidelity of
25 mere *Man*.

I married early, and was happy to find in my wife a disposition not uncon-
genial with my own. Observing my partiality for domestic pets, she lost no
opportunity of procuring those of the most agreeable kind. We had birds, goldfish, a fine dog, rabbits, a small monkey, and *a cat*.
30 This latter was a remarkably large and beautiful animal, entirely black, and
sagacious to an astonishing degree. In speaking of his intelligence, my wife, who
at heart was not a little tinctured with superstition, made frequent allusion to the
ancient popular notion, which regarded all black cats as witches in disguise. Not
that she was ever *serious* upon this point—and I mention the matter at all for no
35 better reason than that it happens, just now, to be remembered.

Pluto—this was the cat's name—was my favourite pet and playmate. I alone fed
him, and he attended me wherever I went about the house. It was even with
difficulty that I could prevent him from following me through the streets.

Our friendship lasted, in this manner, for several years, during which my general
40 temperament and character—through the instrumentality of the fiend Intem-
perance—had (I blush to confess it) experienced a radical alteration for the worse.

I grew, day by day, more moody, more irritable, more regardless of the feelings of others. I suffered myself to use intemperate language to my wife. At length, I even offered her personal violence. My pets, of course, were made to feel the
45 change in my disposition. I not only neglected, but ill-used them. For Pluto, however, I still retained sufficient regard to restrain me from maltreating him, as I made no scruple of maltreating the rabbits, the monkey, or even the dog, when by accident, or through affection, they came in my way. But my disease grew upon me—for what disease is like alcohol?—and at length even Pluto, who was now
50 becoming old, and consequently somewhat peevish—even Pluto began to experience the effects of my ill-temper.

One night, returning home, much intoxicated, from one of my haunts about town, I fancied that the cat avoided my presence. I seized him; when, in his fright at my violence, he inflicted a slight wound upon my hand with his teeth.
55 The fury of a demon instantly possessed me. I knew myself no longer. My original soul seemed, at once, to take its flight from my body; and a more than fiendish malevolence, gin-nurtured, thrilled every fibre of my frame. I took from my waistcoat pocket a pen-knife, opened it, grasped the poor beast by the throat, and deliberately cut one of its eyes from the socket! I blush, I burn, I shudder,
60 while I pen the damnable atrocity.

When reason returned with the morning—when I had slept off the fumes of the night's debauch—I experienced a sentiment half of horror, half of remorse, for the crime of which I had been guilty; but it was, at best, a feeble and equivocal feeling, and the soul remained untouched. I again plunged into excess, and soon
65 drowned in wine all memory of the deed.

In the meantime the cat slowly recovered. The socket of the lost eye presented, it is true, a frightful appearance, but he no longer appeared to suffer any pain. He went about the house as usual, but, as might be expected, fled in extreme terror at my approach. I had so much of my old heart left, as to be at first grieved
70 by this evident dislike on the part of a creature which had once so loved me. But this feeling soon gave place to irritation. And then came, as if to my final and irrevocable overthrow, the spirit of PERVERSENESS. Of this spirit philosophy takes no account. Yet I am not more sure that my soul lives, than I am that perverseness is one of the primitive impulses of the human heart—one of the indivisible pri-
75 mary faculties, or sentiments, which give direction to the character of man. Who has not, a hundred times, found himself committing a vile or a silly action, for no other reason than because he knows he should *not?* Have we not a perpetual inclination, in the teeth of our best judgment, to violate that which is *Law,* merely because we understand it to be such? This spirit of perverseness, I say,
80 came to my final overthrow. It was this unfathomable longing of the soul *to vex itself*—to offer violence to its own nature—to do wrong for the wrong's sake only—that urged me to continue and finally to consummate the injury I had inflicted upon the unoffending brute. One morning, in cool blood, I slipped a noose about its neck and hung it to the limb of a tree—hung it with the tears
85 streaming from my eyes, and with the bitterest remorse at my heart—hung it *because* I knew that it had loved me, and *because* I felt it had given me no reason of offence—hung it *because* I knew that in so doing I was committing a sin—a deadly

sin that would so jeopardise my immortal soul as to place it—if such a thing were possible—even beyond the reach of the infinite mercy of the Most Merciful and Most Terrible God.

90 On the night of the day on which this cruel deed was done, I was aroused from sleep by the cry of 'Fire!' The curtains of my bed were in flames. The whole house was blazing. It was with great difficulty that my wife, a servant, and myself, made our escape from the conflagration. The destruction was complete. My entire worldly wealth was swallowed up, and I resigned myself thenceforward to despair.

95 I am above the weakness of seeking to establish a sequence of cause and effect between the disaster and the atrocity. But I am detailing a chain of facts, and wish not to leave even a possible link imperfect. On the day succeeding the fire, I visited the ruins. The walls, with one exception, had fallen in. This exception was found in a compartment wall, not very thick, which stood about the middle of the house, and against which had rested the head of my bed. The plastering had here, in great measure, resisted the action of the fire—a fact which I attributed to its having been recently spread. About this wall a dense crowd were collected, and many persons seemed to be examining a particular portion of it with very minute and eager attention. The words 'strange!' 'singular!' and other similar expressions, excited my curiosity. I approached and saw, as if graven in bas-relief upon the white surface, the figure of a gigantic *cat*. The impression was given with an accuracy truly marvellous. There was a rope about the animal's neck.

110 When I first beheld this apparition—for I could scarcely regard it as less—my wonder and my terror were extreme. But at length reflection came to my aid. The cat, I remembered, had been hung in a garden adjacent to the house. Upon the alarm of fire, this garden had been immediately filled by the crowd—by some one of whom the animal must have been cut from the tree and thrown, through an open window, into my chamber. This had probably been done with the view of arousing me from sleep. The falling of other walls had compressed the victim of my cruelty into the substance of the freshly-spread plaster; the lime of which, with the flames and the *ammonia* from the carcass, had then accomplished the portraiture as I saw it.

120 Although I thus readily accounted to my reason, if not altogether to my conscience, for the startling fact just detailed, it did not the less fail to make a deep impression upon my fancy. For months I could not rid myself of the phantasm of the cat; and, during this period, there came back into my spirit a half-sentiment that seemed, but was not, remorse. I went so far as to regret the loss of the animal, and to look about me, among the vile haunts which I now habitually frequented, for another pet of the same species, and of somewhat similar appearance, with which to supply its place.

One night as I sat, half-stupefied, in a den of more than infamy, my attention was suddenly drawn to some black object, reposing upon the head of one of the immense hogsheads of gin, or of rum, which constituted the chief furniture of the apartment. I had been looking steadily at the top of this hogshead for some minutes, and what now caused me surprise was the fact that I had not sooner perceived the object thereupon. I approached it, and touched it with my hand.

It was a black cat—a very large one—fully as large as Pluto, and closely
135 resembling him in every respect but one. Pluto had not a white hair upon any
portion of his body; but this cat had a large, although indefinite, splotch of white,
covering nearly the whole region of the breast.

Upon my touching him, he immediately arose, purred loudly, rubbed against
my hand, and appeared delighted with my notice. This, then, was the very creature
140 of which I was in search. I at once offered to purchase it of the landlord; but this
person made no claim to it—knew nothing of it—had never seen it before.

I continued my caresses, and when I prepared to go home, the animal evinced a
disposition to accompany me. I permitted it to do so; occasionally stooping and
patting it as I proceeded. When it reached the house it domesticated itself at once,
145 and became immediately a great favourite with my wife.

For my own part, I soon found a dislike to it arising within me. This was just
the reverse of what I had anticipated; but—I know not how or why it was—its
evident fondness for myself rather disgusted and annoyed me. By slow degrees,
these feelings of disgust and annoyance rose into the bitterness of hatred. I avoided
150 the creature; a certain sense of shame, and the remembrance of my former deed of
cruelty, preventing me from physically abusing it. I did not, for some weeks,
strike, or otherwise violently ill-use it; but gradually—very gradually—I came to
look upon it with unutterable loathing, and to flee silently from its odious
presence, as from the breath of a pestilence.
155 What added, no doubt, to my hatred of the beast, was the discovery, on the
morning after I brought it home, that, like Pluto, it also had been deprived of
one of its eyes. This circumstance, however, only endeared it to my wife, who,
as I have already said, possessed, in a high degree, that humanity of feeling which
had once been my distinguishing trait, and the source of many of my simplest and
160 purest pleasures.

With my aversion to this cat, however, its partiality for myself seemed to
increase. It followed my footsteps with a pertinacity which it would be difficult to
make the reader comprehend. Whenever I sat, it would crouch beneath my chair,
or spring upon my knees, covering me with its loathsome caresses. If I arose to
165 walk, it would get between my feet, and thus nearly throw me down, or, fastening
its long and sharp claws in my dress, clamber, in this manner, to my breast. At
such times, although I longed to destroy it with a blow, I was yet withheld from
so doing, partly by a memory of my former crime, but chiefly—let me confess it
at once—by absolute *dread* of the beast.
170 This dread was not exactly a dread of physical evil—and yet I should be at a
loss how otherwise to define it. I am almost ashamed to own—yes, even in this
felon's cell, I am almost ashamed to own—that the terror and horror with which
the animal inspired me, had been heightened by one of the merest chimeras it
would be possible to conceive. My wife had called my attention, more than once,
175 to the character of the mark of white hair, of which I have spoken, and which
constituted the sole visible difference between the strange beast and the one I had
destroyed. The reader will remember that this mark, although large, had been
originally very indefinite; but, by slow degrees—degrees nearly imperceptible,
and which for a long time my reason struggled to reject as fanciful—it had, at

180 length, assumed a rigorous distinctness of outline. It was now the representation
of an object that I shudder to name—and for this, above all, I loathed, and dread-
ed, and would have rid myself of the monster *had I dared*—it was now, I say, the
image of a hideous—of a ghastly thing—of the GALLOWS!—oh, mournful and
terrible engine of horror and of crime—of agony and of death!

185 And now was I indeed wretched beyond the wretchedness of mere humanity.
And *a brute beast*—whose fellow I had contemptuously destroyed—*a brute beast* to
work out for *me*—for me, a man, fashioned in the image of the High God—so
much of insufferable woe! Alas! neither by day nor by night knew I the blessing
of rest any more! During the former the creature left me no moment alone; and,
190 in the latter, I started, hourly, from dreams of unutterable fear, to find the hot
breath of *the thing* upon my face, and its vast weight—an incarnate nightmare that
I had no power to shake off—incumbent eternally upon my *heart*!

Beneath the pressure of torments such as these, the feeble remnant of the good
within me succumbed. Evil thoughts became my sole intimates—the darkest and
195 most evil of thoughts. The moodiness of my usual temper increased to hatred of
all things and of all mankind; while, from the sudden, frequent, and ungovernable
outbursts of a fury to which I now blindly abondoned myself, my uncomplaining
wife, alas! was the most usual and the most patient of sufferers.

One day she accompanied me, upon some household errand, into the cellar of
200 the old building which our poverty compelled us to inhabit. The cat followed me
down the steep stairs, and, nearly throwing me headlong, exasperated me to
madness. Uplifting an axe, and forgetting, in my wrath, the childish dread which
had hitherto stayed my hand, I aimed a blow at the animal which, of course,
would have proved instantly fatal had it descended as I wished. But this blow
205 was arrested by the hand of my wife. Goaded, by the interference, into a rage
more than demoniacal, I withdrew my arm from her grasp, and buried the axe in
her brain. She fell dead upon the spot, without a groan.

This hideous murder accomplished, I set myself forthwith, and with entire
deliberation, to the task of concealing the body. I knew that I could not remove
210 it from the house, either by day or by night, without the risk of being observed
by the neighbours. Many projects entered my mind. At one period I thought of
cutting the corpse into minute fragments and destroying them by fire. At another,
I resolved to dig a grave for it in the floor of the cellar. Again, I deliberated about
casting it into the well in the yard—about packing it in a box, as if merchandise,
215 with the usual arrangements, and so getting a porter to take it from the house.
Finally I hit upon what I considered a far better expedient than either of these.
I determined to wall it up in the cellar—as the monks of the Middle Ages are
recorded to have walled up their victims.

For a purpose such as this the cellar was well adapted. Its walls were loosely
220 constructed, and had lately been plastered throughout with a rough plaster,
which the dampness of the atmosphere had prevented from hardening. Moreover, in one of the walls was a projection, caused by a false chimney, or fire-place,
that had been filled up and made to resemble the rest of the cellar. I made no doubt
that I could readily displace the bricks at this point, insert the corpse, and wall the
225 whole up as before, so that no eye could detect anything suspicious.

And in this calculation I was not deceived. By means of a crowbar I easily dislodged the bricks, and, having carefully deposited the body against the inner wall, I propped it in that position, while, with little trouble, I relaid the whole structure as it originally stood. Having procured mortar, sand, and hair, with
230 every possible precaution, I prepared a plaster which could not be distinguished from the old, and with this I very carefully went over the new brickwork. When I had finished, I felt satisfied that all was right. The wall did not present the slightest appearance of having been disturbed. The rubbish on the floor was picked up with the minutest care. I looked around triumphantly, and said to
235 myself, 'Here at least, then, my labour has not been in vain.'

My next step was to look for the beast which had been the cause of so much wretchedness; for I had, at length, firmly resolved to put it to death. Had I been able to meet with it at the moment, there could have been no doubt of its fate; but it appeared that the crafty animal had been alarmed at the violence of my previous
240 anger, and forbore to present itself in my present mood. It is impossible to describe, or to imagine, the deep, the blissful sense of relief which the absence of the detested creature occasioned in my bosom. It did not make its appearance during the night—and thus for one night at least, since its introduction into the house I soundly and tranquilly slept; aye, *slept* even with the burden of murder upon
245 my soul!

The second and the third day passed, and still my tormentor came not. Once again I breathed as a free man. The monster, in terror, had fled the premises for ever! I should behold it no more! My happiness was supreme! The guilt of my dark deed disturbed me but little. Some few inquiries had been made, but these
250 had been readily answered. Even a search had been instituted—but of course nothing was to be discovered. I looked upon my future felicity as secured.

Upon the fourth day of the assassination, a party of the police came, very unexpectedly, into the house, and proceeded again to make rigorous investigation of the premises. Secure, however, in the inscrutability of my place of concealment,
255 I felt no embarrassment whatever. The officers bade me accompany them in their search. They left no nook or corner unexplored. At length, for the third or fourth time, they descended into the cellar. I quivered not in a muscle. My heart beat calmly as that of one who slumbers in innocence. I walked the cellar from end to end. I folded my arms upon my bosom, and roamed easily to and fro. The police
260 were thoroughly satisfied, and prepared to depart. The glee at my heart was too strong to be restrained. I burned to say if but one word, by way of triumph, and to render doubly sure their assurance of my guiltlessness.

'Gentlemen,' I said at last, as the party ascended the steps, 'I delight to have allayed your suspicions. I wish you all health, and a little more courtesy. By-the-
265 bye, gentlemen, this—this is a very well-constructed house.' (In the rabid desire to say something easily, I scarcely knew what I uttered at all.) 'I may say an *excellently* well-constructed house. These walls—are you going, gentlemen?—these walls are solidly put together'; and here, through the mere frenzy of bravado, I rapped heavily, with a cane which I held in my hand, upon that very portion of
270 the brickwork behind which stood the corpse of the wife of my bosom.

But may God shield and deliver me from the fangs of the Arch-Fiend! No sooner had the reverberation of my blows sunk into silence, than I was answered by a voice from within the tomb!—by a cry, at first muffled and broken, like the sobbing of a child, and then quickly swelling into one long, loud, and continuous
275 scream, utterly anomalous and inhuman—a howl—a wailing shriek, half of horror and half of triumph, such as might have arisen only out of hell, conjointly from the throats of the damned in their agony and of the demons that exult in the damnation.

Of my own thoughts it is folly to speak. Swooning, I staggered to the opposite
280 wall. For one instant the party upon the stairs remained motionless, through extremity of terror and of awe. In the next, a dozen stout arms were toiling at the wall. It fell bodily. The corpse, already greatly decayed and clotted with gore stood erect before the eyes of the spectators. Upon its head, with red extended mouth and solitary eye of fire, sat the hideous beast whose craft had seduced me
285 into murder, and whose informing voice had consigned me to the hangman. I had walled the monster up within the tomb!

From *Tales* by Edgar Allan Poe. (1843)

Irwin Shaw

38 The Girls in Their Summer Dresses

Fifth Avenue was shining in the sun when they left the Brevoort. The sun was warm, even though it was February, and everything looked like Sunday morning —the buses and the well-dressed people walking slowly in couples and the quiet buildings with the windows closed.

5 Michael held Frances' arm tightly as they walked toward Washington Square in the sunlight. They walked lightly, almost smiling, because they had slept late and had a good breakfast and it was Sunday. Michael unbuttoned his coat and let it flap around him in the mild wind.

"Look out," Frances said as they crossed Eighth Street. "You'll break your
10 neck."

Michael laughed and Frances laughed with him.

"She's not so pretty," Frances said. "Anyway, not pretty enough to take a chance of breaking your neck."

Michael laughed again. "How did you know I was looking at her?"

15 Frances cocked her head to one side and smiled at her husband under the brim of her hat. "Mike, darling," she said.

"O.K.," he said. "Excuse me."

Frances patted his arm lightly and pulled him along a little faster toward Washington Square. "Let's not see anybody all day," she said. "Let's just hang
20 around with each other. You and me. We're always up to the neck with people, drinking their Scotch or drinking our Scotch; we only see each other in bed. I want to go out with my husband all day long. I want him to talk only to me and listen only to me."

"What's to stop us?" Michael asked.

25 "The Stevensons. They want us to drop by around one o'clock and they'll drive us into the country."

"The cunning Stevensons," Mike said. "Transparent. They can whistle. They can go driving in the country by themselves."

"Is it a date?"

30 "It's a date."

Frances leaned over and kissed him on the tip of the ear.

"Darling," Michael said, "this is Fifth Avenue."

"Let me arrange a program," Frances said. "A planned Sunday in New York for a young couple with money to throw away."

35 "Go easy."

"First let's go the Metropolitan Museum of Art," Frances suggested, because Michael had said during the week he wanted to go. "I haven't been there in three years and there're at least ten pictures I want to see again. Then we can take the bus down to Radio City and watch them skate. And later we'll go down to
40 Cavanagh's and get a steak as big as a blacksmith's apron, with a bottle of wine,

and after that there's a French picture at the Filmarte that everybody says—say, are you listening to me?"

"Sure," he said. He took his eyes off the hatless girl with the dark hair, cut dancer-style like a helmet, who was walking past him.

45   "That's the program for the day," Frances said flatly. "Or maybe you'd just rather walk up and down Fifth Avenue."

"No," Michael said. "Not at all."

"You always look at other women," Frances said. "Everywhere. Every damned place we go."

50   "Now, darling," Michael said, "I look at everything. God gave me eyes and I look at women and men and subway excavations and moving pictures and the little flowers of the field. I casually inspect the universe."

"You ought to see the look in your eye," Frances said, "as you casually inspect the universe on Fifth Avenue."

55   "I'm a happily married man." Michael pressed her elbow tenderly. "Example for the whole twentieth century—Mr. and Mrs. Mike Loomis. Hey, let's have a drink," he said, stopping.

"We just had breakfast."

"Now listen, darling," Mike said, choosing his words with care, "it's a nice
60 day and we both felt good and there's no reason why we have to break it up. Let's have a nice Sunday."

"All right. I don't know why I started this. Let's drop it. Let's have a good time."

They joined hands consciously and walked without talking among the baby
65 carriages and the old Italian men in their Sunday clothes and the young women with Scotties in Washington Square Park.

"At least once a year everyone should go to the Metropolitan Museum of Art," Frances said after a while, her tone a good imitation of the tone she had used at breakfast and at the beginning of their walk. "And it's nice on Sunday. There're a
70 lot of people looking at the pictures and you get the feeling maybe Art isn't on the decline in New York City after all—"

"I want to tell you something," Michael said very seriously. "I have not touched another woman. Not once. In all the five years."

"All right," Frances said.

75   "You believe that, don't you?"

"All right."

They walked between the crowded benches under the scrubby city-park trees.

"I try not to notice it," Frances said, "but I feel rotten inside, in my stomach, when we pass a woman and you look at her and I see that look in your eye and
80 that's the way you looked at me the first time. In Alice Maxwell's house. Standing there in the living room, next to the radio, with a green hat on and all those people."

"I remember the hat," Michael said.

"The same look," Frances said. "And it makes me feel bad. It makes me feel
85 terrible."

"Sh-h-h, please, darling, sh-h-h."

"I think I would like a drink now," Frances said.

They walked over to a bar on Eighth Street, not saying anything, Michael automatically helping her over curbstones and guiding her past automobiles.
90 They sat near a window in the bar and the sun streamed in and there was a small, cheerful fire in the fireplace. A little Japanese waiter came over and put down some pretzels and smiled happily at them.

"What do you order after breakfast?" Michael asked.

"Brandy, I suppose," Frances said.

95 "Courvoisier," Michael told the waiter. "Two Courvoisiers."

The waiter came with the glasses and they sat drinking the brandy in the sunlight. Michael finished half his and drank a little water.

"I look at women," he said. "Correct. I don't say it's wrong or right. I look at them. If I pass them on the street and I don't look at them, I'm fooling you, I'm
100 fooling myself."

"You look at them as though you want them," Frances said, playing with her brandy glass. "Every one of them."

"In a way," Michael said, speaking softly and not to his wife, "in a way that's true. I don't do anything about it, but it's true."

105 "I know it. That's why I feel bad."

"Another brandy," Michael called. "Waiter, two more brandies."

He sighed and closed his eyes and rubbed them gently with his finger tips. "I love the way women look. One of the things I like about New York is the battalions of women. When I first came to New York from Ohio that was the
110 first thing I noticed, the million wonderful women, all over the city. I walked around with my heart in my throat."

"A kid," Frances said. "That's a kid's feeling."

"Guess again," Michael said. "Guess again. I'm older now, I'm a man getting near middle age, putting on a little fat and I still love to walk along Fifth Avenue
115 at three o'clock on the east side of the street between Fiftieth and Fifty-seventh Streets. They're all out then, shopping, in their furs and their crazy hats, everything all concentrated from all over the world into seven blocks — the best furs, the best clothes, the handsomest women, out to spend money and feeling good about it."

120 The Japanese waiter put the two drinks down, smiling with great happiness.

"Everything is all right?" he asked.

"Everything is wonderful," Michael said.

"If it's just a couple of fur coats," Frances said, and forty-five-dollar hats—"

"It's not the fur coats. Or the hats. That's just the scenery for that particular
125 kind of woman. Understand," he said, "you don't have to listen to this."

"I want to listen."

"I like the girls in the offices. Neat, with their eyeglasses, smart, chipper, knowing what everything is about. I like the girls on Forty-fourth Street at lunchtime, the actresses, all dressed up on nothing a week. I like the salesgirls in
130 the stores, paying attention to you first because you're a man, leaving lady customers waiting. I got all this stuff accumulated in me because I've been thinking about it for ten years and now you've asked for it and here it is."

"Go ahead," Frances said.

"When I think of New York City, I think of all the girls on parade in the city.
135 I don't know whether it's something special with me or whether every man in the
city walks around with the same feeling inside him, but I feel as though I'm at a
picnic in this city. I like to sit near the women in the theaters, the famous beauties
who've taken six hours to get ready and look it. And the young girls at the
football games, with their red cheeks, and when the warm weather comes, the
140 girls in their summer dresses." He finished his drink. "That's the story."

Frances finished her drink and swallowed two or three times extra. "You say
you love me?"

"I love you."

"I'm pretty, too," Frances said. "As pretty as any of them."
145 "You're beautiful," Michael said.

"I'm good for you," Frances said, pleading. "I've made a good wife, a good
housekeeper, a good friend. I'd do any damn thing for you."

"I know," Michael said. He put his hand out and grasped hers.

"You'd like to be free to—" Frances said.
150 "Sh-h-h."

"Tell the truth." She took her hand away from under his.

Michael flicked the edge of his glass with his finger. "O.K.," he said gently.
"Sometimes I feel I would like to be free."

"Well," Frances said, "any time you say."
155 "Don't be foolish." Michael swung his chair around to her side of the table
and patted her thigh.

She began to cry silently into her handkerchief, bent over just enough so that
nobody in the bar would notice. "Someday," she said, crying, "you're going to
make a move."
160 Michael didn't say anything. He sat watching the bartender slowly peel a
lemon.

"Aren't you?" Frances asked harshly. "Come on, tell me. Talk. Aren't you?"

"Maybe," Michael said. He moved his chair back again. "How the hell do I
know?"
165 "You know," Frances persisted. "Don't you?"

"Yes," Michael said after a while, "I know."

Frances stopped crying then. Two or three snuffles into the handkerchief and
she put it away and her face didn't tell anything to anybody. "At least do me one
favor," she said.
170 "Sure."

"Stop talking about how pretty this woman is or that one. Nice eyes, nice
breasts, a pretty figure, good voice." She mimicked his voice. "Keep it to yourself. I'm not interested."

Michael waved to the waiter. "I'll keep it to myself," he said.
175 Frances flicked the corners of her eyes. "Another brandy," she told the waiter.

"Two," Michael said.

"Yes, ma'am, yes, sir," said the waiter, backing away.

Frances regarded Michael coolly across the table. "Do you want me to call the Stevensons?" she asked. "It'll be nice in the country."

180   "Sure," Michael said. "Call them."

She got up from the table and walked across the room toward the telephone. Michael watched her walk, thinking what a pretty gal, what nice legs.

From *Mixed Company* by Irwin Shaw. (1952)

Alan Sillitoe

39 The Match

Bristol City had played Notts County and won. Right from the kick-off Lennox had somehow known that Notts was going to lose, not through any prophetic knowledge of each homeplayer's performance, but because he himself, a spectator, hadn't been feeling in top form. One-track pessimism had made him godly enough
5 to inform his mechanic friend Fred Iremonger who stood by his side: 'I knew they'd bleddy-well lose, all the time.'

Towards the end of the match, when Bristol scored their winning goal, the players could only just be seen, and the ball was a roll of mist being kicked about the field. Advertising boards above the stands, telling of pork-pies, ales, whisky,
10 cigarettes and other delights of Saturday night, faded with the afternoon visibility.

They stood in the one-and-threes, Lennox trying to fix his eyes on the ball, to follow each one of its erratic well-kicked movements, but after ten minutes going from blurred player to player he gave it up and turned to look at the spectators
15 massed in the rising stands that reached out in a wide arc on either side and joined dimly way out over the pitch. This proving equally futile he rubbed a clenched hand into his weak eyes and squeezed them tight, as if pain would give them more strength. Useless. All it produced was a mass of grey squares dancing before his open lids, so that when they cleared his sight was no better than before. Such
20 an affliction made him appear more phlegmatic at a football match than Fred and most of the others round about, who spun rattles, waved hats and scarves, opened their throats wide to each fresh vacillation in the game.

During his temporary blindness the Notts' forwards were pecking and weaving around the Bristol goal and a bright slam from one of them gave rise to a false
25 alarm, an indecisive rolling of cheers roofed in by a grey heavy sky. 'What's up?' Lennox asked Fred. 'Who scored? Anybody?'

Fred was a younger man, recently married, done up in his Saturday afternoon best of sports coat, gaberdine trousers and rain-mac, dark hair sleeked back with oil. 'Not in a month of Sundays,' he laughed, 'but they had a bleddy good try,
30 I'll tell you that.'

By the time Lennox had focused his eyes once more on the players the battle had moved to Notts' goal and Bristol were about to score. He 'saw a player running down the field, hearing in his imagination the thud of boots on damp introdden turf. A knot of adversaries dribbled out in a line and straggled behind him at
35 a trot. Suddenly the man with the ball spurted forward, was seen to be clear of everyone as if, in a second of time that hadn't existed to any spectator or other player, he'd been catapulted into a hallowed untouchable area before the goal posts. Lennox's heart stopped beating. He peered between two oaken unmovable shoulders that, he thought with anger, had swayed in front purposely to stop him
40 seeing. The renegade centre-forward from the opposing side was seen, like a puppet worked by someone above the low clouds, to bring his leg back, lunge

out heavily with his booted foot. 'No,' Lennox had time to say. 'Get on to him you dozy sods. Don't let him get it in.'

From being an animal pacing within the prescribed area of his defended posts, the goalkeeper turned into a leaping ape, arms and legs outstretched, then became a mere stick that swung into a curve—and missed the ball as it sped to one side and lost itself in folds of net behind him.

The lull in the general noise seemed like silence for the mass of people packed about the field. Everyone had settled it in his mind that the match, as bad as it was, would be a draw, but now it was clear that Notts, the home team, had lost. A great roar of disappointment and joy, from the thirty-thousand spectators who hadn't realized that the star of Bristol City was so close, or who had expected a miracle from their own stars at the last moment, ran up the packed embankments, overflowing into streets outside where groups of people, startled at the sudden noise of an erupting mob, speculated as to which team had scored.

Fred was laughing wildly, jumping up and down, bellowing something between a cheer and a shout of hilarious anger, as if out to get his money's worth on the principle that an adverse goal was better than no goal at all. 'Would you believe it?' he called at Lennox. 'Would you believe it? Ninety-five thousand quid gone up like Scotch mist!'

Hardly knowing what he was doing Lennox pulled out a cigarette, lit it. 'It's no good,' he cursed, 'they've lost. They should have walked away with the game'—adding under his breath that he must get some glasses in order to see things better. His sight was now so bad that the line of each eye crossed and converged some distance in front of him. At the cinema he was forced down to the front row, and he was never the first to recognize a pal on the street. And it spelt ruination for any football match. He could remember being able to pinpoint each player's face, and distinguish every spectator around the field, yet he still persuaded himself that he had no need of glasses and that somehow his sight would begin to improve. A more barbed occurrence connected with such eyes was that people were beginning to call him Cock-eye. At the garage where he worked the men sat down to tea-break the other day, and because he wasn't in the room one of them said: 'Where's owd Cock-eye? 'Is tea'll get cold.'

'What hard lines,' Fred shouted, as if no one yet knew about the goal. 'Would you believe it?' The cheering and booing were beginning to die down.

'That goalie's a bloody fool,' Lennox swore, cap pulled low over his forehead. 'He couldn't even catch a bleeding cold.'

'It was dead lucky,' Fred put in reluctantly, 'they deserved it, I suppose'—simmering down now, the full force of the tragedy seeping through even to his newly wedded body and soul. 'Christ, I should have stayed at home with my missis. I'd bin warm there, I know that much. I might even have cut myself a chunk of hearthrug pie if I'd have asked her right!'

The laugh and wink were intended for Lennox, who was still in the backwater of his personal defeat. 'I suppose that's all you think on these days,' he said wryly ' ' Appen I do, but I don't get all that much of it, I can tell you.' It was obvious though that he got enough to keep him in good spirits at a cold and disappointing football match.

'Well.' Lennox pronounced, 'all that'll alter in a bit. You can bet on that.'

'Not if I know it,' Fred said with a broad smile. 'And I reckon it's better after a
90 bad match than if I didn't come to one.'

'You never said a truer word about bad,' Lennox said. He bit his lip with anger.
'Bloody team. They'd even lose at blow football.' A woman behind, swathed in a
thick woollen scarf coloured white and black like the Notts players, who had been
screaming herself hoarse in support of the home team all the afternoon was
95 almost in tears at the adverse goal. 'Foul! Foul! Get the dirty lot off the field.
Send 'em back to Bristol where they came from. Foul! Foul I tell yer.'

People all around were stamping feet dead from the cold, having for more than
an hour staved off its encroachment into their limbs by the hope of at least one
home-team win before Christmas. Lennox could hardly feel his, hadn't the will to
100 help them back to life, especially in face of an added force to the bitter wind, and
a goal that had been given away so easily. Movement on the pitch was now desultory, for there were only ten minutes of play left to go. The two teams knotted
up towards one goal, then spread out around an invisible ball, and moved down
the field again, back to the other with no decisive result. It seemed that both
105 teams had accepted the present score to be the final state of the game, as though
all effort had deserted their limbs and lungs.

'They're done for,' Lennox observed to Fred. People began leaving the ground,
making a way between those who were determined to see the game out to its
bitter end. Right up to the dull warbling blast of the final whistle the hard core of
110 optimists hoped for a miraculous revival in the worn-out players.

'I'm ready when yo' are,' Fred said.

'Suits me.' He threw his cigarette-end to the floor and, with a grimace of disappointment and disgust, made his way up the steps. At the highest point he
turned a last glance over the field, saw two players running and the rest standing
115 around in deepening mist—nothing doing—so went on down towards the
barriers. When they were on the road a great cheer rose behind, as a whistle blew
the signal for a mass rush to follow.

Lamps were already lit along the road, and bus queues grew quickly in semidarkness. Fastening up his mac Lennox hurried across the road. Fred lagged
120 behind, dodged a trolleybus that sloped up to the pavement edge like a man-
eating monster and carried off a crowd of people to the city-centre with blue
lights flickering from overhead wires. 'Well,' Lennox said when they came close,
'after that little lot I only hope the wife's got summat nice for my tea.'

'I can think of more than that to hope for,' Fred said. 'I'm not one to grumble
125 about my grub.'

' 'Course,' Lennox sneered, 'you're living on love. If you had Kit-E-Kat
shoved in front of you you'd say it was a good dinner.' They turned off by the
recruiting centre into the heart of the Meadows, an ageing suburb of black houses
and small factories. 'That's what yo' think,' Fred retorted, slightly offended yet
130 too full of hope to really mind. 'I'm just not one to grumble a lot about my snap,
that's all.'

'It wouldn't be any good if you was,' Lennox rejoined, 'but the grub's rotten
these days, that's the trouble. Either frozen, or in tins. Nowt natural. The bread's

enough to choke yer.' And so was the fog: weighed down by frost it lingered and
135 thickened, causing Fred to pull up his rain-mac collar. A man who came level
with them on the same side called out derisively: 'Did you ever see such a game?'

'Never in all my born days,' Fred replied.

'It's always the same though,' Lennox was glad to comment, 'the best players
are never on the field. I don't know what they pay 'em for.'

140 The man laughed at this sound logic. 'They'll 'appen get 'em on nex' wik.
That'll show 'em.'

'Let's hope so,' Lennox called out as the man was lost in the fog. 'It ain't a bad
team,' he added to Fred. But that wasn't what he was thinking. He remembered
how he had been up before the gaffer yesterday at the garage for clouting the
145 mash lad who had called him Cock-eye in front of the office-girl, and the manager
said that if it happened again he would get his cards. And now he wasn't sure that
he wouldn't ask for them anyway. He'd never lack a job, he told himself, knowing
his own worth and the sureness of his instinct when dissecting piston from
cylinder, camshaft and connecting-rod and searching among a thousand-and-one
150 possible faults before setting an engine bursting once more with life. A small boy
called from the doorway of a house: 'What's the score, mate?'

'They lost, two-one,' he said curtly, and heard a loud clear-sounding doorslam
as the boy ran in with the news. He walked with hands in pockets, and a
cigarette at the corner of his mouth so that ash occasionally fell on to his mac. The
155 smell of fish-and-chips came from a well-lit shop, making him feel hungry.

'No pictures for me tonight,' Fred was saying. 'I know the best place in
weather like this.' The Meadows were hollow with the clatter of boots behind
them, the muttering of voices hot in discussion about the lost match. Groups
gathered at each corner, arguing and teasing any girl that passed, lighted gas-
160 lamps a weakening ally in the fog. Lennox turned into an entry, where the cold
damp smell of backyards mingled with that of dustbins. They pushed open gates
to their separate houses.

'So long. See you tomorrow at the pub maybe.'

'Not tomorrow,' Fred answered, already at his back door. 'I'll have a job on
165 mending my bike. I'm going to gi' it a coat of enamel and fix in some new brake
blocks. I nearly got flattened by a bus the other day when they didn't work.'

The gate-latch clattered. 'All right then,' Lennox said, 'see you soon'—opening
the back door and going into his house.

He walked through the small living-room without speaking, took off his mac
170 in the parlour. 'You should mek a fire in there,' he said, coming out. 'It smells
musty. No wonder the clo'es go to pieces inside six months.' His wife sat by the
fire knitting from two balls of electric-blue wool in her lap. She was forty, the
same age as Lennox, but gone to a plainness and discontented fat, while he had
stayed thin and wiry from the same reason. Three children, the eldest a girl of
175 fourteen, were at the table finishing tea.

Mrs. Lennox went on knitting. 'I was going to make one today but I didn't
have time.'

'Iris can mek one,' Lennox said, sitting down at the table.

The girl looked up. 'I haven't finished my tea yet, our dad.' The wheedling
180 tone of her voice made him angry. 'Finish it later,' he said with a threatening look.
'The fire needs making now, so come on, look sharp and get some coal from the
cellar.'

She didn't move, sat there with the obstinacy of the young spoiled by a mother.
Lennox stood up. 'Don't let me have to tell you again.' Tears came into her eyes.
185 'Go on,' he shouted. 'Do as you're told.' He ignored his wife's plea to stop picking
on her and lifted his hand to settle her with a blow.

'All right, I'm going. Look'—she got up and went to the cellar door. So he sat
down again, his eyes roaming over the well-set table before him, holding his
hands tightly clenched beneath the cloth. 'What's for tea, then?'
190 His wife looked up again from her knitting. 'There's two kippers in the oven.'

He did not move, sat morosely fingering a knife and fork, 'Well?' he demanded.
'Do I have to wait all night for a bit o' summat t'eat?'

Quietly she took a plate from the oven and put it before him. Two brown kippers lay steaming across it. 'One of these days,' he said, pulling a long strip of
195 white flesh from the bone, 'we'll have a change.'

'That's the best I can do,' she said, her deliberate patience no way to stop his
grumbling—though she didn't know what else would. And the fact that he de-
tected it made things worse.

'I'm sure it is,' he retorted. The coal bucket clattered from the parlour where
200 the girl was making a fire. Slowly, he picked his kippers to pieces without eating
any. The other two children sat on the sofa watching him, not daring to talk.
On one side of his plate he laid bones; on the other, flesh. When the cat rubbed
against his leg he dropped pieces of fish for it on to the lino, and when he
considered that it had eaten enough he kicked it away with such force that its
205 head knocked against the sideboard. It leapt on to a chair and began to lick itself,
looking at him with green surprised eyes.

He gave one of the boys sixpence to fetch a *Football Guardian*. 'And be quick
about it,' he called after him. He pushed his plate away, and nodded towards the
mauled kippers. 'I don't want this, You'd better send somebody out for some
210 pastries. And mash some fresh tea,' he added as an afterthought, 'that pot's
stewed.'

He had gone too far. Why did he make Saturday afternoon such hell on earth?
Anger throbbed violently in her temples. Through the furious beating of her
heart she cried out: 'If you want some pastries you'll fetch 'em yourself. And
215 you'll mash your own tea as well.'

'When a man goes to work all week he wants some tea,' he said, glaring at her.
Nodding at the boy: 'Send him out for some cakes.'

The boy had already stood up. 'Don't go. Sit down,' she said to him. 'Get 'em
yourself,' she retorted to her husband. 'The tea I've already put on the table's
220 good enough for anybody. There's nowt wrong wi' it at all, and then you carry
on like this. I suppose they lost at the match, because I can't think of any other
reason why you should have such a long face.'

He was shocked by such a sustained tirade, stood up to subdue her. 'You what?'
he shouted. 'What do you think you're on wi'?'

225 Her face turned a deep pink. 'You heard,' she called back. 'A few home truths might do you a bit of good.'

He picked up the plate of fish and, with exaggerated deliberation, threw it to the floor. 'There,' he roared. 'That's what you can do with your bleeding tea.'

'You're a lunatic,' she screamed. 'You're mental.'

230 He hit her once, twice, three times across the head, and knocked her to the ground. The little boy wailed, and his sister came running in from the parlour . . .

Fred and his young wife in the house next door heard a commotion through the thin walls. They caught the cadence of voices and shifting chairs, but didn't really

235 think anything amiss until the shriller climax was reached. 'Would you believe it?' Ruby said, slipping off Fred's knee and straightening her skirt. 'Just because Notts have lost again. I'm glad yo' aren't like that.'

Ruby was nineteen, plump like a pear not round like a pudding, already pregnant though they'd only been married a month. Fred held her back by the waist.

240 'I'm not so daft as to let owt like that bother me.'

She wrenched herself free. 'It's a good job you're not; because if you was I'd bosh you one.'

Fred sat by the fire with a bemused, Cheshire-cat grin on his face while Ruby was in the scullery getting them something to eat. The noise in the next house

245 had died down. After a slamming of doors and much walking to and fro outside Lennox's wife had taken the children, and left him for the last time.

From *The Loneliness Of The Long Distance Runner* by Alan Sillitoe. (1958)

Muriel Spark

40 You Should Have Seen the Mess

I am now more than glad that I did not pass into the Grammar School five years ago, although it was a disappointment at the time. I was always good at English, but not so good at the other subjects!!

I am glad that I went to the Secondary Modern School, because it was only
5 constructed the year before. Therefore, it was much more hygienic than the Grammar School. The Secondary Modern was light and airy, and the walls were painted with a bright, washable, gloss. One day, I was sent over to the Grammar School with a note for one of the teachers, and you should have seen the mess! The corridors were dusty, and I saw dust on the window ledges, which were
10 chipped. I saw into one of the classrooms. It was very untidy in there.

I am also glad that I did not go to the Grammar School, because of what it does to one's habits. This may appear to be a strange remark, at first sight. It is a good thing to have an education behind you, and I do not believe in ignorance, but I have had certain experiences, with educated people, since going out into
15 the world.

I am seventeen years of age, and left school two years ago last month. I had my A certificate for typing, so got my first job, as a junior, in a solicitor's office. Mum was pleased at this, and Dad said it was a first-class start, as it was an old-established firm. I must say that when I went for the interview I was surprised at the
20 windows, and the stairs up to the offices were also far from clean. There was a little waiting room, where some of the elements were missing from the gas fire, and the carpet on the floor was worn. However, Mr. Heygate's office, into which I was shown for the interview, was better. The furniture was old, but it was polished, and there was a good carpet, I will say that. The glass of the bookcase
25 was very clean.

I was to start on the Monday, so along I went. They took me to the general office, where there were two senior shorthand-typists, and a clerk, Mr. Gresham, who was for from smart in appearance. You should have seen the mess!! There was no floor covering whatsoever, and so dusty everywhere. There were shelves
30 all round the room, with old box files on them. The box files were falling to pieces, and all the old papers inside them were crumpled. The worst shock of all was the tea cups. It was my duty to make tea, mornings and afternoons. Miss Bewlay showed me where everything was kept. It was kept in an old orange box, and the cups were all cracked. There were not enough saucers to go round, etc. I will not
35 go into the facilities, but they were also far from hygienic. After three days, I told Mum, and she was upset, most of all about the cracked cups. We never keep a cracked cup, but throw it out, because those cracks can harbour germs. So Mum gave me my own cup to take to the office.

Then at the end of the week, when I got my salary, Mr. Heygate said, 'Well,
40 Lorna, what are you going to do with your first pay?' I did not like him saying this, and I nearly passed a comment, but I said, 'I don't know.' He said, 'What do

you do in the evenings, Lorna? Do you watch Telly?' I did take this as an insult, because we call it TV, and his remark made me out to be uneducated. I just stood, and did not answer, and he looked surprised. Next day, Saturday I told Mum
45 and Dad about the facilities, and we decided I should not go back to that job. Also, the desks in the general office were rickety. Dad was indignant, because Mr. Heygate's concern was flourishing, and he had letters after his name.

Everyone admires our flat, because Mum keeps it spotless, and Dad keeps doing things to it. He has done it up all over, and got permission from the
50 Council to re-modernise the kitchen. I well recall the Health Visitor remarking to Mum, 'You could eat off your floor, Mrs. Merrifield.' It is true that you could eat your lunch off Mum's floors, and any hour of the day or night you will find every corner spick and span.

Next, I was sent by the agency to a Publisher's for an interview, because of
55 being good at English. One look was enough!! My next interview was a success, and I am still at Low's Chemical Co. It is a modern block, with a quarter of an hour rest period, morning and afternoon. Mr. Marwood is very smart in appearance. He is well spoken, although he has not got a university education behind him. There is special lighting over the desks, and the typewriters are latest
60 models.

So I am happy at Low's. But I have met other people, of an educated type, in the past year, and it has opened my eyes. It so happened that I had to go to the Doctor's house, to fetch a prescription for my young brother, Trevor, when the epidemic was on. I rang the bell, and Mrs. Darby came to the door. She was
65 small, with fair hair, but too long, and a green maternity dress. But she was very nice to me. I had to wait in their living-room, and you should have seen the state it was in! There were broken toys on the carpet, and the ash trays were full up. There were contemporary pictures on the walls, but the furniture was not contemporary, but old-fashioned, with covers which were past standing up to
70 another wash, I should say. To cut a long story short, Dr. Darby and Mrs. Darby have always been very kind to me, and they meant everything for the best. Dr. Darby is also short and fair, and they have three children, a girl and a boy, and now a baby boy.

When I went that day for the prescription, Dr. Darby said to me, 'You look
75 pale, Lorna. It's the London atmosphere. Come on a picnic with us, in the car, on Saturday.' After that I went with the Darbys more and more. I liked them, but I did not like the mess, and it was a surprise. But I also kept in with them for the opportunity of meeting people, and Mum and Dad were pleased that I had made nice friends. So I did not say anything about the cracked lino, and the paint-
80 work all chipped. The children's clothes were very shabby for a doctor, and she changed them out of their school clothes when they came home from school, into those worn-out garments. Mum always kept us spotless to go out to play, and I do not like to say it, but those Darby children frequently looked like the Leary family, which the Council evicted from our block, as they were far from house-
85 proud.

One day, when I was there, Mavis (as I called Mrs. Darby by then) put her head out of the window, and shouted to the boy, 'John, stop peeing over the

cabbages at once. Pee on the lawn.' I did not know which way to look. Mum
would never say a word like that from the window, and I know for a fact that
90 Trevor would never pass water outside, not even bathing in the sea.

I went there usually at the weekends, but sometimes on weekdays, after supper.
They had an idea to make a match for me with a chemist's assistant, whom they
had taken up too. He was an orphan, and I do not say there was anything wrong
with that. But he was not accustomed to those little extras that I was. He was a
95 good-looking boy, I will say that. So I went once to a dance, and twice to the films
with him. To look at, he was quite clean in appearance. But there was only hot
water at the weekend at his place, and he said that a bath once a week was sufficient. Jim (as I called Dr. Darby by then) said it was sufficient also, and surprised
me. He did not have much money, and I do not hold that against him. But there
100 was no hurry for me, and I could wait for a man in a better position, so that I
would not miss those little extras. So he started going out with a girl from the
coffee bar, and did not come to the Darbys very much then.

There were plenty of boys at the office, but I will say this for the Darbys, they
had lots of friends coming and going, and they had interesting conversation,
105 although sometimes it gave me a surprise, and I did not know where to look.
And sometimes they had people who were very down and out, although there is
no need to be. But most of the guests were different, so it made a comparison
with the boys at the office, who were not so educated in their conversation.

Now it was near the time for Mavis to have her baby, and I was to come in at the
110 weekend, to keep an eye on the children, while the help had her day off. Mavis
did not go away to have her baby, but would have it at home, in their double bed,
as they did not have twin beds, although he was a Doctor. A girl I knew, in our
block, was engaged, but was let down, and even she had her baby in the labour
ward. I was sure the bedroom was not hygienic for having a baby, but I did not
115 mention it.

One day, after the baby boy came along, they took me in the car to the country
to see Jim's mother. The baby was put in a carry-cot at the back of the car. He
began to cry, and without a word of a lie, Jim said to him over his shoulder, 'Oh
shut your gob, you little bastard.' I did not know what to do, and Mavis was
120 smoking a cigarette. Dad would not dream of saying such a thing to Trevor or I.
When we arrived at Jim's mother's place, Jim said, 'It's a fourteenth-century
cottage, Lorna.' I could well believe it. It was very cracked and old, and it made
one wonder how Jim could let his old mother live in this tumble-down cottage,
as he was so good to everyone else. So Mavis knocked at the door, and the old
125 lady came. There was not much anyone could do to the inside. Mavis said, 'Isn't
it charming, Lorna?' If that was a joke, it was going too far. I said to the old Mrs.
Darby, 'Are you going to be re-housed?' but she did not understand this, and I
explained how you have to apply to the Council, and keep at them. But it was
funny that the Council had not done something already, when they go round
130 condemning. Then old Mrs. Darby said, 'My dear, I shall be re-housed in the
Grave.' I did not know where to look.

There was a carpet hanging on the wall, which I think was there to hide a damp
spot. She had a good TV set, I will say that. But some of the walls were bare brick,

and the facilities were outside, through the garden. The furniture was far from
135 new.

One Saturday afternoon, as I happened to go to the Darbys, they were just
going off to a film, and they took me too. It was the Curzon, and afterwards we
went to a flat in Curzon Street. It was a very clean block, I will say that, and there
were good carpets at the entrance. The couple there had contemporary furniture,
140 and they also spoke about music. It was a nice place, but there was no Welfare
Centre to the flats, where people could go for social intercourse, advice and
guidance. But they were well-spoken, and I met Willy Morley, who was an artist.
Willy sat beside me, and we had a drink. He was young, dark, with a dark shirt,
so one could not see right away if he was clean. Soon after this, Jim said to me,
145 'Willy wants to paint you, Lorna. But you'd better ask your Mum.' Mum said it
was all right if he was a friend of the Darbys.

I can honestly say that Willy's place was the most unhygienic place I have seen
in my life. He said I had an unusual type of beauty, which he must capture. This
was when we came back to his place from the restaurant. The light was very dim,
150 but I could see the bed had not been made, and the sheets were far from clean.
He said he must paint me, but I told Mavis I did not like to go back there. 'Don't
you like Willy?' she asked. I could not deny that I liked Willy, in a way. There
was something about him, I will say that. Mavis said, 'I hope he hasn't been
making a pass at you, Lorna.' I said he had not done so, which was almost true,
155 because he did not attempt to go to the full extent. It was always unhygienic
when I went to Willy's place, and I told him so once, but he said, 'Lorna, you are
a joy.' He had a nice way, and he took me out in his car, which was a good one,
but dirty inside, like his place. Jim said one day, 'He has pots of money, Lorna,'
and Mavis said, 'You might make a man of him, as he is keen on you.' They
160 always said Willy came from a good family.

But I saw that one could not do anything with him. He would not change his
shirt very often, or get clothes, but he went around like a tramp, lending people
money, as I have seen with my own eyes. His place was in a terrible mess, with the
empty bottles, and laundry in the corner. He gave me several gifts over the
165 period, which I took, as he would have only given them away, but he never tried
to go to the full extent. He never painted my portrait, as he was painting fruit on
a table all that time, and they said his pictures were marvellous, and thought
Willy and I were getting married.

One night, when I went home, I was upset as usual, after Willy's place. Mum
170 and Dad had gone to bed, and I looked round our kitchen which is done in
primrose and white. Then I went into the living-room, where Dad has done one
wall in a patterned paper, deep rose and white, and the other walls pale rose, with
white wood-work. The suite is new, and Mum keeps everything beautiful. So it
came to me, all of a sudden, what a fool I was, going with Willy. I agree to
175 equality, but as to me marrying Willy, as I said to Mavis, when I recall his place,
and the good carpet gone greasy, not to mention the paint oozing out of the
tubes, I think it would break my heart to sink so low.

From *The Go-Away Bird and Other Stories* by Muriel Spark. (1958)

James Thurber

41 The Catbird Seat

Mr Martin bought the pack of Camels on Monday night in the most crowded cigar store on Broadway. It was theatre time and seven or eight men were buying cigarettes. The clerk didn't even glance at Mr Martin, who put the pack in his overcoat pocket and went out. If any of the staff at F. & S. had seen him buy the
5 cigarettes, they would have been astonished, for it was generally known that Mr Martin did not smoke, and never had. No one saw him.

It was just a week to the day since Mr Martin had decided to rub out Mrs Ulgine Barrows. The term 'rub out' pleased him because it suggested nothing more than the correction of an error—in this case an error of Mr Fitweiler. Mr
10 Martin had spent each night of the past week working out his plan and examining it. As he walked home now he went over it again. For the hundredth time he resented the element of imprecision, the margin of guesswork that entered into the business. The project as he had worked it out was casual and bold, the risks were considerable. Something might go wrong anywhere along the line. And
15 therein lay the cunning of his scheme. No one would ever see in it the cautious, painstaking hand of Erwin Martin, head of the filing department at F. & S., of whom Mr Fitweiler had once said, 'Man is fallible but Martin isn't.' No one would see his hand, that is, unless it were caught in the act.

Sitting in his apartment, drinking a glass of milk, Mr Martin reviewed his case
20 against Mrs Ulgine Barrows, as he had every night for seven nights. He began at the beginning. Her quacking voice and braying laugh had first profaned the halls of F. & S. on 7 March 1941 (Mr Martin had a head for dates). Old Roberts, the personnel chief, had introduced her as the newly appointed special adviser to the president of the firm, Mr Fitweiler. The woman had appalled Mr Martin instantly,
25 but he hadn't shown it. He had given her his dry hand, a look of studious concentration, and a faint smile. 'Well,' she had said, looking at the papers on his desk, 'are you lifting the oxcart out of the ditch?' As Mr Martin recalled that moment, over his milk, he squirmed slightly. He must keep his mind on her crimes as a special adviser, not on her peccadillos as a personality. This he found
30 difficult to do, in spite of entering an objection and sustaining it. The faults of the woman as a woman kept chattering on in his mind like an unruly witness. She had, for almost two years now, baited him. In the halls, in the elevator, even in his own office, into which she romped now and then like a circus horse, she was constantly shouting these silly questions at him. 'Are you lifting the oxcart out
35 of the ditch? Are you tearing up the pea patch? Are you hollering down the rain barrel? Are you scraping around the bottom of the pickle barrel? Are you sitting in the catbird seat?'

It was Joey Hart, one of Mr Martin's two assistants, who had explained what the gibberish meant. 'She must be a Dodger fan,' he had said. 'Red Barber
40 announces the Dodger games over the radio and he uses those expressions— picked 'em up down South.' Joey had gone on to explain one or two. 'Tearing

up the pea patch' meant going on a rampage; 'sitting in the catbird seat' meant sitting pretty, like a batter with three balls and no strikes on him. Mr Martin dismissed all this with an effort. It had been annoying, it had driven him near to
45 distraction, but he was too solid a man to be moved to murder by anything so childish. It was fortunate, he reflected as he passed on to the important charges against Mrs Barrows, that he had stood up under it so well. He had maintained always an outward appearance of polite tolerance. 'Why, I even believe you like the woman,' Miss Paird, his other assistant, had once said to him. He had simply
50 smiled.

A gavel rapped in Mr Martin's mind and the case proper was resumed. Mrs Ulgine Barrows stood charged with wilful, blatant and persistent attempts to destroy the efficiency and system of F. & S. It was competent, material and relevant to review her advent and rise to power. Mr Martin had got the story
55 from Miss Paird, who seemed always able to find things out. According to her, Mrs Barrows had met Mr Fitweiler at a party, where she had rescued him from the embraces of a powerfully built drunken man who had mistaken the president of F. & S. for a famous retired Middle Western football coach. She had led him to a sofa and somehow worked upon him a monstrous magic. The ageing gentle-
60 man had jumped to the conclusion there and then that this was a woman of singular attainments, equipped to bring out the best in him and in the firm. A week later he had introduced her into F. & S. as his special adviser. On that day confusion got its foot in the door. After Miss Tyson, Mr Brundage and Mr Bartlett had been fired and Mr Munson had taken his hat and stalked out, mailing
65 in his resignation later, old Roberts had been emboldened to speak to Mr Fitweiler. He mentioned that Mr Munson's department had been 'a little disrupted' and hadn't they perhaps better resume the old system there? Mr Fitweiler had said certainly not. He had the greatest faith in Mrs Barrows' ideas. 'They require a little seasoning, a little seasoning, is all,' he had added. Mr Roberts had given
70 it up. Mr Martin reviewed in detail all the changes wrought by Mrs Barrows. She had begun chipping at the cornices of the firm's edifice and now she was swinging at the foundation stones with a pickaxe.

Mr Martin came now, in his summing up, to the afternoon of Monday, 2 November 1942—just one week ago. On that day, at 3 p.m., Mrs Barrows had bounced
75 into his office. 'Boo!' she had yelled. 'Are you scraping around the bottom of the pickle barrel?' Mr Martin had looked at her from under his green eyeshade, saying nothing. She had begun to wander about the office, taking it in with her great, popping eyes. 'Do you really need *all* these filing cabinets?' she had demanded suddenly. Mr Martin's heart had jumped. 'Each of these files,' he had
80 said, keeping his voice even, 'plays an indispensable part in the system of F. & S.' She had brayed at him, 'Well, don't tear up the pea patch!' and gone to the door. From there she had bawled, 'But you sure have got a lot of fine scrap in here!' Mr Martin could no longer doubt that the finger was on his beloved department. Her pickaxe was on the upswing, poised for the first blow. It had not come yet;
85 he had received no blue memo from the enchanted Mr Fitweiler bearing nonsensical instructions deriving from the obscene woman. But there was no doubt in Mr Martin's mind that one would be forthcoming. He must act quickly. Already

a precious week had gone by. Mr Martin stood up in his living-room, still holding his milk glass. 'Gentlemen of the jury,' he said to himself, 'I demand the death penalty for this horrible person.'

The next day Mr Martin followed his routine, as usual. He polished his glasses more often and once sharpened an already sharp pencil, but not even Miss Paird noticed. Only once did he catch sight of his victim; she swept past him in the hall with a patronizing 'Hi!' At five-thirty he walked home, as usual, and had a glass of milk, as usual. He had never drunk anything stronger in his life—unless you could count ginger ale. The late Sam Schlosser, the S. of F. & S., had praised Mr Martin at a staff meeting several years before for his temperate habits. 'Our most efficient worker neither drinks nor smokes,' he had said. 'The results speak for themselves.' Mr Fitweiler had sat by, nodding approval.

Mr Martin was still thinking about that red-letter day as he walked over to the Schrafft's on Fifth Avenue near Forty-sixth Street. He got there, as he always did, at eight o'clock. He finished his dinner and the financial page of the *Sun* at a quarter to nine, as he always did. It was his custom after dinner to take a walk. This time he walked down Fifth Avenue at a casual pace. His gloved hands felt moist and warm, his forehead cold. He transferred the Camels from his overcoat to a jacket pocket. He wondered, as he did so, if they did not represent an unnecessary note of strain. Mrs Barrows smoked only Luckies. It was his idea to puff a few puffs on a Camel (after the rubbing-out), stub it out in the ashtray holding her lipstick-stained Luckies, and thus drag a small red herring across the trail. Perhaps it was not a good idea. It would take time. He might even choke, too loudly.

Mr Martin had never seen the house on West Twelfth Street where Mrs Barrows lived, but he had a clear enough picture of it. Fortunately, she had bragged to everybody about her ducky firstfloor apartment in the perfectly darling three-storey red-brick. There would be no doorman or other attendants; just the tenants of the second and third floors. As he walked along, Mr Martin realized that he would get there before nine-thirty. He had considered walking north on Fifth Avenue from Schrafft's to a point from which it would take him until ten o'clock to reach the house. At that hour people were less likely to be coming in or going out. But the procedure would have made an awkward loop in the straight thread of his casualness, and he had abandoned it. It was impossible to figure when people would be entering or leaving the house, anyway. There was a great risk at any hour. If he ran into anybody, he would simply have to place the rubbing-out of Ulgine Barrows in the inactive file forever. The same thing would hold true if there were someone in her apartment. In that case he would just say that he had been passing by, recognized her charming house and thought to drop in.

It was eighteen minutes after nine when Mr Martin turned into Twelfth Street. A man passed him, and a man and a woman talking. There was no one within fifty paces when he came to the house, half-way down the block. He was up the steps and in the small vestibule in no time, pressing the bell under the card that said 'Mrs Ulgine Barrows'. When the clicking in the lock started, he jumped forward against the door. He got inside fast, closing the door behind him. A bulb in a lantern hung from the hall ceiling on a chain seemed to give a monstrously

bright light. There was nobody on the stairs, which went up ahead of him along
135 the left wall. A door opened down the hall in the wall on the right. He went
toward it swiftly, on tiptoe.

'Well, for God's sake, look who's here!' bawled Mrs Barrows, and her braying
laugh rang out like a report of a shotgun. He rushed past her like a football
tackle, bumping her. 'Hey, quit shoving!' she said, closing the door behind them.
140 They were in her living-room, which seemed to Mr Martin to be lighted by a
hundred lamps. 'What's after you?' she said. 'You're as jumpy as a goat.' He
found he was unable to speak. His heart was wheezing in his throat. 'I—yes,' he
finally brought out. She was jabbering and laughing as she started to help him off
with his coat. 'No, no,' he said. 'I'll put it here.' He took it off and put it on a chair
145 near the door. 'Your hat and gloves, too,' she said. 'You're in a lady's house.'
He put his hat on top of the coat. Mrs Barrows seemed larger than he had thought.
He kept his gloves on. 'I was passing by,' he said. 'I recognized—is there anyone
here?' She laughed louder than ever. 'No,' she said, 'we're all alone. You're as
white as a sheet, you funny man. Whatever *has* come over you? I'll mix you a
150 toddy.' She started toward a door across the room. 'Scotch-and-soda be all right?
But say, you don't drink, do you?' She turned and gave him her amused look.
Mr Martin pulled himself together. 'Scotch-and-soda will be all right,' he heard
himself say. He could hear her laughing in the kitchen.

Mr Martin looked quickly around the living-room for the weapon. He had
155 counted on finding one there. There were handirons and a poker and something
in a corner that looked like an Indian club. None of them would do. It couldn't
be that way. He began to pace around. He came to a desk. On it lay a metal paper
knife with an ornate handle. Would it be sharp enough? He reached for it and
knocked over a small brass jar. Stamps spilled out of it and it fell to the floor with
160 a clatter. 'Hey,' Mrs Barrows yelled from the kitchen, 'are you tearing up the pea
patch?' Mr Martin gave a strange laugh. Picking up the knife, he tried its point
against his left wrist. It was blunt. It wouldn't do.

When Mrs Barrows reappeared, carrying two highballs, Mr Martin, standing
there with his gloves on, became acutely conscious of the fantasy he had wrought.
165 Cigarettes in his pocket, a drink prepared for him—it was all too grossly improbable. It was more than that; it was impossible. Somewhere in the back of his mind
a vague idea stirred, sprouted. 'For heaven's sake, take off those gloves,' said
Mrs Barrows. 'I always wear them in the house,' said Mr Martin. The idea began
to bloom, strange and wonderful. She put the glasses on a coffee table in front of
170 a sofa and sat on the sofa. 'Come over here, you odd little man,' she said. Mr Martin went over and sat beside her. It was difficult getting a cigarette out of the pack
of Camels, but he managed it. She held a match for him, laughing. 'Well,' she
said, handing him his drink, 'this is perfectly marvellous. You with a drink and a
cigarette.'
175 Mr Martin puffed, not too awkwardly, and took a gulp of the highball. 'I drink
and smoke all the time,' he said. He clinked his glass against hers. 'Here's nuts to
that old windbag, Fitweiler,' he said, and gulped again. The stuff tasted awful,
but he made no grimace. 'Really, Mr Martin,' she said, her voice and posture
changing, 'you are insulting our employer.' Mrs Barrows was now all special

180 adviser to the president. 'I am preparing a bomb,' said Mr Martin, 'which will blow the old goat higher than hell.' He had only had a little of the drink, which was not strong. It couldn't be that. 'Do you take dope or something?' Mrs Barrows asked coldly. 'Heroin,' said Mr Martin. 'I'll be coked to the gills when I bump that old buzzard off.' 'Mr Martin!' she shouted, getting to her feet. 'That
185 will be all of that. You must go at once.' Mr Martin took another swallow of his drink. He tapped his cigarette out in the ashtray and put the pack of Camels on the coffee table. Then he got up. She stood glaring at him. He walked over and put on his hat and coat. 'Not a word about this,' he said, and laid an index finger against his lips. All Mrs Barrows could bring out was 'Really!' Mr Martin put
190 his hand on the doorknob. 'I'm sitting in the catbird seat,' he said. He stuck his tongue out at her and left. Nobody saw him go.

Mr Martin got to his apartment, walking, well before eleven. No one saw him go in. He had two glasses of milk after brushing his teeth, and he felt elated. It wasn't tipsiness, because he hadn't been tipsy. Anyway, the walk had worn off
195 all effects of the whisky. He got in bed and read a magazine for a while. He was asleep before midnight.

Mr Martin got to the office at eight-thirty the next morning, as usual. At a quarter to nine, Ulgine Barrows, who had never before arrived at work before ten, swept into his office. 'I'm reporting to Mr Fitweiler now!' she shouted. 'If he
200 turns you over to the police, it's no more than you deserve!' Mr Martin gave her a look of shocked surprise. 'I beg your pardon?' he said. Mrs Barrows snorted and bounced out of the room, leaving Miss Paird and Joey Hart staring after her. 'What's the matter with that old devil now?' asked Miss Paird. 'I have no idea,' said Mr Martin, resuming his work. The other two looked at him and then at
205 each other. Miss Paird got up and went out. She walked slowly past the closed door of Mr Fitweiler's office. Mrs Barrows was yelling inside, but she was not braying. Miss Paird could not hear what the woman was saying. She went back to her desk.

Forty-five minutes later, Mrs Barrows left the president's office and went into
210 her own, shutting the door. It wasn't until half an hour later that Mr Fitweiler sent for Mr Martin. The head of the filing department, neat, quiet, attentive, stood in front of the old man's desk. Mr Fitweiler was pale and nervous. He took his glasses off and twiddled them. He made a small, bruffing sound in his throat. 'Martin,' he said, 'you have been with us more than twenty years.' 'Twenty-two
215 sir,' said Mr Martin. 'In that time,' pursued the president, 'your work and your— uh—manner have been exemplary.' 'I trust so, sir,' said Mr Martin. 'I have understood, Martin,' said Mr Fitweiler, 'that you have never taken a drink or smoked.' 'That is correct, sir,' said Mr Martin. 'Ah, yes.' Mr Fitweiler polished his glasses. 'You may describe what you did after leaving the office yesterday, Martin,' he
220 said. Mr Martin allowed less than a second for his bewildered pause. 'Certainly, sir,' he said. 'I walked home. Then I went to Schrafft's for dinner. Afterward I walked home again. I went to bed early, sir, and read a magazine for a while. I was asleep before eleven.' 'Ah, yes,' said Mr Fitweiler again. He was silent for a moment, searching for the proper words to say to the head of the filing depart-
225 ment. 'Mrs Barrows,' he said finally, 'Mrs Barrows has worked hard, Martin,

very hard. It grieves me to report that she has suffered a severe breakdown. It has taken the form of a persecution complex accompanied by distressing hallucinations.' 'I am very sorry, sir,' said Mr Martin. 'Mrs Barrows is under the delusion,' continued Mr Fitweiler, 'that you visited her last evening and behaved yourself

230 in an—uh—unseemly manner.' He raised his hand to silence Mr Martin's little pained outcry. 'It is the nature of these psychological diseases,' Mr Fitweiler said, 'to fix upon the least likely and most innocent party as the—uh—source of persecution. These matters are not for the lay mind to grasp, Martin. I've just had my psychiatrist, Dr Fitch, on the phone. He would not, of course, commit himself,

235 but he made enough generalizations to substantiate my suspicions. I suggested to Mrs Barrows when she had completed her—uh—story to me this morning, that she visit Dr Fitch, for I suspected a condition at once. She flew, I regret to say, into a rage, and demanded—uh—requested that I call you on the carpet. You may not know, Martin, but Mrs Barrows had planned a reorganization of your depart-

240 ment—subject to my approval, of course, subject to my approval. This brought you, rather than anyone else, to her mind—but again that is a phenomenon for Dr Fitch and not for us. So, Martin, I am afraid Mrs Barrow's usefulness here is at an end.' 'I am dreadfully sorry, sir,' said Mr Martin.

It was at this point that the door to the office blew open with the suddenness of

245 a gas-main explosion and Mrs Barrows catapulted through it. 'Is the little rat denying it?' she screamed. 'He can't get away with that!' Mr Martin got up and moved discreetly to a point beside Mr Fitweiler's chair. 'You drank and smoked at my apartment,' she bawled at Mr Martin, 'and you know it! You called Mr Fitweiler an old windbag and said you were going to blow him up when you got

250 coked to the gills on your heroin!' She stopped yelling to catch her breath and a new glint came into her popping eyes. 'If you weren't such a drab, ordinary little man,' she said, 'I'd think you'd planned it all. Sticking your tongue out, saying you were sitting in the catbird seat, because you thought no one would believe me when I told it! My God, it's really too perfect!' She brayed loudly and hysteri-

255 cally, and the fury was on her again. She glared at Mr Fitweiler. 'Can't you see how he has tricked us, you old fool? Can't you see his little game?' But Mr Fitweiler had been surreptitiously pressing all the buttons under the top of his desk and employees of F. & S. began pouring into the room. 'Stockton, said Mr Fitweiler, 'you and Fishbein will take Mrs Barrows to her home. Mrs Powell, you

260 will go with them.' Stockton, who had played a little football in high school, blocked Mrs Barrows as she made for Mr Martin. It took him and Fishbein together to force her out of the door into the hall, crowded with stenographers and office boys. She was still screaming imprecations at Mr Martin, tangled and contradictory imprecations. The hubbub finally died out down the corridor.

265 'I regret that this has happened,' said Mr Fitweiler. 'I shall ask you to dismiss it from your mind, Martin.' 'Yes, sir,' said Mr Martin, anticipating his chief's 'That will be all' by moving to the door. 'I will dismiss it.' He went out and shut the door, and his step was light and quick in the hall. When he entered his department he had slowed down to his customary gait, and he walked quietly across the

270 room to the W20 file, wearing a look of studious concentration.

From *Vintage Thurber* by James Thurber. (1943)

James Thurber

42 The Owl Who Was God

Once upon a starless midnight there was an owl who sat on the branch of an oak tree. Two ground moles tried to slip quietly by, unnoticed. 'You!' said the owl. 'Who?' they quavered, in fear and astonishment, for they could not believe it was possible for anyone to see them in that thick darkness. 'You two!' said the
5 owl. The moles hurried away and told the other creatures of the field and forest that the owl was the greatest and wisest of all animals because he could see in the dark and because he could answer any question. 'I'll see about that,' said a secretary bird, and he called on the owl one night when it was again very dark. 'How many claws am I holding up?' said the secretary bird, 'Two,' said the owl, and that
10 was right. 'Can you give me another expression for "that is to say" or "namely"?' asked the secretary bird. 'To wit,' said the owl. 'Why does a lover call on his love?' asked the secretary bird. 'To woo,' said the owl.

The secretary bird hastened back to the other creatures and reported that the owl was indeed the greatest and wisest animal in the world because he could see
15 in the dark and because he could answer any question. 'Can he see in the day-time, too?' asked a red fox. 'Yes,' echoed a dormouse and a French poodle. 'Can he see in the daytime, too?' All the other creatures laughed loudly at this silly

question, and they set upon the red fox and his friends and drove them out of the region. Then they sent a messenger to the owl and asked him to be their leader.

20   When the owl appeared among the animals it was high noon and the sun was shining brightly. He walked very slowly, which gave him an appearance of great dignity, and he peered about him with large, staring eyes, which gave him an air of tremendous importance. 'He's God!' screamed a Plymouth Rock hen. And the others took up the cry 'He's God!' So they followed him wherever he went and

25 when he began to bump into things they began to bump into things, too. Finally he came to a concrete highway and he started up the middle of it and all the other creatures followed him. Presently a hawk, who was acting as outrider, observed a truck coming toward them at fifty miles an hour, and he reported to the secretary bird and the secretary bird reported to the owl. 'There's danger ahead,' said the

30 secretary bird. 'To wit?' said the owl. The secretary bird told him. 'Aren't you afraid?' He asked. 'Who?' said the owl calmly, for he could not see the truck. 'He's God!' cried all the creatures again, and they were still crying 'He's God!' when the truck hit them and ran them down. Some of the animals were merely injured, but most of them, including the owl, were killed.

35   *Moral: You can fool too many of the people too much of the time.*

(1939)

James Thurber

43 The Unicorn in the Garden

Once upon a sunny morning a man who sat in a breakfast nook looked up from his scrambled eggs to see a white unicorn with a gold horn quietly cropping the roses in the garden. The man went up to the bedroom where his wife was still asleep and woke her. 'There's a unicorn in the garden,' he said. 'Eating roses.' She

5 opened one unfriendly eye and looked at him. 'The unicorn is a mythical beast,' she said, and turned her back on him. The man walked slowly downstairs and out into the garden. The unicorn was still there; he was now browsing among the tulips. 'Here, unicorn,' said the man, and he pulled up a lily and gave it to him. The unicorn ate it gravely. With a high heart, because there was a unicorn in his

10 garden, the man went upstairs and roused his wife again. 'The unicorn,' he said, 'ate a lily.' His wife sat up in bed and looked at him, coldly. 'You are a booby,' she said, 'and I am going to have you put in the booby-hatch.' The man, who had never liked the words 'booby' and 'booby-hatch', and who liked them even less on a shining morning when there was a unicorn in the garden, thought for a

15 moment. 'We'll see about that,' he said. He walked over to the door. 'He has a golden horn in the middle of his forehead,' he told her. Then he went back to the garden to watch the unicorn; but the unicorn had gone away. The man sat down among the roses and went to sleep.

As soon as the husband had gone out of the house, the wife got up and dressed
as fast as she could. She was very excited and there was a gloat in her eye. She
telephoned the police and she telephoned a psychiatrist; she told them to hurry
to her house and bring a strait-jacket. When the police and the psychiatrist arrived
they sat down in chairs and looked at her, with great interest. 'My husband,' she
said, 'saw a unicorn this morning.' The police looked at the psychiatrist and the
psychiatrist looked at the police. 'He told me it ate a lily,' she said. The psychiatrist
looked at the police and the police looked at the psychiatrist. 'He told me it had a
golden horn in the middle of its forehead,' she said. At a solemn signal from the
psychiatrist, the police leaped from their chairs and seized the wife. They had a
hard time subduing her, for she put up a terrific struggle, but they finally subdued
her. Just as they got her into the strait-jacket, the husband came back into the
house.

'Did you tell your wife you saw a unicorn?' asked the police. 'Of course not,'
said the husband. 'The unicorn is a mythical beast.' 'That's all I wanted to know,'
said the psychiatrist. 'Take her away. I'm sorry, sir, but your wife is as crazy as a
jay bird.' So they took her away, cursing and screaming, and shut her up in an
institution. The husband lived happily ever after.

Moral: Don't count your boobies until they are hatched.

(1939)

John Updike

44 Tomorrow and Tomorrow and So Forth

Whirling, talking, 11D began to enter Room 109. From the quality of the class's excitement Mark Prosser guessed it would rain. He had been teaching high school for three years, yet his students still impressed him; they were such sensitive animals. They reacted so infallibly to merely barometric pressure.

5   In the doorway, Brute Young paused while little Barry Snyder giggled at his elbow. Barry's stagey laugh rose and fell, dipping down towards some vile secret that had to be tasted and retasted, then soaring like a rocket to proclaim that he, little Barry, shared such a secret with the school's fullback. Being Brute's stooge was precious to Barry. The fullback paid no attention to him; he twisted his neck
10   to stare at something not yet come through the door. He yielded heavily to the procession pressing him forward.

    Right under Mr Prosser's eyes, like a murder suddenly appearing in an annalistic frieze of kings and queens, someone stabbed a girl in the back with a pencil. She ignored the assault saucily. Another hand yanked out Geoffrey Langer's
15   shirt-tail. Geoffrey, a bright student, was uncertain whether to laugh it off or defend himself with anger, and made a weak, half-turning gesture of compromise, wearing an expression of distant arrogance that Prosser instantly coordinated with baffled feelings he used to have. All along the line, in the glitter of key chains and the acute angles of turned-back shirt cuffs, an electricity was expressed which
20   simple weather couldn't generate.

    Mark wondered if today Gloria Angstrom wore that sweater, an ember-pink angora, with very brief sleeves. The virtual sleevelessness was the disturbing factor, the exposure of those two serene arms to the air, white as thighs against the delicate wool.

25   His guess was correct. A vivid pink patch flashed through the jiggle of arms and shoulders as the final knot of youngsters entered the room.

    'Take your seats,' Mr Prosser said. 'Come on. Let's go.'

    Most obeyed, but Peter Forrester, who had been at the centre of the group around Gloria, still lingered in the doorway with her, finishing some story,
30   apparently determined to make her laugh or gasp. When she did gasp, he tossed his head with satisfaction. His orange hair, preened into a kind of floating bang, bobbed. Mark had always disliked redheaded males, with their white eyelashes and puffy faces and thyroid eyes, and absurdly self-confident mouths. A race of bluffers. His own hair was brown.

35   When Gloria, moving in a considered, stately way, had taken her seat, and Peter had swerved into his, Mr Prosser said, 'Peter Forrester.'

    'Yes?' Peter rose, scrabbling through his book for the right place.

    'Kindly tell the class the exact meaning of the words "Tomorrow, and tomorrow, and tomorrow/Creeps in this petty pace from day to day".'
40   Peter glanced down at the high-school edition of *Macbeth* lying open on his desk. One of the duller girls tittered expectantly from the back of the room. Peter was popular with the girls; girls that age had minds like moths.

'Peter. With your book shut. We have all memorized this passage for today. Remember?' The girl in the back of the room squealed in delight. Gloria laid her
45 own book face-open on her desk, where Peter could see it.

Peter shut his book with a bang and stared into Gloria's. 'Why,' he said at last, 'I think it means pretty much what it says.'

'Which is?'

'Why, that tomorrow is something we often think about. It creeps into our
50 conversation all the time. We couldn't make any plans without thinking about tomorrow.'

'I see. Then you would say that Macbeth is here referring to the, the date-book aspect of life?'

Geoffrey Langer laughed, no doubt to please Mr Prosser. For a moment, he
55 *was* pleased. Then he realized he had been playing for laughs at a student's expense.

His parapharse had made Peter's reading of the lines seem more ridiculous than it was. He began to retract. 'I admit—'

But Peter was going on; redheads never know when to quit. 'Macbeth means
60 that if we quit worrying about tomorrow, and just live for today, we could appreciate all the wonderful things that are going on under our noses.'

Mark considered this a moment before he spoke. He would not be sarcastic. 'Uh, without denying that there is truth in what you say, Peter, do you think it likely that Macbeth, in his situation, would be expressing such'—he couldn't
65 help himself—'such sunny sentiments?'

Geoffrey laughed again. Peter's neck reddened; he studied the floor. Gloria glared at Mr Prosser, the indignation in her face clearly meant for him to see.

Mark hurried to undo his mistake. 'Don't misunderstand me, please,' he told Peter. 'I don't have all the answers myself. But it seems so me the whole speech,
70 down to "Signifying nothing", is saying that life is—well, a *fraud*. Nothing wonderful about it.'

'Did Shakespeare really think that?' Geoffrey Langer asked, a nervous quickness pitching his voice high.

Mark read into Geoffrey's question his own adolescent premonitions of the
75 terrible truth. The attempt he must make was plain. He told Peter he could sit down and looked through the window towards the steadying sky. The clouds were gaining intensity. 'There is,' Mr Prosser slowly began, 'much darkness in Shakespeare's work, and no play is darker than *Macbeth*. The atmosphere is poisonous, oppressive. One critic has said that in this play, humanity suffocates.'
80 He felt himself in danger of suffocating, and cleared his throat.

'In the middle of his career, Shakespeare wrote plays about men like Hamlet and Othello and Macbeth—men who aren't allowed by their society, or bad luck, or some minor flaw in themselves, to become the great men they might have been. Even Shakespeare's comedies of this period deal with a world gone sour.
85 It is as if he had seen through the bright, bold surface of his earlier comedies and histories and had looked upon something terrible. It frightened him, just as some day it may frighten some of you.' In his determination to find the right

words, he had been staring at Gloria, without meaning to. Embarrassed, she nodded, and, realizing what had happened, he smiled at her.

90 He tried to make his remarks gentle, even diffident. 'But then I think Shakespeare sensed a redeeming truth. His last plays are serene and symbolical, as if he had pierced through the ugly facts and reached a realm where the facts are again beautiful. In this way, Shakespeare's total work is a more complete image of life than that of any other writer, except perhaps for Dante, an Italian poet who wrote
95 several centuries earlier.' He had been taken far from the Macbeth soliloquy. Other teachers had been happy to tell him how the kids made a game of getting him 'going'. He looked towards Geoffrey. The boys was doodling on his tablet, indifferent. Mr Prosser concluded, 'The last play Shakespeare wrote is an extraordinary poem called *The Tempest*. Some of you may want to read it for your
100 next book reports—the ones due May 10th. It's a short play.'

The class had been taking a holiday. Barry Snyder was snicking BBs off the blackboard and glancing over at Brute Young to see if he noticed. 'Once more, Barry,' Mr Prosser said, 'and out you go.' Barry blushed, and grinned to cover the blush, his eyeballs sliding towards Brute. The dull girl in the rear of the room
105 was putting on lipstick. 'Put that away, Alice,' Prosser said. 'This isn't a beauty parlour.' Sejak, the Polish boy who worked nights, was asleep at his desk, his cheek white with pressure against the varnished wood, his mouth sagging sidewise. Mr Prosser had an impulse to let him sleep. But the impulse might not be true kindness, but just the self-congratulatory, kindly pose in which he sometimes
110 discovered himself. Besides, one breach of discipline encouraged others. He strode down the aisle and squeezed Sejak's shoulder; the boy awoke. A mumble was growing at the front of the room.

Peter Forrester was whispering to Gloria, trying to make her laugh. The girl's face, though, was cool and solemn, as if a thought had been provoked in her
115 head—as if there lingered there something of what Mr Prosser had been saying. With a bracing sense of chivalrous intercession, Mark said, 'Peter. I gather from this noise that you have something to add to your theories.'

Peter responded courteously. 'No, sir. I honestly don't understand the speech. Please, sir, what *does* it mean?'

120 This candid admission and odd request stunned the class. Every white, round face, eager, for once, to learn, turned towards Mark. He said, 'I don't know. I was hoping *you* would tell *me*.'

In college, when a professor made such a remark, it was with grand effect. The professor's humility, the necessity for creative interplay between teacher and
125 student were dramatically impressed upon the group. But to 11D, ignorance in an instructor was as wrong as a hole in a roof. It was as if Mark had held forty strings pulling forty faces taut towards him and then had slashed the strings. Heads waggled, eyes dropped, voices buzzed. Some of the discipline problems, like Peter Forrester, smirked signals to one another.

130 'Quiet!' Mr Prosser shouted. 'All of you. Poetry isn't arithmetic. There's no single right answer. I don't want to force my own impression on you; that's not why I'm here.' The silent question, *Why are you here?*, seemed to steady the air with suspense. 'I'm here,' he said, 'to let you teach yourselves.'

Whether or not they believed him, they subsided, somewhat. Mark judged he
135 could safely reassume his human-among-humans pose. He perched on the edge
of the desk, informal, friendly, and frankly beseeching. 'Now, honestly. Don't
any of you have some personal feeling about the lines that you would like to
share with the class and me?'

One hand, with a flowered handkerchief balled in it, unsteadily rose. 'Go ahead,
140 Teresa,' Mr Prosser said. She was a timid, sniffly girl whose mother was a Jeho-
vah's Witness.

'It makes me think of cloud shadows,' Teresa said.

Geoffrey Langer laughed. 'Don't be rude, Geoff,' Mr Prosser said sideways,
softly, before throwing his voice forward: 'Thank you, Teresa. I think that's an
145 interesting and valid impression. Cloud movement has something in it of the
slow, monotonous rhythm one feels in the line "Tomorrow, and tomorrow, and
tomorrow". It's a very grey line, isn't it, class?' No one agreed or diagreed.

Beyond the windows actual clouds were bunching rapidly, and erratic sections
of sunlight slid around the room. Gloria's arm, crooked gracefully above her
150 head, turned gold. 'Gloria?' Mr Prosser asked.

She looked up from something on her desk with a face of sullen radiance.
'I think what Teresa said was very good,' she said, glaring in the direction of
Geoffrey Langer. Geoffrey snickered defiantly. 'And I have a question. What does
"petty pace" mean?'
155   'It means the trivial day-to-day sort of life that, say, a bookkeeper or a bank
clerk leads. Or a schoolteacher,' he added, smiling.

She did not smile back. Thought wrinkles irritated her perfect brow. 'But
Macbeth has been fighting wars, and killing kings, and being a king himself, and
all,' she pointed out.
160   'Yes, but it's just these acts Macbeth is condemning as "nothing". Can you see
that?'

Gloria shook her head. 'Another thing I worry about—isn't it silly for Macbeth
to be talking to himself right in the middle of this war, with his wife just dead,
and all?'
165   'I don't think so, Gloria. No matter how fast events happen, thought is faster.'

His answer was weak; everyone knew it, even if Gloria hadn't mused, supposedly to herself, but in a voice the entire class could hear, 'It seems so *stupid*.'

Mark winced, pierced by the awful clarity with which his students saw him.
Through their eyes, how queer he looked with his chalky hands, and his horn-
170 rimmed glasses, and his hair never slicked down, all wrapped up in 'literature',
where, when things get rough, the king mumbles a poem nobody understands.
He was suddenly conscious of a terrible tenderness in the young, a frightening
patience and faith. It was so good of them not to laugh him out of the room. He
looked down and rubbed his finger-tips together, trying to erase the chalk dust.
175 The class noise sifted into unnatural quiet. 'It's getting late,' he said finally. 'Let's
start the recitations of the memorized passage. Bernard Amilson, you begin.'

Bernard had trouble enunciating, and his rendition began ' "T'mau 'n' t'mau
'n' t'mau".' It was reassuring, the extent to which the class tried to repress its
laughter. Mr Prosser wrote 'A' in his marking book opposite Bernard's name.

180 He always gave Bernard A on recitations, despite the school nurse, who claimed there was nothing organically wrong with the boy's mouth.

It was the custom, cruel but traditional, to deliver recitations from the front of the room. Alice, when her turn came, was reduced to a helpless state by the first funny face Peter Forrester made at her. Mark let her hang up there a good minute
185 while her face ripened to cherry redness, and at last relented. 'Alice, you may try it later.' Many of the class knew the passage gratifyingly well, though there was a tendency to leave out the line 'To the last syllable of recorded time' and to turn 'struts and frets' into 'frets and struts' or simply 'struts and struts'. Even Sejak, who couldn't have looked at the passage before he came to class, got through it
190 as far as 'And then is heard no more'.

Geoffrey Langer showed off, as he always did, by interrupting his own recitation with bright questions. ' "Tomorrow, and tomorrow, and tomorrow",' he said, ' "creeps in"—shouldn't that be "*creep* in", Mr Prosser?'

'It is "creeps". The trio is in effect singular. Go on. Without the footnotes.'
195 Mr Prosser was tired of coddling Langer. The boy's black hair, short and stiff, seemed deliberately rat-like.

' "Creep*sss* in this petty pace from day to day, to the last syllable of recorded time and all our yesterdays have lighted fools the way to dusty death. Out, out—" '

200 'No, no!' Mr Prosser jumped out of his chair. 'This is poetry. Don't mush-mouth it! Pause a little after "Fools".' Geoffrey looked genuinely startled this time, and Mark himself did not quite understand his annoyance and, mentally turning to see what was behind him, seemed to glimpse in the humid under-growth the two stern eyes of the indignant look Gloria had thrown Geoffrey.
205 He glimpsed himself in the absurd position of acting as Gloria's champion in her private war with this intelligent boy. He sighed apologetically. 'Poetry is made up of lines,' he began, turning to the class. Gloria was passing a note to Peter Forrester.

The rudeness of it! To pass notes during a scolding that she herself had caused!
210 Mark caged in his hand the girl's frail wrist and ripped the note from her fingers. He read it to himself, letting the class see he was reading it, though he despised such methods of discipline. The note went:
Pete—I think you're *wrong* about Mr Prosser. I think he's wonderful and I get a lot out of his class. He's heavenly with poetry. I think I love him. I really do *love*
215 him. So there.

Mr Prosser folded the note once and slipped it into his side coat pocket. 'See me after class, Gloria,' he said. Then, to Geoffrey, 'Let's try it again. Begin at the beginning.'

While the boy was reciting the passage, the buzzer sounded the end of the
220 period. It was the last class of the day. The room quickly emptied, except for Gloria. The noise of lockers slamming open and books being thrown against metal and shouts drifted in.

'Who has a car?'

'Lend me a cig, pig.'

225 'We can't have practice in this slop.'

Mark hadn't noticed exactly when the rain started, but it was coming down hard now. He moved around the room with the window pole, closing windows and pulling down shades. Spray bounced in on his hands. He began to talk to Gloria in a crisp voice that, like his device of shutting the windows, was intended
230 to protect them both from embarrassment.

'About note-passing.' She sat motionless at her desk in the front of the room, her short, brushed-up hair like a cool torch. From the way she sat, her naked arms folded at her breasts and her shoulders hunched, he felt she was chilly. 'It is not only rude to scribble when a teacher is talking, it is stupid to put one's words
235 down on paper, where they look much more foolish than they might have sounded if spoken.' He leaned the window pole in its corner and walked towards his desk.

'And about love. "Love" is one of those words that illustrate what happens to an old, overworked language. These days, with movie stars and crooners and
240 preachers and psychiatrists all pronouncing the word, it's come to mean nothing but a vague fondness for something. In this sense, I love the rain, this blackboard, these desks, you. It means nothing, you see, whereas once the word signified a quite explicit thing—a desire to share all you own and are with someone else. It is time we coined a new word to mean that, and when you think up the
245 word *you* want to use, I suggest that you be economical with it. Treat it as something you can spend only once—if not for your own sake, for the good of the language.' He walked over to his own desk and dropped two pencils on it, as if to say, 'That's all.'

'I'm sorry,' Gloria said.
250 Rather surprised, Mr Prosser said, 'Don't be.'

'But you don't understand.'

'Of course I don't. I probably never did. At your age, I was like Geoffrey Langer.'

'I bet you weren't.' The girl was almost crying; he was sure of that.
255 'Come on, Gloria. Run along. Forget it.' She slowly cradled her books between her bare arm and her sweater, and left the room with that melancholy shuffling teenage gait, so that her body above her thighs seemed to float over the desktops.

What was it, Mark asked himself, these kids were after? What did they want?
260 Glide, he decided, the quality of glide. To slip along, always in rhythm, always cool, the little wheels humming under you, going nowhere special. If Heaven existed, that's the way it would be there. *He's heavenly with poetry.* They loved the word. Heaven was in half their songs.

'Christ, he's humming.' Strunk, the physical ed teacher, had come into the
265 room without Mark's noticing. Gloria had left the door ajar.

'Ah,' Mark said, 'a fallen angel, full of grit.'

'What the hell makes you so happy?'

'I'm not happy, I'm just heavenly. I don't know why you don't appreciate me.'

270   'Say.' Strunk came up an aisle with a disagreeably effeminate waddle, pregnant
with gossip. 'Did you hear about Murchison?'

    'No.' Mark mimicked Strunk's whisper.

    'He got the pants kidded off him today.'

    'Oh dear.'

275   Strunk started to laugh, as he always did before beginning a story. 'You know
what a goddam lady's man he thinks he is?'

    'You bet,' Mark said, although Strunk said that about every male member of
the faculty.

    'You have Gloria Angstrom, don't you?'

280   'You bet.'

    'Well, this morning Murky intercepts a note she was writing, and the note says
what a damn neat guy she thinks Murchison is and how she *loves* him!' Strunk
waited for Mark to say something, and then, when he didn't, continued, 'You
could see he was tickled pink. But—get this—it turns out at lunch that the same
285 damn thing happened to Fryeburg in history yesterday!' Strunk laughed and
cracked his knuckles viciously. 'The girl's too dumb to have thought it up herself.
We all think it was Peter Forrester's idea.'

    'Probably was,' Mark agreed. Strunk followed him out to his locker, describing
Murchison's expression when Fryeburg (in all innocence, mind you) told what
290 had happened to him.

    Mark turned the combination of his locker, 18-24-3. 'Would you excuse me,
Dave?' he said. 'My wife's in town waiting.'

    Strunk was too thick to catch Mark's anger. 'I got to get over to the gym.
Can't take the little darlings outside in the rain; their mommies'll write notes to
295 teacher.' He waddled down the hall and wheeled at the far end, shouting, 'Now
don't tell You-know-who!'

    Mr Prosser took his coat from the locker and shrugged it on. He placed his hat
upon his head. He fitted his rubbers over his shoes, pinching his fingers painfully,
and lifted his umbrella off the hook. He thought of opening it right there in the
300 vacant hall, as a kind of joke, and decided not to. The girl had been almost crying;
he was sure of that.

From *The Same Door* by John Updike. (1956)

Kurt Vonnegut, Jr.

45 Tomorrow and Tomorrow and Tomorrow

The year was 2158 A.D., and Lou and Emerald Schwartz were whispering on the balcony outside Lou's family's apartment on the seventy-sixth floor of Building 257 in Alden Village, a New York housing development that covered what had once been known as Southern Connecticut. When Lou and Emerald
5 had married, Em's parents had tearfully described the marriage as being between May and December; but now, with Lou one hundred and twelve and Em ninety-three, Em's parents had to admit that the match had worked out well.
But Em and Lou weren't without their troubles, and they were out in the nippy air of the balcony because of them.
10 "Sometimes I get so mad, I feel like just up and diluting his anti-gerasone," said Em.
"That'd be against Nature, Em," said Lou, "it'd be murder. Besides, if he caught us tinkering with his anti-gerasone, not only would he disinherit us, he'd bust my neck. Just because he's one hundred and seventy-two doesn't mean
15 Gramps isn't strong as a bull."
"Against Nature," said Em. "Who knows what Nature's like anymore? Ohhhhh—I don't guess I could ever bring myself to dilute his anti-gerasone or anything like that, but, gosh, Lou, a body can't help thinking Gramps is never going to leave if somebody doesn't help him along a little. Golly—we're so
20 crowded a person can hardly turn around, and Verna's dying for a baby, and Melissa's gone thirty years without one." She stamped her feet. "I get so sick of seeing his wrinkled old face, watching him take the only private room and the best chair and the best food, and getting to pick out what to watch on TV, and running everybody's life by changing his will all the time."
25 "Well, after all," said Lou bleakly, "Gramps *is* head of the family. And he can't help being wrinkled like he is. He was seventy before anti-gerasone was invented. He's going to leave, Em. Just give him time. It's his business. I know he's tough to live with, but be patient. It wouldn't do to do anything that'd rile him. After all, we've got it better'n anybody else, there on the daybed."
30 "How much longer do you think we'll get to sleep on the daybed before he picks another pet? The world's record's two months, isn't it?"
"Mom and Pop had it that long once, I guess."
"When *is* he going to leave, Lou?" said Emerald.
"Well, he's talking about giving up anti-gerasone right after the five-hundred-
35 mile Speedway Race."
"Yes—and before that it was the Olympics, and before that the World's Series, and before that the Presidential Elections, and before that I-don't-know-what. It's been just one excuse after another for fifty years now. I don't think we're ever going to get a room to ourselves or an egg or anything."
40 "All right—call me a failure!" said Lou. "What can I do? I work hard and make good money, but the whole thing, practically, is taxed away for defense and

old age pensions. And if it wasn't taxed away, where you think we'd find a vacant room to rent? Iowa, maybe? Well, who wants to live on the outskirts of Chicago?"

45   Em put her arms around his neck. "Lou, hon, I'm not calling you a failure. The Lord knows you're not. You just haven't had a chance to be anything or have anything because Gramps and the rest of his generation won't leave and let somebody else take over."

"Yeah, yeah," said Lou gloomily. "You can't exactly blame 'em, though, can
50   you? I mean, I wonder how quick we'll knock off the anti-gerasone when we get Gramps' age."

"Sometimes I wish there wasn't any such thing as anti-gerasone!" said Emerald passionately. "Or I wish it was made out of something real expensive and hard-to-get instead of mud and dandelions. Sometimes I wish folks just up and died
55   regular as clockwork, without anything to say about it, instead of deciding themselves how long they're going to stay around. There ought to be a law against selling the stuff to anybody over one hundred and fifty."

"Fat chance of that," said Lou, "with all the money and votes the old people've got." He looked at her closely. "You ready to up and die, Em?"

60   "Well, for heaven's sakes, what a thing to say to your wife. Hon! I'm not even one hundred yet." She ran her hands lightly over her firm, youthful figure, as though for confirmation. "The best years of my life are still ahead of me. But you can bet that when one hundred and fifty rolls around, old Em's going to pour her anti-gerasone down the sink, and quit taking up room, and she'll do it smiling."

65   "Sure, sure," said Lou, "you bet. That's what they all say. How many you heard of doing it?"

"There was that man in Delaware."

"Aren't you getting kind of tired of talking about him, Em? That was five months ago."

70   "All right, then—Gramma Winkler, right here in the same building."

"She got smeared by a subway."

"That's just the way she picked to go," said Em.

"Then what was she doing carrying a six-pack of anti-gerasone when she got it?"

75   Emerald shook her head wearily and covered her eyes. "I dunno, I dunno, I dunno. All I know is, something's just got to be done." She sighed. "Sometimes I wish they'd left a couple of diseases kicking around somewhere, so I could get one and go to bed for a little while. Too many people!" she cried, and her words cackled and gabbled and died in a thousand asphalt-paved, skyscraper-walled
80   courtyards.

Lou laid his hand on her shoulder tenderly. "Aw, hon, I hate to see you down in the dumps like this."

"If we just had a car, like the folks used to in the old days," said Em, "we could go for a drive, and get away from people for a little while. Gee—if *those*
85   weren't the days!"

"Yeah," said Lou, "before they'd used up all the metal."

"We'd hop in, and Pop'd drive up to a filling station and say, 'Fillerup!' "

"That *was* the nuts, wasn't it—before they'd used up all the gasoline."

"And we'd go for a carefree ride in the country."

90 "Yeah—all seems like a fairyland now, doesn't it, Em? Hard to believe there really used to be all that space between cities."

"And when we got hungry," said Em, "we'd find ourselves a restaurant, and walk in, big as you please and say, 'I'll have a steak and French-fries, I believe,' or, 'How are the pork chops today?' " She licked her lips, and her eyes glistened.

95 "Yeah man!" growled Lou. "How'd you like a hamburger with the works, Em?"

"Mmmmmmmmm."

"If anybody'd offered us processed seaweed in those days, we would have spit right in his eye, huh, Em?"

100 "Or processed sawdust," said Em.

Doggedly, Lou tried to find the cheery side of the situation.

"Well, anyway, they've got the stuff so it tastes a lot less like seaweed and sawdust than it did at first; and they say it's actually better for us than what we used to eat."

105 "I felt fine!" said Em fiercely.

Lou shrugged. "Well, you've got to realize, the world wouldn't be able to support twelve billion people if it wasn't for processed seaweed and sawdust. I mean, it's a wonderful thing, really. I guess. That's what they say."

"They say the first thing that pops into their heads," said Em. She closed her
110 eyes. "Golly—remember shopping, Lou? Remember how the stores used to fight to get our folks to buy something? You didn't have to wait for somebody to die to get a bed or chairs or a stove or anything like that. Just went in—bing!—and bought whatever you wanted. Gee whiz, that was nice, before they used up all the raw materials. I was just a little kid then, but I can remember so plain."

115 Depressed, Lou walked listlessly to the balcony's edge, and looked up at the clean, cold, bright stars against the black velvet of infinity. "Remember when we used to be bugs on science fiction, Em? Flight seventeen, leaving for Mars, launching ramp twelve. 'Board! All non-technical personnel kindly remain in bunkers. Ten seconds . . . nine . . . eight . . . seven . . . six . . . five . . . four . . .
120 three . . . two . . . *one! Main Stage! Barrrrrroooom!*"

"Why worry about what was going on on Earth?" said Em, looking up at the stars with him. "In another few years, we'd all be shooting through space to start life all over again on a new planet."

Lou sighed. "Only it turns out you need something about twice the size of the
125 Empire State Building to get one lousy colonist to Mars. And for another couple of trillion bucks he could take his wife and dog. *That's* the way to lick over-population—*emigrate!*"

"Lou—?"

"Hmmm?"

130 "When's the Five-Hundred-Mile Speedway Race?"

"Uh—Memorial Day, May thirtieth."

She bit her lip. "Was that awful of me to ask?"

"Not very, I guess. Everybody in the apartment's looked it up to make sure."

"I don't want to be awful," said Em, "but you've just got to talk over these
135 things now and then, and get them out of your system."

"Sure you do. Feel better?"

"Yes—and I'm not going to lose my temper anymore, and I'm going to be just
as nice to him as I know how."

"That's my Em."

140 They squared their shoulders, smiled bravely, and went back inside.

Gramps Schwartz, his chin resting on his hands, his hands on the crook of his
cane, was staring irascibly at the five-foot television screen that dominated the
room. On the screen, a news commentator was summarizing the day's happenings.
Every thirty seconds or so, Gramps would jab the floor with his cane-tip and
145 shout, "Hell! We did that a hundred years ago!"

Emerald and Lou, coming in from the balcony, were obliged to take seats in
the back row, behind Lou's father and mother, brother and sister-in-law, son and
daughter-in-law, grandson and wife, granddaughter and husband, great-grandson
and wife, nephew and wife, grandnephew and wife, great-grandniece and hus-
150 band, great-grandnephew and wife, and, of course, Gramps, who was in front of
everybody. All, save Gramps, who was somewhat withered and bent, seemed, by
pre-anti-gerasone standards, to be about the same age—to be somewhere in their
late twenties or early thirties.

"*Meanwhile,*" the commentator was saying. "*Council Bluffs, Iowa, was still
155 threatened by stark tragedy. But two hundred weary rescue workers have refused to give up
hope, and continue to dig in an effort to save Elbert Haggedorn, one hundred and eighty-three,
who has been wedged for two days in a . . .*"

"I wish he'd get something more cheerful," Emerald whispered to Lou.

"Silence!" cried Gramps. "Next one shoots off his big bazoo while the TV's
160 on is gonna find hisself cut off without a dollar—" and here his voice suddenly
softened and sweetened "when they wave that checkered flag at the Indianapolis
Speedway, and old Gramps gets ready for the Big Trip Up Yonder." He sniffed
sentimentally, while his heirs concentrated desperately on not making the slightest
sound. For them, the poignancy of the prospective Big Trip had been dulled
165 somewhat by its having been mentioned by Gramps about once a day for fifty
years.

"*Dr. Brainard Keyes Bullard,*" said the commentator, "*President of Wyandotte
College, said in an address tonight that most of the world's ills can be traced to the fact that
Man's knowledge of himself has not kept pace with his knowledge of the physical world.*"

170 "Hell!" said Gramps. "We said that a hundred years ago!"

"*In Chicago tonight,*" said the commentator, "*a special celebration is taking place in
the Chicago Lying-in Hospital. The guest of honor is Lowell W. Hitz, age zero. Hitz,
born this morning, is the twenty-five-millionth child to be born in the hospital.*" The commentator faded, and was replaced on the screen by young Hitz, who squalled
175 furiously.

"Hell," whispered Lou to Emerald, "we said that a hundred years ago."

"I heard that!" shouted Gramps. He snapped off the television set, and his petrified descendants stared silently at the screen. "You, there, boy—"

"I didn't mean anything by it, sir," said Lou.

180 "Get me my will. You know where it is. You kids *all* know where it is. Fetch, boy!"

Lou nodded dully, and found himself going down the hall, picking his way over bedding to Gramps' room, the only private room in the Schwartz apartment. The other rooms were the bathroom, the living room, and the wide, 185 windowless hallway, which was originally intended to serve as a dining area, and which had a kitchenette in one end. Six mattresses and four sleeping bags were dispersed in the hallway and living room, and the daybed, in the living room, accommodated the eleventh couple, the favorites of the moment.

On Gramps' bureau was his will, smeared, dog-eared, perforated, and blotched 190 with hundreds of additions, deletions, accusations, conditions, warnings, advice, and homely philosophy. The document was, Lou reflected, a fifty-year diary, all jammed onto two sheets—a garbled, illegible log of day after day of strife. This day, Lou would be disinherited for the eleventh time, and it would take him perhaps six months of impeccable behavior to regain the promise of a share in 195 the estate.

"Boy!" called Gramps.

"Coming, sir." Lou hurried back into the living room, and handed Gramps the will.

"Pen!" said Gramps.

200 He was instantly offered eleven pens, one from each couple.

"Not *that* leaky thing," he said, brushing Lou's pen aside. "Ah, there's a nice one. Good boy, Willy." He accepted Willy's pen. That was the tip they'd all been waiting for. Willy, then, Lou's father, was the new favorite.

Willy, who looked almost as young as Lou, though one hundred and forty-205 two, did a poor job of concealing his pleasure. He glanced shyly at the daybed, which would become his, and from which Lou and Emerald would have to move back into the hall, back to the worst spot of all by the bathroom door.

Gramps missed none of the high drama he'd authored, and he gave his own familiar role everything he had. Frowning and running his finger along each line, 210 as though he were seeing the will for the first time, he read aloud in a deep, portentous monotone, like a bass tone on a cathedral organ:

"I, Harold D. Schwartz, residing in Building 257 of Alden Village, New York City, do hereby make, publish, and declare this to be my last Will and Testament, hereby revoking any and all former wills and codicils by me at any time heretofore 215 made." He blew his nose importantly, and went on, not missing a word, and repeating many for emphasis—repeating in particular his ever-more-elaborate specifications for a funeral.

At the end of these specifications, Gramps was so choked with emotion that Lou thought he might forget why he'd gotten out the will in the first place. But 220 Gramps heroically brought his powerful emotions under control, and, after erasing for a full minute, he began to write and speak at the same time. Lou could have spoken his lines for him, he'd heard them so often.

"I have had many heartbreaks ere leaving this vale of tears for a better land," Gramps said and wrote. "But the deepest hurt of all has been dealt me by—"

225 He looked around the group, trying to remember who the malefactor was.

Everyone looked helpfully at Lou, who held up his hand resignedly.

Gramps nodded, remembering, and completed the sentence: "my great-grandson, Louis J. Schwartz."

"Grandson, sir," said Lou.

230 "Don't quibble. You're in deep enough now, young man," said Gramps, but he changed the trifle. And from there he went without a misstep through the phrasing of the disinheritance, causes for which were disrespectfulness and quibbling.

In the paragraph following, the paragraph that had belonged to everyone in the

235 room at one time or another, Lou's name was scratched out and Willy's substituted as heir to the apartment and, the biggest plum of all, the double bed in the private bedroom. "So!" said Gramps, beaming. He erased the date at the foot of the will, and substituted a new one, including the time of day. "Well—time to watch the McGarvey Family." The McGarvey Family was a television serial that

240 Gramps had been following since he was sixty, or for one hundred and twelve years. "I can't wait to see what's going to happen next," he said.

Lou detached himself from the group and lay down on his bed of pain by the bathroom door. He wished Em would join him, and he wondered where she was.

245 He dozed for a few moments, until he was disturbed by someone's stepping over him to get into the bathroom. A moment later, he heard a faint gurgling sound, as though something were being poured down the washbasin drain. Suddenly, it entered his mind that Em had cracked up, and that she was in there doing something drastic about Gramps.

250 "Em—!" he whispered through the panel. There was no reply, and Lou pressed against the door. The worn lock, whose bolt barely engaged its socket, held for a second, then let the door swing inward.

"Morty!" gasped Lou.

Lou's great-grandnephew, Mortimer, who had just married and brought his

255 wife home to the Schwartz menage, looked at Lou with consternation and surprise. Morty kicked the door shut, but not before Lou had glimpsed what was in his hand—Gramps' enormous economy-size bottle of anti-gerasone, which had been half-emptied, and which Morty was refilling to the top with tap water.

A moment later, Morty came out, glared defiantly at Lou, and brushed past him

260 wordlessly to rejoin his pretty bride.

Shocked, Lou didn't know what on earth to do. He couldn't let Gramps take the mousetrapped anti-gerasone; but if he warned Gramps about it, Gramps would certainly make life in the apartment, which was merely insufferable now, harrowing.

265 Lou glanced into the living room, and saw that the Schwartzes, Emerald among them, were momentarily at rest, relishing the botches that McGarveys had made of *their* lives. Stealthily, he went into the bathroom, locked the door as well as he could, and began to pour the contents of Gramps' bottle down the

drain. He was going to refill it with full-strength anti-gerasone from the twenty-
270 two smaller bottles on the shelf. The bottle contained a half-gallon, and its neck
was small, so it seemed to Lou that the emptying would take forever. And the
almost imperceptible smell of anti-gerasone, like Worcestershire sauce, now
seemed to Lou, in his nervousness, to be pouring out into the rest of the apartment through the keyhole and under the door.

275   "*Gloog-gloog-gloog-gloog-*," went the bottle monotonously. Suddenly, up came
the sound of music from the living room, and there were murmurs and the scraping of chair legs on the floor. "*Thus ends,*" said the television announcer, "*the
29,121st chapter in the life of your neighbours and mine, the McGarveys.*" Footsteps were
coming down the hall. There was a knock on the bathroom door.

280   "Just a sec," called Lou cheerily. Desperately, he shook the big bottle, trying
to speed up the flow. His palms slipped on the wet glass, and the heavy bottle
smashed to splinters on the tile floor.

The door sprung open, and Gramps, dumfounded, stared at the mess.

Lou grinned engagingly through his nausea, and, for want of anything remotely
285 resembling a thought, he waited for Gramps to speak.

"Well, boy," said Gramps at last, "looks like you've got a little tidying up to
do."

And that was all he said. He turned around, elbowed his way through the
crowd, and locked himself in his bedroom.

290   The Schwartzes contemplated Lou in icredulous silence for a moment longer,
and then hurried back to the living room, as though some of his horrible guilt
would taint them, too, if they looked too long. Morty stayed behind long enough
to give Lou a quizzical, annoyed glance. Then he, too, went into the living room,
leaving only Emerald standing in the doorway.

295   Tears streamed over her cheeks. "Oh, you poor lamb—please don't look so
awful. It was my fault. I put you up to this."

"No," said Lou, finding his voice, "really you didn't. Honest, Em, I was
just—"

"You don't have to explain anything to me, hon. I'm on your side no matter
300 what." She kissed him on his cheek, and whispered in his ear. "It wouldn't have
been murder, hon. It wouldn't have killed him. It wasn't such a terrible thing to
do. It just would have fixed him up so he'd be able to go any time God decided
He wanted him."

"What's gonna happen next, Em?" said Lou hollowly. "What's he gonna do?"

305   Lou and Emerald stayed fearfully awake almost all night, waiting to see what
Gramps was going to do. But not a sound came from the sacred bedroom. At
two hours before dawn, the pair dropped off to sleep.

At six o'clock they arose again, for it was time for their generation to eat breakfast in the kitchenette. No one spoke to them. They had twenty minutes in which
310 to eat, but their reflexes were so dulled by the bad night that they had hardly
swallowed two mouthfuls of egg-type processed seaweed before it was time to
surrender their places to their son's generation.

Then, as was the custom for whomever had been most recently disinherited,
they began preparing Gramps' breakfast, which would presently be served to
315 him in bed, on a tray. They tried to be cheerful about it. The toughest part of the
job was having to handle the honest-to-God eggs and bacon and oleomargarine
on which Gramps spent almost all of the income from his fortune.

"Well," said Emerald, "I'm not going to get all panicky until I'm sure there's
something to be panicky about."

320 "Maybe he doesn't know what it was I busted," said Lou hopefully.

"Probably thinks it was your watch crystal," said Eddie, their son, who was
toying apathetically with his buckwheat-type processed sawdust cakes.

"Don't get sarcastic with your father," said Em, "and don't talk with your
mouth full, either."

325 "I'd like to see anybody take a mouthful of this stuff and *not* say something,"
said Eddie, who was seventy-three. He glanced at the clock. "It's time to take
Gramps his breakfast, you know."

"Yeah, it is, isn't it," said Lou weakly. He shrugged. "Let's have the tray,
Em."

330 "We'll both go."

Walking slowly, smiling bravely, they found a large semicircle of long-faced
Schwartzes standing around the bedroom door.

Em knocked. "Gramps," she said brightly, "break-fast is rea-dy."

There was no reply, and she knocked again, harder.

335 The door swung open before her fist. In the middle of the room, the soft,
deep, wide, canopied bed, the symbol of the sweet by-and-by to every Schwartz,
was empty.

A sense of death, as unfamiliar to the Schwartzes as Zoroastrianism or the
causes of the Sepoy Mutiny, stilled every voice and slowed every heart. Awed,
340 the heirs began to search gingerly under the furniture and behind the drapes for
all that was mortal of Gramps, father of the race.

But Gramps had left not his earthly husk but a note, which Lou finally found
on the dresser, under a paperweight which was a treasured souvenir from the
2000 World's Fair. Unsteadily, Lou read it aloud:

345 "'Somebody who I have sheltered and protected and taught the best I know
how all these years last night turned on me like a mad dog and diluted my anti-
gerasone, or tried to. I am no longer a young man. I can no longer bear the
crushing burden of life as I once could. So, after last night's bitter experience, I say
goodbye. The cares of this world will soon drop away like a cloak of thorns, and
350 I shall know peace. By the time you find this, I will be gone.'"

"Gosh," said Willy brokenly, "he didn't even get to see how the Five-Hundred-
Mile Speedway Race was going to come out."

"Or the World's Series," said Eddie.

"Or whether Mrs. McGarvey got her eyesight back," said Morty.

355 "There's more," said Lou, and he began reading aloud again: "'I, Harold D.
Schwartz . . . do hereby make, publish and declare this to be my last Will and
Testament, hereby revoking any and all former wills and codicils by me at any
time heretofore made.'"

"No!" cried Willy. "Not another one!"

360 " 'I do stipulate' " read Lou, " 'that all of my property, of whatsoever kind and nature, not be divided, but do devise and bequeath it to be held in common by my issue, without regard for generation, equally, share and share alike.' "

"Issue?" said Emerald.

Lou included the multitude in a sweep of his hand. "It means we all own the 365 whole damn shootin' match."

All eyes turned instantly to the bed.

"Share and share alike?" said Morty.

"Actually," said Willy, who was the oldest person present, "it's just like the old system, where the oldest people head up things with their headquarters in 370 here, and—"

"I like *that!*" said Em. "Lou owns as much of it as you do, and I say it ought to be for the oldest one who's still working. You can snooze around here all day, waiting for your pension check, and poor Lou stumbles in here after work, all tuckered out, and—"

375 "How about letting somebody who's never had any privacy get a little crack at it?" said Eddie hotly. "Hell, you old people had plenty of privacy back when you were kids. I was born and raised in the middle of the goddam barracks in the hall! How about—"

"Yeah?" said Morty. "Sure, you've all had it pretty tough, and my heart bleeds 380 for you. But try honeymooning in the hall for a real kick."

"Silence!" shouted Willy imperiously. "The next person who opens his mouth spends the next six months by the bathroom. Now clear out of my room. I want to think."

A vase shattered against the wall, inches above his head. In the next moment, 385 a free-for-all was underway, with each couple battling to eject every other couple from the room. Fighting coalitions formed and dissolved with the lightning changes of the tactical situation. Em and Lou were thrown into the hall, where they organized others in the same situation, and stormed back into the room.

After two hours of struggle, with nothing like a decision in sight, the cops 390 broke in.

For the next half-hour, patrol wagons and ambulances hauled away Schwartzes, and then the apartment was still and spacious.

An hour later, films of the last stages of the riot were being televised to 500,000,000 delighted viewers on the Eastern Seaboard.

395 In the stillness of the three-room Schwartz apartment on the 76th floor of Building 257, the television set had been left on. Once more the air was filled with the cries and grunts and crashes of the fray, coming harmlessly now from the loudspeaker.

The battle also appeared on the screen of the television set in the police station, 400 where the Schwartzes and their captors watched with professional interest.

Em and Lou were in adjacent four-by-eight cells, and were stretched out peacefully on their cots.

"Em—" called Lou through the partition, "you got a washbasin all your own too?"

405 "Sure. Washbasin, bed, light—the works. Ha! And we thought Gramps' room was something. How long's this been going on?" She held out her hand. "For the first time in forty years, hon, I haven't got the shakes."

"Cross your fingers," said Lou, "the lawyer's going to try to get us a year."

"Gee," said Em dreamily, "I wonder what kind of wires you'd have to pull to
410 get solitary?"

"All right, pipe down," said the turnkey, "or I'll toss the whole kit and ca-boodle of you right out. And first one who lets on to anybody outside how good jail is ain't never getting back in!"

The prisoners instantly fell silent.

415 The living room of the Schwartz apartment darkened for a moment, as the riot scenes faded, and then the face of the announcer appeared, like the sun coming from behind a cloud. "*And now, friends,*" he said, "*I have a special message from the makers of anti-gerasone, a message for all you folks over one hundred and fifty. Are you hampered socially by wrinkles, by stiffness of joints and discoloration or loss of hair, all*
420 *because these things came upon you before anti-gerasone was developed? Well, if you are, you need no longer suffer, need no longer feel different and out of things.*

"*After years of research, medical science has now developed* super-anti-gerasone! *In weeks, yes weeks, you can look, feel, and act as young as your great-great-grandchildren! Wouldn't you pay $5,000 to be indistinguishable from everybody else? Well, you don't have*
425 *to. Safe, tested super-anti-gerasone costs you only dollars a day. The average cost of regaining all the sparkle and attractiveness of youth is less than fifty dollars.*

"*Write now for your free trial carton. Just put your name and address on a dollar post-card, and mail it to 'Super,' Box 500,000, Schenectady, N. Y. Have you got that? I'll repeat it. 'Super.' Box . . .*" Underlining the announcer's words was the scratch-
430 ing of Gramps' fountain-pen, the one Willy had given him the night before. He had come in a few minutes previous from the Idle Hour Tavern, which com-manded a view of Building 257 across the square of asphalt known as the Alden Village Green. He had called a cleaning woman to come straighten the place up, and had hired the best lawyer in town to get his descendants a conviction. Gramps had
435 then moved the daybed before the television screen so that he could watch from a reclining position. It was something he'd dreamed of doing for years.

"Schen-*ec*-ta-dy," mouthed Gramps. "Got it." His face had changed remark-ably. His facial muscles seemed to have relaxed, revealing kindness and equani-mity under what had been taut, bad-tempered lines. It was almost as though his
440 trial package of *Super*-anti-gerasone had already arrived. When something amused him on television, he smiled easily, rather than barely managing to lengthen the thin line of his mouth a millimeter. Life was good. He could hardly wait to see what was going to happen next.

From *Welcome To the Monkey House* by Kurt Vonnegut Jr. (1953). Originally appeared in *Galaxy* as 'The Big Trip Up Yonder'.

John Wain

46 Manhood

Swiftly free-wheeling, their breath coming easily, the man and the boy steered their bicycles down the short dip which led them from woodland into open country. Then they looked ahead and saw that the road began to climb.

'Now, Rob,' said Mr Willison, settling his plump haunches firmly on the saddle, 'just up that rise and we'll get off and have a good rest.'

'Can't we rest now?' the boy asked. 'My legs feel all funny. As if they're turning to water.'

'Rest at the top,' said Mr Willison firmly. 'Remember what I told you? The first thing any athlete has to learn is to break the fatigue barrier.'

'I've broken it already. I was feeling tired when we were going along the main road and I—'

'When fatigue sets in, the thing to do is to keep going until it wears off. Then you get your second wind and your second endurance.'

'I've already done that.'

'Up we go,' said Mr Willison, 'and at the top we'll have a good rest.' He panted slightly and stood on his pedals, causing his machine to sway from side to side in a laboured manner. Rob, falling silent, pushed doggedly at his pedals. Slowly, the pair wavered up the straight road to the top. Once there, Mr Willison dismounted with exaggerated steadiness, laid his bicycle carefully on its side, and spread his jacket on the ground before sinking down to rest. Rob slid hastily from the saddle and flung himself full-length on the grass.

'Don't lie there,' said his father. 'You'll catch cold.'

'I'm all right. I'm warm.'

'Come and sit on this. When you're over-heated, that's just when you're prone to—'

'I'm all *right*, Dad. I want to lie here. My back aches.'

'Your back needs strengthening, that's why it aches. It's a pity we don't live near a river where you could get some rowing.'

The boy did not answer, and Mr Willison, aware that he was beginning to sound like a nagging, over-anxious parent, allowed himself to be defeated and did not press the suggestion about Rob's coming to sit on his jacket. Instead, he waited a moment and then glanced at his watch.

'Twenty to twelve. We must get going in a minute.'

'*What?* I thought we were going to have a rest.'

'Well, we're having one, aren't we?' said Mr Willison reasonably. 'I've got my breath back, so surely you must have.'

'My back still aches. I want to lie here a bit.'

'Sorry,' said Mr Willison, getting up and moving over to his bicycle. 'We've got at least twelve miles to do and lunch is at one.'

'Dad, why did we have to come so far if we've got to get back for one o'clock? I know, let's find a telephone box and ring up Mum and tell her we—'

'Nothing doing. There's no reason why two fit men shouldn't cycle twelve miles in an hour and ten minutes.'

'But we've already done about a million miles.'

45 'We've done about fourteen, by my estimation,' said Mr Willison stiffly. 'What's the good of going for a bike ride if you don't cover a bit of distance?'

He picked up his bicycle and stood waiting. Rob, with his hand over his eyes, lay motionless on the grass. His legs looked thin and white among the rich grass.

'Come on, Rob.'

50 The boy showed no sign of having heard. Mr Willison got on to his bicycle and began to ride slowly away. 'Rob,' he called over his shoulder, 'I'm going.'

Rob lay like a sullen corpse by the roadside. He looked horribly like the victim of an accident, unmarked but dead from internal injuries. Mr Willison cycled fifty yards, then a hundred, then turned in a short, irritable circle and came back 55 to where his son lay.

'Rob, is there something the matter or are you just being awkward?'

The boy removed his hand and looked up into his father's face. His eyes were surprisingly mild: there was no fire of rebellion in them.

'I'm tired and my back aches. I can't go on yet.'

60 'Look, Rob,' said Mr Willison gently, 'I wasn't going to tell you this, because I meant it to be a surprise, but when you get home you'll find a present waiting for you.'

'What kind of present?'

'Something very special I've bought for you. The man's coming this morning 65 to fix it up. That's one reason why I suggested a bike ride this morning. He'll have done it by now.'

'What is it?'

'Aha. It's a surprise. Come on, get on your bike and let's go home and see.'

Rob sat up, then slowly clambered to his feet. 'Isn't there a short cut home?'

70 'I'm afraid not. It's only twelve miles.'

Rob said nothing.

'And a lot of that's downhill,' Mr Willison added brightly. His own legs were tired and his muscles fluttered unpleasantly. In addition, he suddenly realized he was very thirsty. Rob, still without speaking, picked up his bicycle, and they 75 pedalled away.

'Where is he?' Mrs Willison asked, coming into the garage.

'Gone up to his room,' said Mr Willison. He doubled his fist and gave the punch-ball a thudding blow. 'Seems to have fixed it pretty firmly. You gave him the instructions, I suppose.'

80 'What's he doing up in his room? It's lunch-time.'

'He said he wanted to rest a bit.'

'I hope you're satisfied,' said Mrs Willison. 'A lad of thirteen, nearly fourteen years of age, just when he should have a really big appetite, and when the lunch is put on the table he's *resting*—'

85 'Now look, I know what I'm—'

'Lying down in his room, resting, too tired to eat because you've dragged him up hill and down dale on one of your—'

'We did nothing that couldn't be reasonably expected of a boy of his age.'

'How do you know?' Mrs Willison demanded. 'You never did anything of that
90 kind when you were a boy. How do you know what can be reasonably—'

'Now look,' said Mr Willison again. 'When I was a boy, it was study, study, study all the time, with the fear of unemployment and insecurity in everybody's mind. I was never even given a bicycle. I never boxed, I never rowed, I never did anything to develop my physique. It was just work, work, work, pass this exam,
95 get that certificate. Well, I did it and now I'm qualified and in a secure job. But you know as well as I do that they let me down. Nobody encouraged me to build myself up.'

'Well, what does it matter? You're all right—'

'Grace!' Mr Willison interrupted sharply. 'I am not all right and you know it.
100 I am under average height, my chest is flat and I'm—'

'What nonsense. You're taller than I am and I'm—'

'No son of mine is going to grow up with the same wretched physical heritage that I—'

'No, he'll just have heart disease through overtaxing his strength, because you
105 haven't got the common sense to—'

'His heart is one hundred per cent all right. Not three weeks have gone by since the doctor looked at him.'

'Well, why does he get so over-tired if he's all right? Why is he lying down now instead of coming to the table, a boy of his age?'

110 A slender shadow blocked part of the dazzling sun in the doorway. Looking up simultaneously, the Willisons greeted their son.

'Lunch ready, Mum? I'm hungry.'

Ready when you are,' Grace Willison beamed. 'Just wash your hands and come to the table.'

115 'Look, Rob,' said Mr Willison. 'If you hit it with your left hand and then catch it on the rebound with your right, it's excellent ring training.' He dealt the punch-ball two amateurish blows. 'That's what they call a right cross,' he said.

'I think it's fine. I'll have some fun with it,' said Rob. He watched mildly as his father peeled off the padded mittens.

120 'Here, slip these on,' said Mr Willison. 'They're just training gloves. They harden your fists. Of course, we can get a pair of proper gloves later. But these are specially for use with the ball.'

'Lunch,' called Mrs Willison from the house.

'Take a punch at it,' Mr Willison urged.

125 'Let's go and eat.'

'Go on. One punch before you go in. I haven't seen you hit it yet.'

Rob took the gloves, put on the right-hand one, and gave the punch-ball one conscientious blow, aiming at the exact centre. 'Now let's go in,' he said.

'Lunch!'

130 'All right. We're coming . . .'

'Five feet eight, Rob,' said Mr Willison, folding up the wooden ruler. 'You're taller than I am. This is a great landmark.'

'Only *just* taller.'

'But you're growing all the time. Now all you have to do is to start growing
135 outwards as well as upwards. We'll have you in the middle of that scrum. The heaviest forward in the pack.'

Rob picked up his shirt and began uncertainly poking his arms into the sleeves.

'When do they pick the team?' Mr. Willison asked. 'I should have thought they'd have done it by now.'

140 'They have done it,' said Rob. He bent down to pick up his socks from under a chair.

'They have? And you—'

'I wasn't selected,' said the boy, looking intently at the socks as if trying to detect minute differences in colour and weave.

145 Mr. Willison opened his mouth, closed it again, and stood for a moment looking out of the window. Then he gently laid his hand on his son's shoulder. 'Bad luck,' he said quietly.

'I tried hard,' said Rob quickly.

'I'm sure you did.'

150 'I played my hardest in the trial games.'

'It's just bad luck,' said Mr. Willison. 'It could happen to anybody.'

There was silence as they both continued with their dressing. A faint smell of frying rose into the air, and they could hear Mrs. Willison laying the table for breakfast.

155 'That's it, then, for this season,' said Mr. Willison, as if to himself.

'I forgot to tell you, though,' said Rob. 'I was selected for the boxing team.'

'You *were?* I didn't know the school had one.'

'It's new. Just formed. They had some trials for it at the end of last term. I found my punching was better than most people's because I'd been getting plenty
160 of practice with the ball.'

Mr. Willison put out a hand and felt Rob's biceps. 'Not bad, not bad at all,' he said critically. 'But if you're going to be a boxer and represent the school, you'll need more power up there. I tell you what. We'll train together.'

'That'll be fun,' said Rob. 'I'm training at school too.'

165 'What weight do they put you in?'

'It isn't weight, it's age. Under fifteen. Then when you get over fifteen you get classified into weights.'

'Well,' said Mr. Willison, tying his tie, 'you'll be in a good position for the under-fifteens. You've got six months to play with. And there's no reason why
170 you shouldn't steadily put muscle on all the time. I suppose you'll be entered as a team, for tournaments and things?'

'Yes. There's a big one at the end of next term. I'll be in that.'

Confident, joking, they went down to breakfast. 'Two eggs for Rob, Mum,' said Mr Willison. 'He's in training. He's going to be a heavyweight.'

175 'A heavyweight what?' Mrs Willison asked, teapot in hand.

'Boxer,' Rob smiled.

120

Grace Willison put down the teapot, her lips compressed, and looked from one to the other. '*Boxing?*' she repeated.

'Boxing,' Mr. Willison replied calmly.

180 'Over my dead body,' said Mrs. Willison. 'That's one sport I'm definite that he's never going in for.'

'Too late. They've picked him for the under-fifteens. He's had trials and everything.

'Is this true, Rob?' she demanded.

185 'Yes,' said the boy, eating rapidly.

'Well, you can just tell them you're dropping it. Baroness Summerskill—'

'To hell with Baroness Summerskill!' her husband shouted. 'The first time he gets a chance to do something, the first time he gets picked for a team and given a chance to show what he's made of, and you have to bring up Baroness
190 Summerskill.'

'But it injures their brains! All those blows on the front of the skull. I've read about it—'

'Injures their brains!' Mr. Willison snorted. 'Has it injured Ingemar Johansson's brain? Why, he's one of the acutest business men in the world!'

195 'Rob,' said Mrs. Willison steadily, 'when you get to school, go and see the sports master and tell him you're giving up boxing.'

'There isn't a sports master. All the masters do bits of it at different times.'

'There must be one who's in charge of the boxing. All you have to do is tell him—'

200 'Are you ready, Rob?' said Mr. Willison. 'You'll be late for school if you don't go.'

'I'm in plenty of time, Dad. I haven't finished my breakfast.'

'Never mind, push along, old son. You've had your egg and bacon, that's what matters. I want to talk to your mother.'

205 Cramming a piece of dry toast into his mouth, the boy picked up his satchel and wandered from the room. Husband and wife sat back, glaring hot-eyed at each other.

The quarrel began, and continued for many days. In the end it was decided that Rob should continue boxing until he had represented the school at the tourna-
210 ment in March of the following year, and should then give it up.

'Ninety-six, ninety-seven, ninety-eight, ninety-nine, a hundred,' Mr. Willison counted. 'Right, that's it. Now go and take your shower and get into bed.'

'I don't feel tired, honestly,' Rob protested.

'Who's manager here, you or me?' Mr. Willison asked bluffly. 'I'm in charge of
215 training and you can't say my methods don't work. Fifteen solid weeks and you start questioning my decisions on the very night of the fight?'

'It just seems silly to go to bed when I'm not—'

'My dear Rob, please trust me. No boxer ever went into a big fight without spending an hour or two in bed, resting, just before going to his dressing-
220 room.'

'All right. But I bet none of the others are bothering to do all this.'

'That's exactly why you're going to be better than the others. Now go and get your shower before you catch cold. Leave the skipping-rope, I'll put it away.'

After Rob had gone, Mr Willison folded the skipping-rope into a neat ball and
225 packed it away in the case that contained the boy's gloves, silk dressing gown, lace-up boxing boots, and trunks with the school badge sewn into the correct position on the right leg. There would be no harm in a little skipping, to limber up and conquer his nervousness while waiting to go on. Humming, he snapped down the catches of the small leather case and went into the house.

230 Mrs Willison did not lift her eyes from the television set as he entered. 'All ready now, Mother,' said Mr Willison. 'He's going to rest in bed now, and go along at about six o'clock. I'll go with him and wait till the doors open to be sure of a ringside seat.' He sat down on the sofa beside his wife, and tried to put his arm round her. 'Come on, love,' he said coaxingly. 'Don't spoil my big night.'

235 She turned to him and he was startled to see her eyes brimming with angry tears. 'What about my big night?' she asked, her voice harsh. 'Fourteen years ago, remember? When he came into the world.'

'Well, what about it?' Mr Willison parried, uneasily aware that the television set was quacking and signalling on the fringe of his attention, turning the scene
240 from clumsy tragedy into a clumsier farce.

'Why didn't you tell me then?' she sobbed. 'Why did you let me have a son if all you were interested in was having him punched to death by a lot of rough bullet-headed louts who—'

'Take a grip on yourself, Grace. A punch on the nose won't hurt him.'

245 'You're an unnatural father,' she keened. 'I don't know how you can bear to send him into that ring to be beaten and thumped—Oh, why can't you stop him now? Keep him at home? There's no *law* that compels us to—'

'That's where you're wrong, Grace,' said Mr Willison sternly. 'There is a law. The unalterable law of nature that says that the young males of the species indulge
250 in manly trials of strength. Think of all the other lads who are going into the ring tonight. D'you think their mothers are sitting about crying and kicking up a fuss? No—they're proud to have strong, masculine sons who can stand up in the ring and take a few punches.'

'Go away, please,' said Mrs Willison, sinking back with closed eyes. 'Just go
255 right away and don't come near me until it's all over.'

'Grace!'

'Please. Please leave me alone. I can't bear to look at you and I can't bear to hear you.'

'You're hysterical,' said Mr Willison bitterly. Rising, he went out into the
260 hall and called up the stairs. 'Are you in bed, Rob?'

There was a slight pause and then Rob's voice called faintly, 'Could you come up, Dad?'

'Come up? Why? Is something the matter?'

'Could you come up?'

265 Mr Willison ran up the stairs. 'What is it?' he panted. 'D'you want something?'

'I think I've got appendicitis,' said Rob. He lay squinting among the pillows, his face suddenly narrow and crafty.

'I don't believe you,' said Mr Willison shortly. 'I've supervised your training for fifteen weeks and I know you're as fit as a fiddle. You can't possibly have
270   anything wrong with you.'

'I've got a terrible pain in my side,' said Rob. 'Low down on the right-hand side. That's where appendicitis comes, isn't it?'

Mr Willison sat down on the bed. 'Listen, Rob,' he said. 'Don't do this to me. All I'm asking you to do is to go into the ring and have one bout. You've been
275   picked for the school team and everyone's depending on you.'

'I'll die if you don't get the doctor,' Rob suddenly hissed. 'Mum!' he shouted.

Mrs Willison came bounding up the stairs. 'What is it, my pet?'

'My stomach hurts. Low down on the right-hand side.'
280   'Appendicitis!' She whirled to face Mr Willison. 'That's what comes of your foolishness!'

'I don't believe it,' said Mr Willison. He went out of the bedroom and down the stairs. The television was still jabbering in the living-room, and for fifteen minutes Mr Willison forced himself to sit staring at the strident puppets, glis-
285   tening in metallic light, as they enacted their Lilliputian rituals. Then he went up to the bedroom again. Mrs Willison was bathing Rob's forehead.

'His temperature's normal,' she said.

'Of course his temperature's normal,' said Mr Willison. 'He doesn't want to fight, that's all.'
290   'Fetch the doctor,' said a voice from under the cold flannel that swathed Rob's face.

'We will, pet, if you don't get better very soon,' said Mrs Willison, darting a murderous glance at her husband.

Mr Willison slowly went downstairs. For a moment he stood looking at the
295   telephone, then picked it up and dialled the number of the grammar school. No one answered. He replaced the receiver, went to the foot of the stairs and called, 'What's the name of the master in charge of this tournament?'

'I don't know,' Rob called weakly.

'You told me you'd been training with Mr Granger,' Mr Willison called.
300   'Would he know anything about it?'

Rob did not answer, so Mr Willison looked up all the Grangers in the telephone book. There were four in the town, but only one was M.A. 'That's him,' said Mr Willison. With lead in his heart and ice in his fingers, he dialled the number.
305   Mrs Granger fetched Mr Granger. Yes, he taught at the school. He was the right man. What could he do for Mr Willison?

'It's about tonight's boxing tournament.'

'Sorry, what? The line's bad.'

'*Tonight's boxing tournament.*'
310   'Have you got the right person?'

'You teach my son, Rob—we've just agreed on that. Well, it's about the boxing tournament he's supposed to be taking part in tonight.'

'Where?'

'Where? At the school, of course. He's representing the under-fifteens.'

315   There was a pause. 'I'm not quite sure what mistake you're making, Mr Willison, but I think you've got hold of the wrong end of at least one stick.' A hearty, defensive laugh. 'If Rob belongs to a boxing-club it's certainly news to me, but in any case it can't be anything to do with the school. We don't go in for boxing.'

'Don't go in for it?'

320   'We don't offer it. It's not in our curriculum.'

'Oh,' said Mr Willison. 'Oh. Thank you. I must have—well, thank you.'

'Not at all. I'm glad to answer any queries. Everything's all right, I trust?'

'Oh, yes,' said Mr Willison, 'yes, thanks. Everything's all right.'

He put down the telephone, hesitated, then turned and began slowly to climb
325 the stairs.

From *Death of the Hindlegs and Other Stories* by John Wain. (1966)

Edward Albee

47 The Sandbox

The Players:

THE YOUNG MAN	25.	A good-looking, well-built boy in a bathing suit.
MOMMY	55.	A well-dressed, imposing woman.
DADDY	60.	A small man; gray, thin.
GRANDMA	86.	A tiny, wizened woman with bright eyes.
THE MUSICIAN		No particular age, but young would be nice.

Note:

When, in the course of the play, MOMMY and DADDY call each other by these names, there should be no suggestion of regionalism. These names are of empty affection and point up the pre-senility and vacuity of their characters.

The Scene:

5 A bare stage, with only the following: Near the footlights, far stage-right, two simple chairs set side by side, facing the audience; near the footlights, far stage-left, a chair facing stage-right with a music stand before it; farther back, and stage-center, slightly elevated and raked, a large child's sandbox with a toy pail and shovel; the background is the sky, which alters from
10 brightest day to deepest night.

At the beginning, it is brightest day; the YOUNG MAN is alone on stage, to the rear of the sandbox, and to one side. He is doing calisthenics; he does calisthenics until quite at the very end of the play. These calisthenics, employing the arms only, should suggest the beating and fluttering of
15 wings. The YOUNG MAN is, after all, the Angel of Death.

MOMMY *and* DADDY *enter from stage-left,* MOMMY *first.*

MOMMY

(*Motioning to* DADDY) Well, here we are; this is the beach.

DADDY (*Whining*)

I'm cold.

MOMMY

(*Dismissing him with a little laugh*) Don't be silly; it's as warm as toast. Look at that nice young man over there: *he* doesn't think it's cold. (*Waves to the* YOUNG
20 MAN) Hello.

YOUNG MAN

(*With an endearing smile*) Hi!

MOMMY (*Looking about*)

This will do perfectly ... don't you think so, Daddy? There's sand there ... and the water beyond. What do you think, Daddy?

DADDY (*Vaguely*)

Whatever you say, Mommy.

MOMMY

25 (*With the same little laugh*) Well, of course ... whatever I say. Then, it's settled, is it?

DADDY (*Shrugs*)

She's *your* mother, not mine.

MOMMY

I know she's my mother. What do you take me for? (*A pause*) All right, now; let's get on with it. (*She shouts into the wings, stage-left*) You! Out there! You can 30 come in now.

> (*The* MUSICIAN *enters, seats himself in the chair, stage-left, places music on the music stand, is ready to play.* MOMMY *nods approvingly*)

MOMMY

Very nice; very nice. Are you ready, Daddy? Let's go get Grandma.

DADDY

Whatever you say, Mommy.

MOMMY

(*Leading the way out, stage-left*) Of course, whatever I say. (*To the* MUSICIAN) You can begin now.

> (*The* MUSICIAN *begins playing;* MOMMY *and* DADDY *exit; the* MUSICIAN, *all the while playing, nods to the* YOUNG MAN)

YOUNG MAN

35 (*With the same endearing smile*) Hi!

> (*After a moment,* MOMMY *and* DADDY *re-enter, carrying* GRANDMA. *She is borne in by their hands under her armpits; she is quite rigid; her legs are drawn up; her feet do not touch the ground; the expression on her ancient face is that of puzzlement and fear*)

DADDY

Where do we put her?

MOMMY

(*The same little laugh*) Wherever I say, of course. Let me see ... well ... all right, over there ... in the sandbox. (*Pause*) Well, what are you waiting for, Daddy? ... The sandbox!

> (*Together they carry* GRANDMA *over to the sandbox and more or less dump her in*)

GRANDMA

(*Righting herself to a sitting position; her voice a cross between a baby's laugh and cry*)
40 Ahhhhhh! Graaaaa!

DADDY (*Dusting himself*)

What do we do now?

MOMMY

(*To the* MUSICIAN) You can stop now.
> (*The* MUSICIAN *stops*)

(*Back to* DADDY) What do you mean, what do we do now? We go over there and sit down, of course. (*To the* YOUNG MAN) Hello there.

YOUNG MAN

45 (*Again smiling*) Hi!
> (MOMMY *and* DADDY *move to the chairs, stage-right, and sit down. A pause*)

GRANDMA

(*Same as before*) Ahhhhhh! Ah-haaaaaa! Graaaaaa!

DADDY

Do you think ... do you think she's ... comfortable?

MOMMY (*Impatiently*)

How would I know?

DADDY

(*Pause*) What do we do now?

MOMMY

50 (*As if remembering*) We ... wait. We ... sit here ... and we wait ... that's what we do.

DADDY

(*After a pause*) Shall we talk to each other?

MOMMY

(*With that little laugh; picking something off her dress*) Well, *you* can talk, if you want to ... if you can think of anything to *say* ... if you can think of anything *new*.

DADDY (*Thinks*)

55 No ... I suppose not.

MOMMY

(*With a triumphant laugh*) Of course not!

GRANDMA

(*Banging the toy shovel against the pail*) Haaaaaa! Ah-haaaaaa!

MOMMY

(*Out over the audience*) Be quiet, Grandma ... just be quiet, and wait.
 (GRANDMA *throws a shovelful of sand at* MOMMY)

MOMMY

(*Still out over the audience*) She's throwing sand at me! You stop that, Grandma;
60 you stop throwing sand at Mommy! (*To* DADDY) She's throwing sand at me.
 (DADDY *looks around at* GRANDMA, *who screams at him*)

GRANDMA

GRAAAAA!

MOMMY

Don't look at her. Just ... sit here ... be very still ... and wait. (*To the*
MUSICIAN) You ... uh ... you go ahead and do whatever it is you do.
 (*The* MUSUCIAN *plays*)
 (MOMMY *and* DADDY *are fixed, staring out beyond the audience.* GRANDMA *looks
at them, looks at the* MUSICIAN, *looks at the sandbox, throws down the shovel*)

GRANDMA

Ah-haaaaaa! Graaaaaa! (*Looks for reaction; gets none. Now ... directly to the audience*)
65 Honestly! What a way to treat an old woman! Drag her out of the house ...
stick her in a car ... bring her out here from the city ... dump her in a pile of
sand ... and leave her here to set. I'm eighty-six years old! I was married when
I was seventeen. To a farmer. He died when I was thirty. (*To the* MUSICIAN) Will
you stop that, please?
 (*The* MUSICIAN *stops playing*)
70 I'm a feeble old woman ... how do you expect anybody to hear me over that
peep! peep! peep! (*To herself*) There's no respect around here. (*To the* YOUNG
MAN) There's no respect around here!

YOUNG MAN

(*Same smile*) Hi!

GRANDMA

(*After a pause, a mild double-take, continues, to the audience*) My husband died when
75 I was thirty (*indicates* MOMMY), and I had to raise that big cow over there all by

my lonesome. You can imagine what *that was like*. Lordy! (*To the* YOUNG MAN) Where'd they get *you?*

YOUNG MAN

Oh ... I've been around for a while.

GRANDMA

I'll bet you have! Heh, heh, heh. Will you look at you!

YOUNG MAN

80 (*Flexing his muscles*) Isn't that something? (*Continues his calisthenics*)

GRANDMA

Boy, oh boy; I'll say. Pretty good.

YOUNG MAN (*Sweetly*)

I'll say.

GRANDMA

Where ya from?

YOUNG MAN

Southern California.

GRANDMA (*Nodding*)

85 Figgers; figgers. What's your name, honey?

YOUNG MAN

I don't know. ...

GRANDMA

(*To the audience*) Bright, too!

YOUNG MAN

I mean ... I mean, they haven't given me one yet ... the studio ...

GRANDMA

(*Giving him the once-over*) You don't say ... you don't say. Well ... uh, I've got
90 to talk some more ... don't you go 'way.

YOUNG MAN

Oh, no.

GRANDMA

(*Turning her attention back to the audience*) Fine; fine. (*Then, once more, back to the*
YOUNG MAN) You're ... you're an actor, hunh?

129

YOUNG MAN (*Beaming*)

Yes. I am.

GRANDMA

95 (*To the audience again; shrugs*) I'm smart that way. *Anyhow*, I had to raise ... *that* over there all by my lonesome; and what's next to her there ... that's what she married. Rich? I tell you ... money, money, money. They took me off the *farm* ... which was real decent of them ... and they moved me into the big town house with *them* ... fixed a nice place for me under the stove ... gave me an
100 army blanket ... and my own dish ... my very own dish! So, what have I got to complain about? Nothing, of course. I'm not complaining. (*She looks up at the sky, shouts to someone off stage*) Shouldn't it be getting dark now, dear?
    (*The lights dim; night comes on. The* MUSICIAN *begins to play; it becomes deepest night. There are spots on all the players including the* YOUNG MAN, *who is, of course, continuing his calisthenics*)

DADDY (*Stirring*)

It's nighttime.

MOMMY

Shhhh. Be still ... wait.

DADDY (*Whining*)

105 It's so hot.

MOMMY

Shhhhhh. Be still ... wait.

GRANDMA

(*To herself*) That's better. Night. (*To the* MUSICIAN) Honey, do you play all through this part?
    (*The* MUSICIAN nods)
Well, keep it nice and soft; that's a good boy.
    (*The* MUSICIAN *nods again; plays softly*)
110 That's nice.
    (*There is an off-stage rumble*)

DADDY (*Starting*)

What was that?

MOMMY

(*Beginning to weep*) It was nothing.

DADDY

It was ... it was ... thunder ... or a wave breaking ... or something.

130

MOMMY

(*Whispering, through her tears*) It was an off-stage rumble ... and you know what
115   *that* means. ...

DADDY

I forget. ...

MOMMY

(*Barely able to talk*) It means the time has come for poor Grandma ... and I can't
bear it!

DADDY (*Vacantly*)

I ... I suppose you've got to be brave.

GRANDMA (*Mocking*)

120   That's right, kid; be brave. You'll bear up; you'll get over it.
(*Another off-stage rumble ... louder*)

MOMMY

Ohhhhhhhhhh ... poor Grandma ... poor Grandma. ...

GRANDMA (*To* MOMMY)

I'm fine! I'm all right! It hasn't happened yet!
        (*A violent off-stage rumble. All the lights go out, save the spot on the* YOUNG MAN;
        the MUSICIAN *stops playing*)

MOMMY

Ohhhhhhhhhh. ... Ohhhhhhhhhh. ...
        (*Silence*)

GRANDMA

Don't put the lights up yet ... I'm not ready; I'm not quite ready. (*Silence*) All
125   right, dear ... I'm about done.
        (*The lights come up again, to brightest day; the* MUSICIAN *begins to play.* GRANDMA
        *is discovered, still in the sandbox, lying on her side, propped up on an elbow, half
        covered, busily shoveling sand over herself*)

GRANDMA (*Muttering*)

I don't know how I'm supposed to do anything with this goddam toy shovel. ...

DADDY

Mommy! It's daylight!

MOMMY (*Brightly*)

So it is! Well! Our long night is over. We must put away our tears, take off our
mourning ... and face the future. It's our duty.

GRANDMA

130 (*Still shoveling; mimicking*) ... take off our mourning ... face the future. ...
Lordy!

> (MOMMY *and* DADDY *rise, stretch.* MOMMY *waves to the* YOUNG MAN)

YOUNG MAN

(*With that smile*) Hi!

> (GRANDMA *plays dead.* (!) MOMMY *and* DADDY *go over to look at her; she is a*
> *little more than half buried in the sand; the toy shovel is in her hands, which are*
> *crossed on her breast*)

MOMMY

(*Before the sandbox; shaking her head*) Lovely! It's ... it's hard to be sad ... she
looks ... so happy. (*With pride and conviction*) It pays to do things well. (*To the*
135 MUSICIAN) All right, you can stop now, if you want to I mean, stay around for a
swim, or something; it's all right with us. (*She sighs heavily*) Well, Daddy ... off
we go.

DADDY

Brave Mommy!

MOMMY

Brave Daddy!

> (*They exit, stage-left*)

GRANDMA

140 (*After they leave; lying quite still*) It pays to do things well. ... Boy, oh boy! (*She*
tries to sit up) ... well, kids ... (*but she finds she can't*) ... I ... I can't get up.
I ... I can't move. ...

> (*The* YOUNG MAN *stops his calisthenics, nods to the* MUSICIAN, *walks over to*
> GRANDMA, *kneels down by the sandbox*)

GRANDMA

I ... can't move. ...

YOUNG MAN

Shhhh ... be very still. ...

GRANDMA

145 I ... I can't move. ...

YOUNG MAN

Uh ... ma'am; I ... I have a line here.

GRANDMA

Oh, I'm sorry, sweetie; you go right ahead.

YOUNG MAN

I am ... uh ...

GRANDMA

Take your time, dear.

YOUNG MAN

150 (*Prepares; delivers the line like a real amateur*) I am the Angel of Death. I am ... uh ... I am come for you.

GRANDMA

What ... wha ... (*Then, with resignation*) ... ohhhh ... ohhhh, I see.
(*The* YOUNG MAN *bends over, kisses* GRANDMA *gently on the forehead*)

GRANDMA

(*Her eyes closed, her hands folded on her breast again, the shovel between her hands, a sweet smile on her face*)
Well ... that was very nice, dear. ...

YOUNG MAN

(*Still kneeling*) Shhhhhh ... be still. ...

GRANDMA

155 What I meant was ... you did that very well, dear. ...

YOUNG MAN (*Blushing*)

... oh ...

GRANDMA

No; I mean it. You've got that ... you've got a quality.

YOUNG MAN

(*With his endearing smile*) Oh ... thank you; thank you very much ... ma'am.

GRANDMA

(*Slowly; softly—as the* YOUNG MAN *puts his hands on top of* GRANDMA'S) You're ...
160 you're welcome ... dear.
(*Tableau. The* MUSICIAN *continues to play as the curtain slowly comes down*)

CURTAIN

From *Zoo Story And Other Plays* by Edward Albee. (1959)

Samuel Beckett

48 Come and Go

(A Dramaticule)

Characters:

VI

RU

FLO

Ages undeterminable

Sitting centre side by side stage right to left FLO, VI *and* RU. *Very erect, facing front, hands clasped in laps.*

Silence.

VI: When did we three last meet?
5 RU: Let us not speak.
  Silence.
  Exit VI *right.*
  Silence.
FLO: Ru.
10 RU: Yes.
FLO: What do you think of Vi?
RU: I see little change. (FLO *moves to centre seat, whispers in* RU's *ear. Appalled.*) Oh! (*They look at each other.* FLO *puts her finger to her lips.*) Does she not realize?
FLO: God grant not.
15 *Enter* VI. FLO *and* RU *turn back front, resume pose.* VI *sits right.*
  Silence.
FLO: Just sit together as we used to, in the playground at Miss Wade's.
RU: On the log.
  Silence.
20 *Exit* FLO *left.*
  Silence.
RU: Vi.
VI: Yes.
RU: How do you find Flo?
25 VI: She seems much the same. (RU *moves to centre seat, whispers in* VI's *ear. Appalled.*) Oh! (*They look at each other.* RU *puts her finger to her lips.*) Has she not been told?
RU: God forbid.
  Enter FLO. RU *and* VI *turn back front, resume pose.*
30 FLO *sits left.*
RU: Holding hands ... that way.

FLO: Dreaming of ... love.
Silence.
Exit RU *right.*
35 *Silence.*
VI: Flo.
FLO: Yes.
VI: How do you think Ru is looking?
FLO: One sees little in this light. (VI *moves to centre seat, whispers in* FLO'*s ear. Ap-*
40 *palled.*) Oh! (*They look at each other.* VI *puts her finger to her lips.*) Does she not
know?

VI: Please God not.
Enter RU. VI *and* FLO *turn back front, resume pose.*
RU *sits right.*
45 *Silence.*
VI: May we not speak of the old days? (*Silence.*) Of what came after? (*Silence.*)
Shall we hold hands in the old way?
After a moment they join hands as follows: VI'*s right hand with* RU'*s right hand,*
VI'*s left hand with* FLO'*s left hand,* FLO'*s right hand with* RU'*s left hand,* VI'*s arms*
50 *being above* RU'*s left arm and* FLO'*s right arm. The three pairs of clasped hands rest*
on the three laps.
Silence.
FLO: I can feel the rings.
Silence.
55 CURTAIN

NOTES

Successive positions

1	FLO	VI	RU
2	⎰ FLO		RU
		FLO	RU
3	VI	FLO	RU
4	⎰ VI		RU
	⎱ VI	RU	
5	VI	RU	FLO
6	⎰ VI		FLO
		VI	FLO
7	RU	VI	FLO

Hands

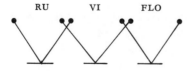

135

Lighting

Soft, from above only and concentrated on playing area. Rest of stage as dark as possible.

Costume

Full-length coats, buttoned high, dull violet (Ru), dull red (Vi), dull yellow (Flo).
70 Drab nondescript hats with enough brim to shade faces. Apart from colour differentiation three figures as alike as possible. Light shoes with rubber soles. Hands made up to be as visible as possible. No rings apparent.

Seat

Narrow benchlike seat, without back, just long enough to accommodate three figures almost touching. As little visible as possible. It should not be clear what
75 they are sitting on.

Exits

The figures are not seen to go off stage. They should disappear a few steps from lit area. If dark not sufficient to allow this, recourse should be had to screens or drapes as little visible as possible. Exits and entrances slow, without sound of feet.

Ohs

80 Three very different sounds.

Voices

As low as compatible with audibility. Colourless except for three "ohs" and two lines following.

From '*Come and Go*' by Samuel Beckett. (1965)

Eugene O'Neill

49 Before Breakfast

SCENE. *A small room serving both as kitchen and dining room in a flat on Christopher Street, New York City. In the rear, to the right, a door leading to the outer hallway. On the left of the doorway, a sink, and a two-burner gas stove. Over the stove, and extending to the left wall, a wooden closet for dishes, etc. On the left, two windows looking out on a fire*
5   *escape where several potted plants are dying of neglect. Before the windows, a table covered with oilcloth. Two cane-bottomed chairs are placed by the table. Another stands against the wall to the right of door in rear. In the right wall, rear, a doorway leading into a bedroom. Farther forward, different articles of a man's and a woman's clothing are hung on pegs. A clothes line is strung from the left corner, rear, to the right wall, forward.*
10   *It is about eight-thirty in the morning of a fine, sunshiny day in the early fall.*

MRS. ROWLAND *enters from the bedroom, yawning, her hands still busy putting the finishing touches on a slovenly toilet by sticking hairpins into her hair which is bunched up in a drab-colored mass on top of her round head. She is of medium height and inclined to a shapeless stoutness, accentuated by her formless blue dress, shabby and worn. Her face is*
15   *characterless, with small regular features and eyes of a nondescript blue. There is a pinched expression about her eyes and nose and her weak, spiteful mouth. She is in her early twenties but looks much older.*

She comes to the middle of the room and yawns, stretching her arms to their full length. Her drowsy eyes stare about the room with the irritated look of one to whom a long sleep
20   *has not been a long rest. She goes wearily to the clothes hanging on the right and takes an apron from a hook. She ties it about her waist, giving vent to an exasperated "damn" when the knot fails to obey her clumsy fingers. Finally gets it tied and goes slowly to the gas stove and lights one burner. She fills the coffee pot at the sink and sets it over the flame. Then slumps down into a chair by the table and puts a hand over her forehead as if she*
25   *were suffering from headache. Suddenly her face brightens as though she had remembered something, and she casts a quick glance at the dish closet; then looks sharply at the bedroom door and listens intently for a moment or so.*

MRS. ROWLAND. (*in a low voice*) Alfred! Alfred! (*There is no answer from the next room and she continues suspiciously in a louder tone*) You needn't pretend you're
30   asleep. (*There is no reply to this from the bedroom, and, reassured, she gets up from her chair and tiptoes cautiously to the dish closet. She slowly opens one door, taking great care to make no noise, and slides out, from their hiding place behind the dishes, a bottle of Gordon gin and a glass. In doing so she disturbs the top dish, which rattles a little. At this sound she starts guiltily and looks with sulky defiance at the doorway to the next room.*)
35   (*Her voice trembling*) Alfred!

(*After a pause, during which she listens for any sound, she takes the glass and pours out a large drink and gulps it down; then hastily returns the bottle and glass to their hiding place. She closes the closet door with the same care as she had opened it, and, heaving a great sigh of relief, sinks down into her chair again. The large dose of alcohol she has taken*
40   *has an almost immediate effect. Her features become more animated, she seems to gather*

energy, and she looks at the bedroom door with a hard, vindictive smile on her lips. Her eyes glance quickly about the room and are fixed on a man's coat and vest which hang from a hook at right. She moves stealthily over to the open doorway and stands there, out of sight of anyone inside, listening for any movement.)

45 *(Calling in a half-whisper)* Alfred!

(Again there is no reply. With a swift movement she takes the coat and vest from the hook and returns with them to her chair. She sits down and takes the various articles out of each pocket but quickly puts them back again. At last, in the inside pocket of the vest, she finds a letter.)

50 *(Looking at the handwriting—slowly to herself)* Hmm! I knew it.

(She opens the letter and reads it. At first her expression is one of hatred and rage, but as she goes on to the end it changes to one of triumphant malignity. She remains in deep thought for a moment, staring before her, the letter in her hands, a cruel smile on her lips. Then she puts the letter back in the pocket of the vest, and still careful not to awaken the sleeper,

55 *hangs the clothes up again on the same hook, and goes to the bedroom door and looks in.)*

(In a loud, shrill voice) Alfred! *(Still louder)* Alfred! *(There is a muffled, yawning groan from the next room).* Don't you think it's about time you got up? Do you want to stay in bed all day? *(Turning around and coming back to her chair)* Not that I've got any doubts about your being lazy enough to stay in bed forever. *(She sits*

60 *down and looks out of the window, irritably)* Goodness knows what time it is. We haven't even got any way of telling the time since you pawned your watch like a fool. The last valuable thing we had, and you knew it. It's been nothing but pawn, pawn, pawn, with you—anything to put off getting a job, anything to get off going to work like a man. *(She taps the floor with her foot nervously, biting*

65 *her lips.)*

(After a short pause) Alfred! Get up, do you hear me? I want to make that bed before I go out. I'm sick of having this place in a continual mess on your account. *(With a certain vindictive satisfaction)* Not that we'll be here long unless you manage to get some money some place. Heaven knows I do my part—and

70 more—going out to sew every day while you play the gentleman and loaf around barrooms with that good-for-nothing lot of artists from the Square.

(A short pause during which she plays nervously with a cup and saucer on the table.)

And where are you going to get money, I'd like to know? The rent's due this week and you know what the landlord is. He won't let us stay a minute over

75 our time. You say you *can't* get a job. That's a lie and you know it. You never even look for one. All you do is moon around all day writing silly poetry and stories that no one will buy—and no wonder they won't. I notice I can always get a position, such as it is; and it's only that which keeps us from starving to death.

80 *(Gets up and goes over to the stove—looks into the coffee pot to see if the water is boiling; then comes back and sits down again.)*

You'll have to get money today some place. I can't do it all, and I won't do it all. You've got to come to your senses. You've got to beg, borrow, or steal it somewhere. *(With a contemptuous laugh)* But where, I'd like to know? You're too

85 proud to beg, and you've borrowed the limit, and you haven't the nerve to steal.

(*After a pause—getting up angrily*) Aren't you up yet, for heaven's sake? It's just like you to go to sleep again, or pretend to. (*She goes to the bedroom door and looks in*) Oh, you are up. Well, it's about time. You needn't look at me like that. Your
90 airs don't fool me a bit any more. I know you too well—better than you think I do—you and your goings-on. (*Turning away from the door—meaningly*) I know a lot of things, my dear. Never mind what I know, now. I'll tell you before I go, you needn't worry. (*She comes to the middle of the room and stands there, frowning.*)
(*Irritably*) Hmm! I suppose I might as well get breakfast ready—not that there's
95 anything much to get. (*Questioningly*) Unless you have some money? (*She pauses for an answer from the next room which does not come*) Foolish question! (*She gives a short, hard laugh*) I ought to know you better by this time. When you left here in such a huff last night I knew what would happen. You can't be trusted for a second. A nice condition you came home in! The fight we had was only an
100 excuse for you to make a beast of yourself. What was the use pawning your watch if all you wanted with the money was to waste it in buying drink?
(*Goes over to the dish closet and takes out plates, cups, etc., while she is talking.*)
Hurry up! It don't take long to get breakfast these days, thanks to you. All we got this morning is bread and butter and coffee; and you wouldn't even have
105 that if it wasn't for me sewing my fingers off. (*She slams the loaf of bread on the table with a bang.*)
The bread's stale. I hope you'll like it. *You* don't see why *I* should suffer.
(*Going over to the stove*) The coffee'll be ready in a minute, and you needn't expect me to wait for you.
110 (*Suddenly with great anger*) What on earth are you doing all this time? (*She goes over to the door and looks in*) Well, you're *almost* dressed at any rate. I expected to find you back in bed. That'd be just like you. How awful you look this morning! For heaven's sake, shave! You're disgusting! You look like a tramp. No wonder no one will give you a job. I don't blame them—when you don't even look
115 half-way decent. (*She goes to the stove*) There's plenty of hot water right here. You've got no excuse. (*Gets a bowl and pours some of the water from the coffee pot into it*) Here.
(*He reaches his hand into the room for it. It is a sensitive hand with slender fingers. It trembles and some of the water spills on the floor.*)
120 (*Tauntingly*) Look at your hand tremble! You'd better give up drinking. You can't stand it. It's just your kind that get the D.T.'s. That would be the last straw! (*Looking down at the floor*) Look at the mess you've made of this floor— cigarette butts and ashes all over the place. Why can't you put them on a plate? No, you wouldn't be considerate enough to do that. You never think of me.
125 You don't have to sweep the room and that's all you care about.
(*Takes the broom and commences to sweep viciously, raising a cloud of dust. From the inner room comes the sound of a razor being stropped.*)
(*Sweeping*) Hurry up! It must be nearly time for me to go. If I'm late I'm liable to lose my position, and then I couldn't support you any longer. (*As an after-
130 thought she adds sarcastically*) And then you'd have to go to work or something dreadful like that. (*Sweeping under the table*) What I want to know is whether you're going to look for a job to-day or not. You know your family won't help

us any more. They've had enough of you too. (*After a moment's silent sweeping*).
I'm about sick of all this life. I've a good notion to go home, if I wasn't too
135 proud to let them know what a failure you've been—you, the millionaire
Rowland's only son, the Harvard graduate, the poet, the catch of the town-
Huh! (*With bitterness*) There wouldn't be many of them now envy my catch if
they knew the truth. What has our marriage been, I'd like to know? Even
before your *millionaire* father died owing everyone in the world money, you
140 certainly never wasted any of your time on your wife. I suppose you thought I
ought to be glad you were *honorable* enough to marry me—after getting me into
trouble. You were ashamed of me with your fine friends because my father's
only a grocer, that's what you were. At least he's honest, which is more than
anyone could say about yours. (*She is sweeping steadily toward the door. Leans on,*
145 *her broom for a moment.*)
You hoped everyone'd think you'd been forced to marry me, and pity you,
didn't you? You didn't hesitate much about telling me you loved me, and making me believe your lies, before it happened, did you? You made me think you
didn't want your father to buy me off as he tried to do. I know better now.
150 I haven't lived with you all this time for nothing. (*Somberly*) It's lucky the poor
thing was born dead, after all. What a father you'd have been!
(*Is silent, brooding moodily for a moment—then she continues with a sort of savage joy.*)
But I'm not the only who's got you to thank for being unhappy. There's one
other, at least, and *she* can't hope to marry you now. (*She puts her head into the*
155 *next room*) How about Helen? (*She starts back from the doorway, half frightened.*)
Don't look at me that way! Yes, I read her letter. What about it? I got a right to.
I'm your wife. And I know all there is to know, so don't lie. You needn't stare
at me so. You can't bully me with your superior airs any longer. Only for me
you'd be going without breakfast this very morning. (*She sets the broom back in the*
160 *corner—whiningly*) You never did have any gratitude for what I've done. (*She*
comes to the stove and puts the pot) The coffee's ready. I'm not going to wait for
you. (*She sits down in her chair again.*)
(*After a pause—puts her hand to her head—fretfully*) My head aches so this morning.
It's a shame I've got to go to work in a stuffy room all day in my condition. And
165 I wouldn't if you were half a man. By rights I ought to be lying on my back
instead of you. You know how sick I've been this last year; and yet you object
when I take a little something to keep up my spirits. You even didn't want me
to take that tonic I got at the drugstore. (*With a hard laugh*) I know you'd be
glad to have me dead and out of your way; then you'd be free to run after all
170 these silly girls that think you're such a wonderful, misunderstood person—this
Helen and the others. (*There is a sharp exclamation of pain from the next room.*)
(*With satisfaction*) There! I knew you'd cut yourself. It'll be a lesson to you.
You know you oughtn't to be running around nights drinking with your nerves
in such an awful shape. (*She goes to the door and looks in.*) What makes you so
175 pale? What are you staring at yourself in the mirror that way for? For goodness'
sake, wipe that blood off your face! (*With a shudder*) It's horrible. (*In relieved*
tones) There, that's better. I never could stand the sight of blood. (*She shrinks*
back from the door a little) You better give up trying and go to a barber shop.

Your hand shakes dreadfully. Why do you stare at me like that? (*She turns away*
180 *from the door*) Are you still mad at me about that letter? (*Defiantly*) Well, I had a
right to read it. I'm your wife. (*She comes to the chair and sits down again. After a*
pause.)

I knew all the time you were running around with someone. Your lame excuses
about spending the time at the library didn't fool me. Who is this Helen, any-
185 way? One of those artists? Or does she write poetry, too? Her letter sounds
that way. I'll bet she told you your things were the best ever, and you believed
her, like a fool. Is she young and pretty? I was young and pretty, too, when you
fooled me with your fine, poetic talk; but life with you would soon wear anyone
down. What I've been through!

190 (*Goes over and takes the coffee off the stove*) Breakfast is ready. (*With a contemptuous*
glance) Breakfast! (*Pours out a cup of coffee for herself and puts the pot on the table.*)
Your coffee'll be cold. What are you doing—still shaving, for heaven's sake?
You'd better give it up. One of these mornings you'll give yourself a serious cut.
(*She cuts off bread and butters it. During the following speeches she eats and sips her coffee.*)
195 I'll have to run as soon as I've finished eating. One of us has got to work.
(*Angrily*) Are you going to look for a job today or aren't you? I should think
some of your fine friends would help you, if they really think you're so much.
But I guess they just like to hear you talk. (*Sits in silence for a moment.*)
I'm sorry for this Helen, whoever she is. Haven't you got any feelings for other
200 people? What will her family say? I see she mentions them in her letter. What is
she going to do—have the child—or go to one of those doctors? That's a nice
thing, I must say. Where can she get the money? Is she rich? (*She waits for some*
answer to this volley of questions.)
Hmm! You won't tell me anything about her, will you? Much I care. Come to
205 think of it, I'm not so sorry for her after all. She knew what she was doing.
She isn't any schoolgirl, like I was, from the looks of her letter. Does she know
you're married? Of course, she must. All your friends know about your unhappy marriage. I know they pity you, but they don't know my side of it.
They'd talk different if they did.
210 (*Too busy eating to go on for a second or so.*)
This Helen must be a fine one, if she knew you were married. What does she
expect, then? That I'll divorce you and let her marry you? Does she think I'm
crazy enough for that—after all you've made me go through? I guess not!
And you can't get a divorce from me and you know it. No one can say I've
215 ever done anything wrong. (*Drinks the last of her cup of coffee.*)
She deserves to suffer, that's all I can say. I'll tell you what I think; I think your
Helen is no better than a common streetwalker, that's what I think. (*There is a*
stifled groan of pain from the next room.)
Did you cut yourself again? Serves you right. (*Gets up and takes off her apron.*)
220 Well, I've got to run along. (*Peevishly*) This is a fine life for me to be leading!
I won't stand for you loafing any longer. (*Something catches her ear and she pauses*
and listens intently) There! You've overturned the water all over everything.
Don't say you haven't. I can hear it dripping on the floor. (*A vague expression of*
fear comes over her face) Alfred! Why don't you answer me?

225 (*She moves slowly toward the room. There is the noise of a chair being overturned and something crashes heavily to the floor. She stands, trembling with fright.*)

Alfred! Alfred! Answer me! What is it you knocked over? Are you still drunk? (*Unable to stand the tension a second longer she rushes to the door of the bedroom.*)

Alfred!

230 (*She stands in the doorway looking down at the floor of the inner room, transfixed with horror. Then she shrieks wildly and runs to the other door, unlocks it and frenziedly pulls it open, and runs shrieking madly into the outer hallway.*)

CURTAIN

From *The Plays Of Eugene O'Neill* by Eugene O'Neill. (1916)

William Shakespeare

50 Julius Caesar: Brutus's Speech

Scene II. The Forum.[1]
Enter BRUTUS *and* CASSIUS, *with a crowd of* Plebeians.

PLEBEIANS

We will be satisfied; let us be satisfied.
BRUTUS

Then follow me, and give me audience,[2] friends.
Cassius, go you into the other street,
And part the numbers:[3]
5 Those that will hear me speak, let them stay here;
Those that will follow Cassius, go with him,
And public reasons shall be rendered
Of Caesar's death.[4]

I PLEBEIAN

I will hear Brutus speak.

2 PLEBEIAN

10 I will hear Cassius, and compare their reasons,
When severally[5] we hear them rendered.

[*Exit* CASSIUS *with some of the* Plebeians;
BRUTUS *goes into the pulpit*

3 PLEBEIAN

The noble Brutus is ascended. Silence!

BRUTUS

Be patient till the last.[6]
Romans, countrymen, and lovers, hear me for my cause,[7] and be silent, that you
15 may hear. Believe me for mine honour, and have respect to mine honour, that[8]
you may believe. Censure me in your wisdom, and awake your sense,[9] that you
may the better judge. If there be any in this assembly, any dear friend of Caesar's,
to him I say, that Brutus' love to Caesar was no less than his. If then, that friend
demand why Brutus rose against Caesar, this is my answer: Not that I loved
20 Caesar less, but that I loved Rome more. Had you rather Caesar were living, and
die all slaves, than that Caesar were dead, to live all free men? As[10] Caesar loved
me, I weep for him; as he was fortunate,[11] I rejoice at it; as he was valiant, I
honour him; but, as he was ambitious, I slew him. There is tears for his love:
joy for his fortune: honour for his valour: and death for his ambition. Who is
25 here so base that would be a bondman? If any, speak, for him have I offended.[12]

Who is here so rude[13] that would not be a Roman? If any, speak, for him have I offended. Who is here so vile that will not love his country? If any, speak, for him have I offended. I pause for a reply.

ALL

None, Brutus, none.

BRUTUS

30 Then none have I offended. I have done no more to Caesar than you shall do to Brutus. The question of his death is enrolled in the Capitol, his glory not extenuated, wherein he was worthy, nor his offences enforced,[14] for which he suffered death.

Enter MARK ANTONY *and others, with Casear's body*

Here comes his body, mourned by Mark Antony who, though he had no hand in
35 his death, shall receive the benefit of his dying,[15] a place in the Commonwealth,— as which of you shall not? With this I depart,[16]—that, as I slew my best lover[17] for the good of Rome, I have the same dagger for myself, when it shall please my country to need my death.

ALL

Live, Brutus, live, live!

I PLEBEIAN

40 Bring him with triumph[18] home unto his house.

2 PLEBEIAN

Give him a statue with[19] his ancestors.

3 PLEBEIAN

Let him be Caesar!

4 PLEBEIAN

Caesar's better parts[20]
Shall be crowned in Brutus.

I PLEBEIAN

45 We'll bring him to his house
With shouts and clamours.

BRUTUS

My countrymen,—

2 PLEBEIAN

Peace! Silence! Brutus speaks.

I PLEBEIAN

Peace, ho!

BRUTUS

50 Good countrymen, let me depart alone,
And, for my sake, stay here with Antony.
Do grace²¹ to Caesar's corpse, and grace his speech
Tending to²² Caesar's glories, which Mark Antony,
By our permission, is allowed to make.
55 I do entreat you, not a man depart
Save I alone, till Antony have spoke.

Exit

I PLEBEIAN

Stay, ho, and let us hear Mark Antony!

3 PLEBEIAN

Let him go up into the public chair.²³
We'll hear him. Noble Antony, go up.

ANTONY

60 For Brutus' sake I am beholding to you.²⁴

[*Goes into the pulpit*

4 PLEBEIAN

What does he say of Brutus?

3 PLEBEIAN

He says, for Brutus' sake
He finds himself beholding to us²⁵ all.

4 PLEBEIAN

'T were best he speak no harm of Brutus here!

I PLEBEIAN

65 This Caesar was a tyrant.

3 PLEBEIAN

Nay,²⁶ that's certain;
We are blest²⁷ that Rome is rid of him.

2 PLEBEIAN

Peace! Let us hear what Antony can say.

ANTONY

You gentle²⁸ Romans,—

ALL

70 Peace ho, let us hear him!

145

51 Julius Caesar: Antony's Speech

ANTONY

Friends, Romans, countrymen, lend me your ears.
I come to bury Caesar, not to praise him.
The evil that men do lives after them;
The good is oft interréd with their bones,
75 So let it be with Caesar. The noble Brutus
Hath told you Caesar was ambitious.
If it were so, it was a grievous[29] fault,
And grievously[30] hath Caesar answered[31] it.
Here, under leave of Brutus, and the rest,—
80 For Brutus is an honourable man,
So are they all; all honourable men,—
Come I to speak in Caesar's funeral.
He was my friend, faithful, and just[32] to me;
But Brutus says he was ambitious,
85 And Brutus is an honourable man.
He hath brought many captives home to Rome,
Whose ransoms did the general coffers fill:[33]
Did this in Caesar seem ambitious?
When that the poor have cried,[34] Caesar hath wept.
90 Ambition should be made of sterner stuff,
Yet Brutus says he was ambitious,
And Brutus is an honourable man.
You all did see that, on the Lupercal,
I thrice presented him a kingly crown,
95 Which he did thrice refuse. Was this ambition?
Yet Brutus says he was ambitious,
And, sure, he is an honourable man.
I speak not to disprove what Brutus spoke,
But here I am, to speak what I do know.
100 You all did love him once, not without cause;
What cause withholds you then to mourn for him?[35]
O judgement! Thou art fled to brutish beasts,[36]
And men have lost their reason! Bear with me,[37]
My heart is in the coffin there with Caesar,
105 And I must pause, till it come back to me.

I PLEBEIAN

Methinks there is much reason in his sayings.[38]

2 PLEBEIAN

If thou consider rightly of the matter,
Caesar has had great wrong.[39]

3 PLEBEIAN

Has he, masters?[40]
110   I fear there will a worse[41] come in his place.

4 PLEBEIAN

Marked ye his words? He would not take the crown,
Therefore 't is certain, he was not ambitious.

1 PLEBEIAN

If it be found so, some will dear abide it.[42]

2 PLEBEIAN

Poor soul, his eyes are red as fire with weeping.

3 PLEBEIAN

115   There's not a nobler man in Rome than Antony.

4 PLEBEIAN

Now mark him; he begins again to speak.

ANTONY

But yesterday the word of Caesar might
Have stood against the world;[43] now lies he there,
And none so poor to do him reverence.[44]
120   O, masters, if I were disposed to stir
Your hearts and minds to mutiny and rage,
I should do Brutus wrong, and Cassius wrong,
Who, you all know, are honourable men.
I will not do them wrong; I rather choose
125   To wrong the dead, to wrong myself and you,
Than I will wrong such honourable men.
But here's a parchment, with the seal of Caesar;
I found it in his closet;[45] 't is his will;
Let but the commons hear this testament,[46]
130   Which, pardon me, I do not mean to read,
And they would go and kiss dead Caesar's wounds,
And dip their napkins[47] in his sacred blood,
Yea, beg a hair of him for memory,[48]
And dying, mention it within their wills,
135   Bequeathing it as a rich legacy
Unto their issue.[49]

4 PLEBEIAN

We'll hear the will; read it, Mark Antony.

ALL

The will, the will! We will hear Caesar's will.

ANTONY

Have patience, gentle friends; I must not⁵⁰ read it.
140 It is not meet you know how Caesar loved you.
You are not wood, you are not stones, but men;
And being men, hearing the will of Caesar,
It will inflame you, it will make you mad.
'T is good you know not that you are his heirs,
145 For if you should, O what would come of it?

4 PLEBEIAN

Read the will! We'll hear it, Antony:
You shall read us the will, Caesar's will.

ANTONY

Will you be patient? Will you stay awhile?
I have o'ershot myself⁵¹ to tell you of it;
150 I fear I wrong the honourable men
Whose daggers have stabbed Caesar; I do fear it.

4 PLEBEIAN

They were traitors. Honourable men!

ALL

The will, the testament!

2 PLEBEIAN

They were villains, murderers! The will, read the will!

ANTONY

155 You will compel me then to read the will?
Then make a ring about the corpse of Caesar,
And let me show you him that made the will.
Shall I descend? And will you give me leave?

ALL

Come down.

2 PLEBEIAN

160 Descend.

[*He comes down from the pulpit*

3 PLEBEIAN

You shall have leave.

4 PLEBEIAN

A ring! Stand round!

I PLEBEIAN

Stand from the hearse; stand from the body!

2 PLEBEIAN

Room for Antony, most noble Antony!

ANTONY

165 Nay, press not so upon me; stand far off.

ALL

Stand back; room, bear back![52]

ANTONY

If you have tears, prepare to shed them now.
You all do know this mantle.[53] I remember
The first time ever Caesar put it on.
170 'T was on a summer's evening in his tent,
That day he overcame the Nervii.[54]
Look, in this place ran Cassius' dagger through;
See what a rent the envious Casca made;
Through this, the well-belovéd Brutus stabbed,
175 And, as he plucked his curséd steel away,
Mark how the blood of Caesar followed it,
As rushing out of doors, to be resolved
If Brutus so unkindly knocked, or no;[55]
For Brutus, as you know, was Caesar's angel.[56]
180 Judge, O you gods, how dearly Caesar loved him!
This was the most unkindest cut[57] of all.
For when the noble Caesar saw him stab,
Ingratitude, more strong than traitors' arms,
Quite vanquished him; then burst his mighty heart,
185 And in his mantle muffling up his face,
Even at the base of Pompey's statue,
Which all the while ran blood, great Caesar fell.[58]
O what a fall was there, my countrymen!
Then I, and you, and all of us fell down,
190 Whilst bloody treason flourished over us.[59]
O now you weep, and I perceive you feel
The dint[60] of pity. These are gracious[61] drops.
Kind souls, what weep you, when you but behold
Our Caesar's vesture wounded? Look you here!
195 Here is himself, marred, as you see, with traitors.[62]

I PLEBEIAN

O piteous spectacle!

2 PLEBEIAN

O noble Caesar!

3 PLEBEIAN

O woeful day!

4 PLEBEIAN

O traitors, villains!

1 PLEBEIAN

200 O most bloody sight!

2 PLEBEIAN

We will be revenged! Revenge,
About, seek,[63] burn, fire, kill, slay!
Let not a traitor live!

ANTONY

Stay, countrymen!

1 PLEBEIAN

205 Peace, there! Hear the noble Antony.

2 PLEBEIAN

We'll hear him, we'll follow him, we'll die with him!

ANTONY

Good friends, sweet friends, let me not stir you up
To such a sudden flood of mutiny.[64]
They that have done this deed are honourable.
210 What private griefs[65] they have, alas, I know not,
That made them do it; they are wise, and honourable,
And will, no doubt, with reasons answer you.
I come not, friends, to steal away your hearts;
I am no orator, as Brutus is.
215 But, as you know me all, a plain blunt man
That love my friend; and that they know full well,
That gave me public leave to speak of him;[66]
For I have neither writ, nor words, nor worth,
Action, nor utterance, nor the power of speech,
220 To stir men's blood. I only speak right on.[67]
I tell you that which you yourselves do know,
Show you sweet Caesar's wounds, poor, poor dumb mouths,[68]
And bid them speak for me; but were I Brutus,
And Brutus Antony, there were an Antony
225 Would ruffle up your spirits, and put a tongue
In every wound of Caesar,[69] that should move
The stones of Rome to rise and mutiny.

ALL

We'll mutiny.

1 PLEBEIAN

We'll burn the house of Brutus.

3 PLEBEIAN

230 Away then, come, seek the conspirators!

ANTONY

Yet hear me, countrymen, yet hear me speak.

ALL

Peace, ho, hear Antony, most noble Antony!

ANTONY

Why, friends, you go to do you know not what.
Wherein [70] hath Caesar thus deserved your loves?
235 Alas, you know not. I must tell you then;
You have forgot the will I told you of.

ALL

Most true; the will; let's stay and hear the will!

ANTONY

Here is the will, and under [71] Caesar's seal:
To every Roman citizen he gives,
240 To every several man, seventy-five drachmas. [72]

2 PLEBEIAN

Most noble Caesar! We'll revenge his death.

3 PLEBEIAN

O royal Caesar!

ANTONY

Hear me with patience.

ALL

Peace, ho!

ANTONY

245 Moreover, he hath left you all his walks,
His private arbours and new-planted orchards,
On this side Tiber; [73] he hath left them you,
And to your heirs for ever, common pleasures
To walk abroad, and recreate yourselves. [74]
250 Here was a Caesar! When comes such another? [75]

I PLEBEIAN

Never, never! Come, away, away!
We'll burn his body in the holy place,[76]
And with the brands fire the traitors' houses.[77]
Take up the body.

2 PLEBEIAN

255 Go, fetch fire!

3 PLEBEIAN

Pluck down benches!

4 PLEBEIAN

Pluck down forms, windows, anything!

[*Exeunt* Plebeians *with the body*

ANTONY

Now let it work! Mischief, thou art afoot,
Take thou what course thou wilt![78]

Enter a Servant

260 How now, fellow?

SERVANT

Sir, Octavius is already come to Rome.

ANTONY

Where is he?

SERVANT

He and Lepidus are at Caesar's house.

ANTONY

And thither will I straight, to visit him:
265 He comes upon a wish. Fortune is merry,[79]
And in this mood will give us any thing.

SERVANT

I heard him say, Brutus and Cassius
Are rid like madmen through the gates of Rome.

ANTONY

Belike they had some notice[80] of the people,
270 How I had moved them. Bring me to Octavius.

[*Exeunt*

(1623)

William Shakespeare

52 Macbeth's Last Great Monologue (V, 5)

She should have died hereafter:
There would have been a time for such a word.—
Tomorrow, and tomorrow, and tomorrow,
Creeps in this petty pace from day to day,
5 To the last syllable of recorded time;
And all our yesterdays have lighted fools
The way to dusty death. Out, out, brief candle!
Life's but a walking shadow, a poor player
That struts and frets his hour upon the stage,
10 And then is heard no more: it is a tale
Told by an idiot, full of sound and fury,
Signifying nothing.

(1623)

Muriel Spark

53 The Party Through the Wall

NARRATOR (DR FELL): Most of the houses in Romney Terrace are bomb damage, they lie open to the Kensington weather like the decayed hollow teeth of some prone—or do I mean supine?—monster. Two of the houses at the end of the Terrace have been repaired and made over into flats. Some months ago Miss
5 Ethel Carson came to live in the last but one, number ten, on the third floor. I myself live next door in number eleven.

You will wonder how it is that I, with my secluded habits, came to know so much about Miss Carson. But, as you will see, I had unique opportunities to study this lady, even before she told me all about herself.
10 One of the first things Miss Carson asked the housekeeper when she came to look over the flat was a question which she always asked in these circumstances.

MISS CARSON: Is it quiet?

HOUSEKEEPER: Too quiet, miss. Too quiet.
15 MISS CARSON: It can't be too quiet for me. No wirelesses? No babies? I sleep badly. I suffer from my nerves. No late parties in the house?

HOUSEKEEPER: No, no parties, miss.

MISS CARSON: It looks rather small. Is it damp?

HOUSEKEEPER: No, miss, no damp. See for yourself, miss.
20 MISS CARSON: Don't call me miss, it gets on my nerves. My name is Miss Carson, Ethel Carson—you won't have heard of me but I am known in certain circles. Where's the bedroom? Is it facing the back? It has to face the back of the house. I can't stand traffic. I suffer from sleeplessness.

HOUSEKEEPER: In here. It looks out on the back.
25 MISS CARSON: It's rather small. Who lives on the other side of the wall?

HOUSEKEEPER: That's number eleven. All made over into flats.

MISS CARSON: The wall is very thin. Are they noisy at number eleven? Shall I hear them at night having parties or quarrelling and screaming? Do they have the wireless on late at night? The wall is rather thin.
30 HOUSEKEEPER: It's a quiet place. Ideal for anyone that's getting on in life.

MISS CARSON: It must be ideal for *you*. Tell me, do you think it odd that I am wearing these clothes at my age? Where's the kitchen? Does it smell?

HOUSEKEEPER: Do you want the flat? There's another party after it.

MISS CARSON: Oh, must I make up my mind right away? How disturbing.
35 HOUSEKEEPER: There's another party wants it that's out all day.

NARRATOR: Miss Carson took the flat and moved in the following week. I believe she was generally satisfied, though, in the first month of her stay, I understand there was some trouble about mice.

MISS CARSON: Mice in my kitchen. I am a vegetarian, which attracts mice. I mean
40 the cheese, I use a lot of cheese. I cannot have mice.

HOUSEKEEPER: I'll set a trap, miss.

MISS CARSON: No, no. I should be unable to sleep at night because of the squeaking of mice in the trap. And don't call me miss, it gets on my nerves.

HOUSEKEEPER: I'll put a cat in the kitchen at night, then.

45 MISS CARSON: Oh, I call that very cruel. I couldn't bear it. How disturbing.

NARRATOR: Eventually the mice were eliminated by means of a powdered preparation which killed them silently and without evidence.
For at least three months I watched Miss Carson's comings and goings, and noted her special times and habits. Really I conceived an interest in her. Of

50 course, it was a detached interest, as becomes my position in life.
I observed that, for a woman in her fifties, she looked, I will not say young, but neat and unusual. She must have been a little unusual from the time of her youth.

MISS CARSON: I have been an unusual person from the time of my youth. My

55 earliest memories—

HOUSEKEEPER: I can see that, miss.

.

.

.

MISS CARSON: I took a couple of phenobarbitones at dawn, and slept late into the morning. Then I rose and dressed and went downstairs to speak to the housekeeper.

60 HOUSEKEEPER: Did you call me, miss?

MISS CARSON: I shall have to leave this house.

HOUSEKEEPER: I should, miss.

MISS CARSON: I have to complain about a frightful noise.

HOUSEKEEPER: I did hear you, miss. You give a scream. I suppose it was night-

65 mares, miss.

MISS CARSON: Don't call me miss, it shatters my nerves. I have to complain about the house next door. It is disorderly. The people are irresponsible. I shall see my lawyer and inform the police.

HOUSEKEEPER: Number eleven, miss? They are all very quiet and respectable

70 people there. Too quiet. No gramophones, no wirelesses, no babies. It belongs to a private company that won't have anyone in the house except old retired parties.

MISS CARSON: You are misinformed. It belongs to a Dr Fell. He has been deliberately causing a disturbance these past two nights. I shall give him in

75 charge.

HOUSEKEEPER: I shouldn't do anything to provoke anyone, miss.

NARRATOR: My scientific curiosity mounted as Miss Carson came up the front-door steps of our house at eleven o'clock that morning.
[*Bell.*]
She seemed very incensed—didn't you, Ethel?
[*Bell.*]

80 Why did you ring the bell in that frantic fashion?
[*Door opens.*]

155

MISS CARSON: Oh, who opened the door?

NARRATOR: You see, Miss Carson was surprised—weren't you, Ethel?—when the door opened apparently by itself.

MISS CARSON: Dr Fell, come downstairs at once! I have had enough of your
85   irresponsible tricks; I wish to speak to you.

NARRATOR: I am downstairs. I am standing beside you. I'm glad to see you have come promptly for your treatment.

MISS CARSON: I can't see you. Where are you? I hear your voice, Dr Fell, but I can't see you. It is disgraceful, a nerve specialist upsetting a woman's nerves.
90   You will be sued for heavy damages. You will be struck off the medical register. Come out of hiding and face me!

NARRATOR: Well, I didn't care to face her on that occasion. Why should I? The treatment was free. And, as I explained to Miss Carson, I have nothing to lose. I'm dead. So is my sister. I strangled her, as a matter of fact. (Didn't I, Ethel?—
95   you heard the screams last night. That was a good fifty years ago.) Now, won't you come up to my attic, Ethel, and we shall get to the bottom of this. Come to the attic and we shall continue with your nerve treatment. Don't mind my being invisible.

MISS CARSON: I'm being haunted! I shall see my solicitor! I shall call the police!
100   I am haunted!

NARRATOR: Precisely my diagnosis, you must admit. I specialize in hauntings, I am sensitive to the life of the spirit around us.

[*Pause.*]

Miss Carson has left number ten. Just as well, she was getting frightfully on my nerves, she gave me the creeps. Didn't you, Ethel? Didn't you give me the
105   creeps? Didn't you get on my nerves?

From *Voices At Play* by Muriel Spark. (1961)

Non-fiction

KYR

Richard Flaste

54 From the Cradle to the Olympics

It can cost a lot to produce an athlete these days. In tennis, for instance, one coach estimated that it cost "in the area of $ 35,000" to turn a six-year-old into a
5 nationally recognized twelve-year-old.

Then there is the tension, even the agony, many parents feel as they watch their children attempt to climb to the top.
10 Yet all across the United States, thousands of parents are waking up with their children at 4:30 or 5:00 a.m. to drive them to that first early-morning practice – the first two hours in the pool,
15 or on the courts, or in the gym – before school starts.

The individual sports – especially swimming, tennis, gymnastics, skating, and track – often absorb children from
20 an early age. The child, parents, and coach become a quartet that may stick together for a decade or so, sharing the same goal.

Centerpiece

The sport becomes the centerpiece of
25 the family. When one boy gets involved in gymnastics, the father tells the mother there won't be much social life any more. "Don't plan anything for the next ten years," he says. And they don't. "After
30 all, where there is a competition every week-end," the mother says, "that's what you do."

It is obvious from interviews with people in several states that parents are
35 often aware of the danger of too much pressure on their children. But once in the sport, parents find it hard to control themselves.

Television gets much of the credit – or
40 the blame – for the growth of highly organized individual sports in the United States. "It is television," a spokesman for the Amateur Athletic Union said, "that made the swimmer, Mark Spitz, into a kind of hero at the Munich Olympics."

Television also gave us the Russian gymnast, Olga Korbut. Graceful children everywhere began to emulate her. And
50 it has been possible to watch Jimmy Conners become famous and rich as he hit a ball with a racket on television.

The Numbers

The Junior Olympics, sponsored by the Amateur Athletic Union, give an indication of how many children are devoting
55 their lives to a single sport. In 1973, there were 600 participants; in 1975, there were 2,000. And these were the best of two million or so children from ages eight to eighteen who began in local
60 competitions.

The determination in some of these children is amazing. In Fort Lauderdale, Florida, Sherri Hanna, thirteen, and her sister Tracy, ten, are swimmers who are
65 both aiming for the Olympics in 1980 or 1984.

"Yes, I will make the Olympics. I'm so determined," Sherri said. "I don't think about not making it."
70 But sometimes the determination has a soft edge to it, especially when a child is too young to understand such catchwords as *national recognition* and *greatness*.
75 Jodi Thompson is a nine-year-old gymnast who began training in earnest when she was five. Her father would drive Jodi twice a week from their home to East Lansing for lessons at Michigan
80 State University. It is a sixty-five-mile ride, but it paid off. Jodi won state championships in the nine-and-under age-group in 1973, 1974, and 1975.

To end the drudgery of all that
85 driving, Mr. Thompson started his own gymnastics school. But even now he fears his daughter is not getting all the training she needs. He said, "She will probably have to go to Colorado or
90 somewhere for more concentrated training if she wants to win the Gold Medal."

Normal Childhood?

Jodi has times when she tires of gymnastics, and she has had a distinctly abnormal childhood. But her father
95 contends that after the 1984 Olympics, Jodi will have plenty of time to grow up normally.

The loss of a normal childhood has disturbed many of those involved in these sports. Mitch Ivy, of the Santa Clara Swim Club in California, says: "The kids have to give up everything. You have to give up a social life as other kids have it. You have to give up other sports. People, especially parents, find it difficult to handle. "They don't like to see their kids tired all the time and missing out on fun things at school."

Gardnar Mulloy, a swimming coach in Miami Beach, said that children often start too early and work too hard. "They burn out," he said, "they lose the desire."

The work is considerable. All of these sports many begin with just three or four hours a week when the child is five or six. But the workload climbs to thirty or forty hours a week as the child reaches adolescence.

Looking back on the work, Tim McKee who won two Olympic medals in 1972 as a swimmer, observed that few children could succeed as he did. Yet they try.

"It's really demanding to go to the pool four and five hours a day and swim back and forth, looking at a black line," he said. "You have to make a yoga out of it. You have to not mind the pain. It does things to your brain. It's unpleasant."

Extract from article reprinted from *The New York Times* (1976).

(unabridged)

Alex Valentine

55 You Can't Help Yourself, Can You Madam?

Make no mistake about it—the modern supermarket is a scientifically-designed human mousetrap. And you, the customer, are the mouse. If you don't believe that, consider this fact: the average supermarket shopper, even armed with a full shopping list, will buy an extra 40p of goods for every £1 they had originally
5 intended to spend.

Ask for an explanation and they'll say something like, 'Oh, I just happened to see something that caught my fancy.' The truth is they didn't just 'happen' to see that extra item—the supermarket men had planned it that way. The human mice had fallen for the bait.

10 See how the supermarket man goes about his business which, like any other business, is simply to sell you as many of his goods as possible.

Nothing wrong with that. But there is one great difference between self-service trading and personal salesmanship. If a salesman at the door is handing out a line of patter, you *know* he is trying to sell you something and you know what
15 that something is. You are on your guard.

The supermarket men don't use patter and warm, friendly smiles. More often than not you never even see them. But they are still giving you a hard sell. So how do they go about it? Just what are the tricks of the trade to get those extra pence we had not intended to spend?

20 The first aim of the supermarket man is to get you into the supermarket, *his* supermarket. And the main ways of doing this are by advertising cut-price bargains and—not so obviously—the careful projection of special 'images'. These images are designed to make you think a particular supermarket group has its own special virtues.

25 Some supermarkets trade by the use of brash 'special offer' campaigns, some do it with trading stamps. Others foster the 'image' of scrupulous cleanliness or of guaranteed quality without gimmicks. Think of the supermarkets you know and see how they will fall into one or other of these categories.

Once you have swallowed the ground bait and have been tempted inside, the
30 selling really begins. Now each supermarket operator has his own system, worked out as a result of scientific surveys on how human beings—and housewives particularly—think and behave when they are shopping.

But one way or the other, the same general methods are used.

Let's step inside a supermarket, to the pile of wire baskets and trolleys by the
35 door. The trolleys may even have a seat for the youngster. You take a trolley—and already you have fallen into the first trap. Of course the trolley is nice and convenient but it also helps to prevent you realising just how much you are buying. You don't feel the weight that could serve as an early warning that maybe you are spending more than you intended.

40 You hum a merry little tune to yourself, echoing the music on the loudspeakers —and that is exactly what you are meant to do. For the music along with the

carefully-chosen bright colours and gay displays, is there to suggest that shopping is fun. It relaxes you into the shopping mood.

It's a big supermarket and yet, somehow, you feel nice and cosy. The floor
45 pattern could be helping there, since supermarket scientists have found that when the customers feel overpowered by the vastness of their surrounds they tend to 'freeze up'—and they don't spend. So often a floor pattern is used to create the illusion of compactness, cosiness and friendliness.

All very well, but so far you haven't actually *bought* anything. Don't worry, they
50 are ahead of you on that one, too. For the head-shrinkers who work out super-market methods have discovered that there's a curious reluctance to make the *first* purchase, to break the ice.

So, very likely, as you go in there will be a prominent display near the door of something you were almost certain to buy, say, bread or tea, or a tempting cut-
55 price offer. That is to get you into the shopping mood and just in case you are using a shopping basket and not a trolley, it's usually something light so that, again, you don't become conscious of the weight too early.

Right, now you're inside the supermarket and they've started you on your shopping. The next ploy is simple enough—it's how to make you buy as much
60 as possible.

What do the supermarket boffins regard as the ideal human mousetrap? It is simply one long straight aisle where you see everything that is on display. You can't get side-tracked or take any short cuts and eventually you arrive at the check-outs where the nice woman with the nice smile takes your money.

65 This might be ideal but it's not practical. Stores are built as either squares or rectangles and the check-outs are not at the far end of a mythical corridor. In fact, they tend to be right next to the very door you went in.

The problem now is to make you 'wander' through the whole shop, for the supermarket men have one maxim in common: 'If you don't see it, you won't buy
70 it.' They have to make sure that you see it, to make you wander as if by accident all over the store so that you do see—and are tempted by—as many goodies as possible.

And to get you to wander around they use a device known in the trade jargon as 'playing the winners'. The object, again in their own peculiar jargon, is to
75 make you 'shop the store'. To make you do this, the supermarket men divide their goods into three categories which they call 'Demand', 'Semi-demand' and 'Impulse'. 'Demand' items are things like tea, sugar, butter, bacon, baked beans, toilet paper and detergents which figure high on any usual household shopping list.

80 The 'Semi-demand' category includes marginal luxuries like a more expensive brand of tea or coffee, canned vegetables, chocolate biscuits, ready-baked cakes, paper napkins and so on. And 'Impulse' goods could be canned asparagus tips, deodorant aerosols, deep-frozen scampi, cake toppings and Chow Mein—all of which might make life a bit more pleasant but without which you could survive.

Shopper's guide to the super-trap

Here is a typical supermarket scene, showing the floor-to-ceiling bait that traps you into spending more than you intended... 5

Music: to lull the shopper into a euphoric mood in which buying will be a pleasure

Arrows: to guide you along the route the supermarket 10 planners want you to take

Impulse: high-profit 'impulse-buying' goods are placed strategically at the shopper's eye level 15

Meat: backed by pink lighting to make sure it catches your eye, the meat is placed as far from the entrance as possible. So you have to walk the full 20 length of the store to get this essential item. Then you're led on to the foods that go with it

Eyecatchers: this time for the children. The idea is that they 25 pester Mum and she's too busy to argue. Result: more sales

Trolley: so easy to pile more and more things into it. And you don't feel the cost piling up 30

Flooring: the pattern is broken up so that the customer feels more cosy—and more like spending

Extract from article in *Mirror Colour Magazine* (Dec. 1969) *(unabridged)*

Margaret Morrison

56 In Only Four Weeks

The ads and labels may promise a new shape almost overnight, but the devices and treatment programs being ballyhooed often fail to deliver what they promise, or deliver results the user would rather do without.

"In only 6 days I lost 4 inches off my waist and 7 pounds of weight."

"In only 5 weeks I added 2 inches to my bust line."

5 "Two full inches in the first 3 days!"

These are the kinds of testimonials used in magazine, newspaper, radio, and television ads, promising new shapes, new looks, and new happiness to those 10 who buy the preparation, the device, or the prescribed program of action. The promotors of such products claim they can develop the bust, shape the legs, wipe out double chins. build muscles, 15 eradicate wrinkles, or in some other way enhance beauty or desirability.

Often such devices or treatments are nothing more than money-making schemes for their promoters. The results 20 they produce are questionable, and some are hazardous to health.

To understand how these products can be legally promoted to the public, it is necessary to understand something of the laws covering their regulation. If the 25 product is a drug, FDA can require proof under the Food, Drug, and Cosmetic (FD&C) Act that it is safe and effective before it is put on the market. But if the product is a device, FDA has no 30 authority to require premarketing proof of safety or effectiveness. If a product already on the market is a hazard to health, FDA can request the manufacturer or distributor to remove it from 35 the market voluntarily, or the Agency can resort to legal actions, including seizure of the product. In such cases, FDA must prove that the device is adulterated or misbranded. A product may be consi- 40 dered misbranded if the directions for use on the label are inadequate, or if the

Promotions for the Iso-Tensor, a plastic tube containing a spring, claimed that exercising with the device would develop the breasts. FDA had the device banned from the market by establishing in court that it would have no effect on the size or shape of the breasts.

product is dangerous to health when used in the dosage or manner or with the frequency or duration prescribed, recommended, or suggested in the labeling.

Obviously, most of the devices on the market have never been the subject of court proceedings, and new devices appear on the scene continually. Before buying, it is up to the consumer to judge the safety or effectiveness of such items. It may be useful to consumers to know about some of the cases in which FDA has taken legal action.

One notable case a few years ago involved an electrical device called the Relaxacisor, which had been sold for reducing the waistline. The Relaxacisor produced electrical shocks to the body through contact pads. FDA brought suit against the distributor in 1970 to halt sales of the device on the grounds that it was dangerous to health and life.

During the five-month trial, about 40 witnesses testified that they suffered varying degrees of injury while using the machine, and U.S. District Court Judge William P. Gray issued a permanent injunction prohibiting the sale of the device to the general public.

It is to be hoped that all owners of Relaxacisors have destroyed the device so there is no longer a possibility of harm to a user who might not be aware of the danger. Also, this case should serve as a reminder to consumers to be cautious of similar devices they may see on the market. . . .

Among the many kinds of devices or programs promoted to improve the looks in some way, bust developers are always among the best sellers. While exercise devices of one kind or another may not be useful, they usually are not harmful. But one method of bust enlargement – the injection of liquid silicone into the breasts – has had tragic results.

Silicone injections became something of a craze in the 1960's with the advent of "topless" dancers. A highly publicized San Francisco topless dancer increased her bustline from 36 to 44 inches by the injection of liquid silicone, and housewives as well as show girls began to follow suit. Many of them are now paying for it in illness, disfiguration, even death. . . .

While FDA has prohibited the injection of liquid silicone into human breasts, its use as an investigational new drug has been approved for other purposes on a limited trial basis. FDA has authorized eight highly qualified doctors to use silicone on an experimental basis for cosmetic or reconstructive purposes. Included are such uses as filling out conspicuously sunken, scarred areas of the

165

face, and injection into the eye for
110 detached retina. The Dow Corning
Corporation, of Midland, Michigan,
which manufactures the medical silicone,
is required to restrict its sales to these
approved physicians or to qualified
115 researchers.

In spite of the injuries and disfiguration that have occurred, some doctors are
continuing the practice of breast injections, using an industrial grade silicone,
120 which is available to anyone. Also, breast
injections of silicone are available in
Mexico, and medical grade silicone from
Mexico can be purchased by unethical
U.S. practitioners.
125 Women who are seeking some kind of

bust development treatment should be
aware that unlawful and unethical practices do exist, and that they feed on the
uninformed. Women who have had silicone injections should seek qualified 130
medical help at the first sign of trouble.

When it comes to any treatment,
device, program, or product being
promoted to make the body beautiful,
buyers should beware. They should learn 135
all the facts – potential hazards as well
as potential benefits. They should be
especially leery of products or treatments
that promise amazing results in a very
short time. The human body cannot be 140
reshaped overnight.

Extract from article from *HEW*, (June 1975). Publication of the United States Food and Drug Administration (FDA).

57 What is luxury?

"Let me tell you how it will be: There's one for you, nineteen for me. 'Cos I'm the tax man; yeah, I'm the tax man."
    (from *Taxman* by George Harrison)

If poverty is relative, so is luxury. How do you pinpoint an 'inessential'? Is it what people will do without in a crisis?

5 We all think we know what luxuries are: luxuries are what other people buy (we buy essentials). But in Britain, if we need a more objective checklist, we could refer – until April 1976 – to the list of
10 goods which attracted the higher rate of value-added-tax (commonly called VAT) which was then 25 per cent. The Customs authorities set out a VAT catalogue of 'inessentials'. These were goods that, in a time of galloping inflation and economic
15 recession, we were penalised for buying. They were – and still are – implicitly, luxuries.

By analysing this grouping, it should be possible to discover what it is that
20 makes something a luxury. Furs: no problems here; a traditional luxury defined by its uncommonness and price. Jewellery, gold and silver: again no problems; they are traditional, 'absolute'
25 luxuries. Domestic electrical appliances: here the difficulties begin. It should be possible for a housewife in *ordinary* circumstances to do without a washing-machine. But what if the circumstances
30 are extraordinary? If she has an invalid child, an aged parent, or if she works *and* has a large family, for example, a washing-machine becomes an essential.

Luxury is relative in the way that
35 poverty is relative. For George Orwell, the supreme irony lay in the situation in which "20 million people are unfed but literally everyone in England has access to a radio. What we have lost in food we
40 have gained in electricity." Logically, in a time of recession (and we are constantly reminded that we have never been nearer than we are now to Orwell's England) the balance should be righted. And 25 per

cent VAT on electrically operated goods 45
was an attempt to do this. To an extent, it has worked.

The idea of luxury is thus tied to our view of our own and other people's needs. There is a basic catalogue of human 50
needs; but it tells us very little about being human. Take clothes. We don't actually *need* clothes that fit really well. Yet who would deny people's right to feel good in well-cut clothes? And al- 55
though the category 'food' might at first appear to fall wholly into the category of essential spending, we spend between four-and-a-half times and five times more on food than we need to. We quite 60
legitimately regard food as more than a life-support essential.

Likewise, the 'genuine luxuries' extreme is unreal. Psychologists have discovered that for us to yearn for some- 65
thing, there has to be the possibility that we could get it. Hence, few people can be expected to hanker after an expensive yacht or a private jet aeroplane. Luxury, for most people, is the small upward 70
adjustment of their living standards: one more bedroom, a larger garden, a second car.

The psychologist, Abraham Maslow, put forward the idea that the gratifica- 75
tion of lower needs leads us on to gratify successively higher needs (for example, the lower need for food, once satisfied, leads up to the higher need for love). "In this way *all* human needs are 'essen- 80
tial' as steps towards 'self-actualization'. Even our lower needs are not really animal. The average Western European is experiencing appetite rather than hunger when he says 'I am hungry'. He 85
is likely to experience sheer life-and-death hunger only by accident, and then only a few times through his entire life."

So what *are* people cutting back on at a time when prices are rising? In the 90
cosmetic market, for example, women are hunting around for cheaper brands of

toothpaste but refusing to change the brand of their favourite lipstick or
95 perfume. Superficially, it might seem that here is a perverse refusal to economize on luxuries to protect essentials. But what has happened is this: the housewife hasn't in any way questioned the
100 *need* for toothpaste. She has merely refused to pay more for it. Hanging on to a personal and favourite brand of lipstick, in spite of inflation, is certainly something that economists would not have pre
105 dicted. One psychologist sees this refusal to give up the 'little' luxuries as a sign of hope and survival. People will deliberately seek out luxuries. Cheap bars of chocolate may suffer in a time of reces
110 sion, but there is often a boom in the sale of expensive after-dinner mints and other confectionery.

If people can't buy *un*sensible things occasionally – if the stress of shopping in
115 inflationary times gets through to them – they can develop symptoms quite unrelated to spending. In a survey of doctors' prescribing habits, it was found that doctors were treating patients for a
120 'depression' that could be attributed only to inflation and rising prices. This has been christened the 'economic malaise'.

Bullmore, the psychologist, believes
125 that 'the right to waste one's money' is an important one. What is the fundamental difference between people who earn money to show it off and people who earn money to save it ? Is it any worse

for one stratum of society to spend its
130 loose money on beer, alcohol and gambling while cutting down on 'services' than for another stratum to spend its money on plumbers, builders, gardeners and decorators ? Luxury is in the
135 eye of the beholder and the ways in which people spend their money vary enormously. "If you are an old-age pensioner," says Bullmore, "you *have* to do without. But the middle classes can still
140 find ways of indulging themselves." Another psychologist foresees a generation of retired people who won't accept the low living standards of today's old people: this new generation will have
145 experienced a high level of need gratification which they're not likely to drop. The determination of people to allow a part of their everyday life to become a luxury puzzles economists.
150

Within the broad pattern, there have been changes, however. Housewives are cutting down on chocolate biscuits, canned fruit and canned fish, for example. These have become luxuries
155 once again. And now the luxury of a *replacement* car, fridge or washing-machine is forgone. "The very last thing people will give up is their car," says one market researcher. "Through it, they've
160 established relationships with friends, supermarkets, out-of-town activities. They've built up a life-style that makes the need for a car essential. Suddenly things are becoming a luxury only if they
165 don't answer deep-felt needs. Polythene dustbin liners, oddly enough, will remain. They are part of a total attitude to cleanliness and hygiene that has built up."
170

Eating in restaurants, however, *can* be dropped (and has been).

We can never quite do without those luxuries we have acquired a need for. And this is perhaps because they are part
175 of a process of widening of human choice. The new dictum might be, "I choose, therefore I am."

Think carefully about what you, your friends and relatives regard as luxuries.
180 How do these luxuries stand the test of economic recession ? In fact, why does money matter ?

Extract from the article in *Current* 4/76 Series 2. (1976) *(unabridged)*

58 What is Your Opinion, Mr Nader?

(The following text is part of an 'NBC Today Show' interview. It was shown in April, 1970, in a five-day series during "Earth Week" and subsequently published in book form.)

Downs
We will begin the day talking with Ralph Nader. Mr. Nader, who began his public career by battling for safer construction in automobiles, has expanded his con-
5 sumer investigation into environmental problems, the most pervasive of which remains the automobile. We invited Mr. Nader to be our guest and we also invited all four of the major automobile manu-
10 facturers to send representatives to dis-cuss the entire subject of the automo-bile in its relationship to the environ-ment. No such representatives were available for today's interview. So today
15 we will be talking to Mr. Nader alone. Welcome to "Today", Ralph Nader. Let me start right off by asking you, flat out, are we winning the fight against pollu-tion?

Nader
20 I don't think we are gaining appreciably at all. The Federal Air Quality Act of 1967 has not reduced smokestack emis-sions one iota. It hasn't even gone into effect yet. Automobiles coming off the
25 production lines consistently and fla-grantly violate the Federal Air Pollution standards and standards are very weak.

Downs
The standards that are now in exis-tence?

Nader
30 That's right, on hydrocarbons and carbon monoxide.

Downs
One other thing, on the matter of both smokestack emissions and the exhaust pipes, what about the technical feasi-
35 bility? Is it technically possible now to suppress most of the pollution that is going into the air?

Nader
There are two answers to that. One is that the available technology is far
40 greater than is actually being used, and second that with some investments, technology could be developed very

rapidly . . . But the full story has never been told to the American people. The technology has been suppressed, it has
45 not been developed even to minimum perfection levels.

Downs
Much money goes into persuasion in the form of paid advertisements. To give an indication according to the text that
50 industry is making an attempt to better things, or at least making an attempt to have people believe they are on the ball with it. What about these ads, that talk about what industry is doing?
55

Nader
It is the latest in public relations. If you won't do it, at least you talk about it, and of course, we are not organized as a society to impeach consistently with nationwide authoritative voices the
60 false, so-called pollution control claims of industry. Clean gasoline is a fraud. The fact that auto exhausts have been controlled is a fraud. There are still five major pollutants coming out of the auto-
65 mobile . . .

Downs
In other words, the money spent for this propaganda you think would be bet-ter spent in correcting the errors.

Nader
Of course. Consolidated Edison, which
70 likes to put on a forward image in New York City, spends more on ads than they do on research. Their annual basic research budget is trivial compared to all the ballyhoo. And it is the same with
75 General Motors. Between 1967 and 1969 they spent 250 million dollars just to change their signs around the country and the world to GM MARK OF EXCELLENCE. They haven't spent
80 30 million dollars in research to find a new alternative propulsion system that isn't polluting.

Downs
Mr. Nader, you have been a crusader on behalf of the consumer, on behalf of the
85 human being, really, to see that he is informed on subjects that are in his interest. Nobody really much questioned the safety of American automobiles until you began looking into them. What
90

made you first decide that there was some unsafety involved and that it would be a good idea to sound the alarm?

Nader

First of all, the technology if it is not
95 designed safely can produce an awful lot of violence. Unsafe cars are violent beings. Environmental pollution is a very serious form of violence leading to emphysema, cancer, shortened life. Now
100 when you look at it that way, and then you look at the marvellous achievements that our engineers and technologists have obtained in space and many other areas, you begin to ask questions. Who
105 decides where the life-gaining technology is distributed and applied? Who decides how fast it gets to two hundred million Americans in their everyday life? The purpose of the law is to generate preven-
110 tive activities, to speed up technology and science for people's health and well-being and safety, and that is the critical point. People must realize that all this modernism they watch on television,
115 going off to the moon and elsewhere, can be applied to the problems at home: hospital services, educational institutions, mass transit, air and water pollution control, safer cars and highways,
120 and many many better ways of doing things. We are a rich country, but we are not distributing [our riches] for our major public needs.

Downs

How do you see the future now? There
tends to be polarization. Nobody says he 125
is against the fight to end pollution. Nobody says he wants to breathe polluted air, or drink polluted water. But there are people who wish to focus on other issues. How do you feel it is going 130 to come out? Will public education rise to a level where industry and government will be forced into responsible action?

Nader

I think that depends on several things. 135
It depends mainly on how much support goes into antipollution groups or private groups ... We are seeing a combination of many forces, conservationists, consumer forces, campus forces, and then 140 pretty soon it will be ghetto forces too, because black people, minority groups, get the worst pollution. They live in the major pollution zones. I have never seen a President or a Chairman of the Board 145 of any of the large pollutors in this country live anywhere but far from their plants and pollution zones.

Extract from article in *New World Or No World*, edited by F. Herbert (1970)   (*slightly abridged*)

Geoffrey Leech and Jan Svartvik

59 Varieties of English

Variety labels

1

To use a language properly, we of course have to know the grammatical struc-
tures of the language and their meanings. But we also have to know what forms
of language are appropriate for given situations, and for this purpose we use
5 'variety labels' such as ‹AmE› (for American English), ‹BrE› (for British English),
‹RP› (for Received Pronunciation), ‹formal›, ‹informal›, ‹polite›, ‹familiar›.
These labels are reminders that the English language is, in a sense, not a single
language, but many languages, each of which belongs to a particular geographical
area or to a particular kind of situation. The English used in the United States is
10 somewhat different from the English used in Great Britain; the English used in
formal written communications is in some ways different from the English used
in informal conversation.

The 'common core'

2

Luckily for the learner, many of the features of English are found in all, or nearly
15 all varieties. We say that general features of this kind belong to the 'common
core' of the language. Take, for instance, the three words *children, offspring*, and
kids. Children is a 'common core' term; *offspring* is rather formal (and used of
animals as well as human beings); *kids* is informal and familiar. It is safest, when
in doubt, to use the 'common core' term; thus *children* is the word you would
20 want to use most often. But part of 'knowing English' is knowing in what circumstances it would be possible to use *offspring* or *kids* instead of *children*. Let us
take another illustration, this time from grammar:

     Feeling tired, John went to bed early.   [1]

     John went to bed early because he felt tired.   [2]

25   John felt tired, so he went to bed early.   [3]

Sentence [2] is a 'common core' construction. It could (for example) be used in
both speech and writing. [1] is rather formal in construction, typical of written
exposition; [3] is informal, and is likely to occur in a relaxed conversation.

Geographical and national varieties: ‹BrE› ‹AmE›

3

30 English is spoken as a native language by nearly three hundred million people:
in the United States of America, Canada, Britain, Ireland, Australia, the Carib-
bean, and many other places. But the varieties of English used in the United
States and in Britain are the most important in terms of population and influence.
The grammatical differences between the two varieties (in comparison with
35 differences of pronunciation and vocabulary) are not very great.

Here are some brief examples of how ‹AmE› and ‹BrE› can differ:

4

(A) ‹AmE› has two past participle forms of *get: gotten* and *got*, whereas ‹BrE› has only one: *got*. (The past tense form is *got* in both varieties.)
For example:

40   ‹AmE›: Have you *gotten/got* the tickets for the match?
    ‹BrE›: Have you *got* the tickets for the match?

5

(B) There is also a difference in the repeated subject after *one*. In ‹AmE› we can say:

    One cannot succeed unless *he* tries hard.

45 In ‹BrE› we have to say:

    One cannot succeed unless *one* tries hard.

6

(C) The normal complement after *different* is *than* in ‹AmE› but *from* (or sometimes *to*) in ‹BrE›.

    ‹AmE›: Their house is different *than* ours.
50   ‹BrE›: Their house is different *from* ours.

7

(D) The use of the subjunctive after verbs like *demand, require, insist, suggest, etc,* is more common in ‹AmE› than ‹BrE›, where the construction is restricted to rather formal contexts:

    They suggested that Smith *be* dropped from the team.
55   ‹chiefly AmE›
    They suggested that Smith *should be* dropped from the team.
                  ‹AmE› and ‹BrE›

Written and spoken English ‹written› ‹spoken›

8

The English of speech tends to be different from the English of writing in some
60 fairly obvious ways. For example, in writing we usually have time to plan our message, to think about it carefully while writing, and to revise it afterwards if necessary. In speech (unless it is, say, a lecture prepared in advance), we have no time to do this, but must shape our message as we go:

    Well I've just come back from New York where it was pretty clear
65   that . this was a general trend with young people there . and er I um
    I'm worried though because you see . it seems that . you're kind of
    putting the whole blame on the family instead of on the conditions a
    family's being forced to live in these days . look . if you took er I
    mean monkeys are very good parents aren't they . rhesus monkeys
70   and so on . they look after their young marvellously—now you put
    them together you crowd them . and they're extremely bad
    parents. . .

Often we use in speech words and phrases like *well, you see,* and *kind of* which add little information, but tell us something of the speaker's attitude to his audience
75 and to what he is saying. We also often hesitate, or fill in gaps with 'hesitation fillers' like *er* /ə:ʳ/ and *um* /əm/ while we think of what next to say. We may fail to

complete a sentence, or lose track of our sentence and mix up one grammatical construction with another. All these features do not normally occur in writing.

9

In general, the grammar of spoken sentences is simpler and less strictly con-
80 structed than the grammar of written sentences. It is difficult to divide a spoken conversation into separate sentences, and the connections between one clause and another are less clear because the speaker relies more on the hearer's under-standing of context and on his ability to interrupt if he fails to understand. But in 'getting across' his message, the speaker is able to rely on features of intonation
85 which tell us a great deal that cannot be given in written punctuation.

Formal and informal English ⟨formal⟩ ⟨informal⟩
10
Formal language is the type of language we use publicly for some serious purpose, for example in official reports, business letters and regulations. Formal English is nearly always written. Exceptionally it is used in speech, for example in formal
90 public speeches.

Informal language (*ie* colloquial language) is the language of private conver-sation, of personal letters, *etc*. It is the first type of language that a native-speaking child becomes familiar with. Because it is generally easier to understand than formal English, it is often used nowadays in public communication of a popular
95 kind: for example, advertisements and popular newspapers mainly employ a colloquial or informal style.

11

There are various degrees of formality, as these examples show:

When his dad died, Pete had to get another job. [4]

After his father's death, Peter had to change his job. [5]

100 On the decease of his father, Mr Brown was obliged to seek
alternative employment. [6]

These sentences mean *roughly* the same thing, but would occur in different situa-tions. Sentence [4] could be part of a casual conversation between friends of Peter Brown. [5] is of fairly neutral ('common core') style. [6] is very formal, in
105 fact stilted, and would only occur in a written report.

12

In English there are many differences of vocabulary between formal and informal language. Much of the vocabulary of formal English is of French, Latin, and Greek origin; and we can often 'translate' these terms into informal language by replacing them by words or phrases of Anglo-Saxon origin: compare *commence,*
110 *continue, conclude* ⟨formal⟩ with *begin, keep (up), end:*

The meeting will { commence at 4 p.m. ⟨formal⟩
{ begin at 4 o'clock.

115 The government is { continuing its struggle against inflation.
{ ⟨formal⟩
{ keeping up its fight against inflation.
{ ⟨rather informal⟩

The concert concluded with a performance of Beethoven's 5th
120   symphony. ‹formal›
They ended the concert with Beethoven's 5th. ‹informal›

Many phrasal and prepositional verbs are characteristic of informal style:

‹FORMAL› OR COMMON CORE WORD	‹INFORMAL› EQUIVALENT
discover	*find out*
explode	*blow up*
encounter	*come across*
invent	*make up*
enter	*go in (to)*
tolerate	*put up with*
investigate	*look into*
surrender	*give in*

But there is not always a direct 'translation' between formal and informal English.
This may be because an informal term has emotive qualities not present in formal
135   language, or because formal language often insists on greater preciseness. The
informal word *job*, for instance, has no formal equivalent: instead, we have to
choose a more precise and restricted term, according to the context: *employment*,
post (esp ‹BrE›), position, appointment, profession, vocation, etc.

13

There are also some grammatical differences between formal and informal Eng-
140   lish: for example, the use of *who* and *whom*, and the placing of a preposition at the
beginning or at the end of a clause:

= { She longed for a friend *in whom* she could confide. ‹formal›
    { She longed for a friend (*who*) she could confide *in*. ‹informal›

= { *In what* country was he born? ‹formal›
145   { *What* country was he born *in*? ›informal›

Impersonal style ‹impersonal›
14

Formal written language often goes with an impersonal style; *ie* one in which the
speaker does not refer directly to himself or his readers, but avoids the pronouns
I, you, we. Some of the common features of impersonal language are passives,
150   sentences beginning with introductory *it*, and abstract nouns. Each of these
features is illustrated in:

Announcement from the librarian
It has been noted with concern that the stock of books in the library
has been declining alarmingly. Students are asked to remind them-
155   selves of the rules for the borrowing and return of books, and to
bear in mind the needs of other students. Penalties for overdue
books will in the future be strictly enforced.

The author of this notice could have written a more informal and less impersonal
message on these lines:

174

160 The number of books in the library has been going down. Please make sure you know the rules for borrowing, and don't forget that the library is for *everyone's* convenience. So from now on, we're going to enforce the rules strictly. *You have been warned!*

Polite and familiar language ⟨polite⟩ ⟨familiar⟩
15

165 Our language tends to be more polite when we are talking to a person we do not know well, or a person senior to ourselves in terms of age or social position.

The opposite of 'polite' is 'familiar'. When we know someone well or intimately, we tend to drop polite forms of language. For example, instead of using the polite vocative *Mr Brown*, we use a first name (*Peter*) or a short name (*Pete*) or

170 even a nickname (*Shortie*). English has no special familiar pronouns, like some languages (*eg* French *tu*, German *du*), but familiarity can be shown in other ways. Compare, for example, these requests:

Shut the dòor, wíll you? ⟨familiar⟩

Would you please shut the dóor? ⟨polite⟩

175 I wonder if you would mind shutting the dòor? ⟨more polite⟩

Words like *please* and *kindly* have the sole function of indicating politeness. One can also be familiar in referring to a third person:

Pete's old woman hit the roof when he came home with that
doll from the disco. ⟨very familiar⟩   [7]

180 Peter's wife was very angry when he came home with the girl
from the discotheque. ⟨common core⟩   [8]

We might judge [7] to be ⟨impolite⟩ in that it fails to show proper respect to Peter's wife and the girl. In other words, impoliteness is normally a question of being familiar in the wrong circumstances.

16

185 Sentence [7] is also an example of slang. Slang is language which is very familiar in style, and is usually restricted to the members of a particular social group, for example 'teenage slang', 'army slang', 'theatre slang'. Slang is not usually fully understood by people outside a particular social group, and so has a value of showing the intimacy and solidarity of its members. Because of its restricted use

190 we shall not be concerned with slang here (See diagram on p. 176).

From *A Communicative Grammar of English* by G. Leech and J. Svartvik. (1975)
(slighlty abridged)

Alvin Toffler

60 The Odds Against Love — Temporary Marriage

Minorities experiment; majorities cling to the forms of the past. It is safe to say that large numbers of people will refuse to jettison the conventional idea of marriage or the familiar family forms. They will, no doubt, continue searching for happiness within the orthodox format. Yet, even they will be forced to inno-
5 vate in the end, for the odds against success may prove overwhelming.

The orthodox format presupposes that two young people will 'find' one another and marry. It presupposes that the two will fulfil certain psychological needs in one another, and the two personalities will develop over the years, more or less in tandem, so that they continue to fulfil each other's needs. It further presupposes
10 that this process will last 'until death do us part'.

These expectations are built deeply into our culture. It is no longer respectable, as it once was, to marry for anything but love. Love has changed from a peripheral concern of the family into its primary justification. Indeed, the pursuit of love through family life has become, for many, the very purpose of life itself.

15 Love, however, is defined in terms of this notion of shared growth. It is seen as a beautiful mesh of complementary needs, flowing into and out of one another, fulfilling the loved ones, and producing feelings of warmth, tenderness and devotion. Unhappy husbands often complain that they have 'left their wives behind' in terms of social, educational or intellectual growth. Partners in successful
20 marriages are said to 'grow together'.

This 'parallel development' theory of love carries endorsement from marriage counsellors, psychologists and sociologists. Thus, says sociologist Nelson Foote, a specialist on the family, the quality of the relationship between husband and wife is dependent upon 'the degree of matching in their phases of distinct but
25 comparable development'.

If love is a product of shared growth, however, and we are to measure success in marriage by the degree to which matched development actually occurs, it becomes possible to make a strong and ominous prediction about the future.

It is possible to demonstrate that, even in a relatively stagnant society, the
30 mathematical odds are heavily stacked against any couple achieving this ideal of parallel growth. The odds for success positively plummet, however, when the rate of change in society accelerates, as it now is doing. In a fast-moving society, in which many things change, not once, but repeatedly, in which the husband moves up and down a variety of economic and social scales, in which the family is
35 again and again torn loose from home and community, in which individuals move further from their parents, further from the religion of origin, and further from traditional values, it is almost miraculous if two people develop at anything like comparable rates.

If, at the same time, average life expectancy rises from, say, fifty to seventy
40 years, thereby lengthening the term during which this acrobatic feat of matched development is supposed to be maintained, the odds against success become

absolutely astronomical. Thus, Nelson Foote writes with wry understatement: 'To expect a marriage to last indefinitely under modern conditions is to expect a lot.' To ask love to last indefinitely is to expect even more. Transience and novelty
45 are both in league against it.

It is this change in the statistical odds against love that accounts for the high divorce and separation rate in most of the techno-societies. The faster the rate of change and the longer the life span, the worse these odds grow. Something has to crack.
50 In point of fact, of course, something has already cracked—and it is the old insistence on permanence. Millions of men and women now adopt what appears to them to be a sensible and conservative strategy. Rather than opting for some offbeat variety of the family, they marry conventionally, they attempt to make it 'work', and then, when the paths of the partners diverge beyond an acceptable
55 point, they divorce or depart. Most of them go on to search for a new partner whose developmental stage, at that moment, matches their own.
As human relationships grow more transient and modular, the pursuit of love becomes, if anything, more frenzied. But the temporal expectations change. As conventional marriage proves itself less and less capable of delivering on its
60 promise of lifelong love, therefore, we can anticipate open public acceptance of temporary marriages. Instead of wedding 'until death do us part', couples will enter into matrimony knowing from the first that the relationship is likely to be short-lived.
They will know, too, that when the paths of husband and wife diverge, when
65 there is too great a discrepancy in developmental stages, they may call it quits—without shock or embarrassment, perhaps even without some of the pain that goes with divorce today. And when the opportunity presents itself, they will marry again...and again...and again.
Serial marriage—a pattern of successive temporary marriages—is cut to order
70 for the Age of Transience in which all man's relationships, all his ties with the environment, shrink in duration. It is the natural, the inevitable outgrowth of a social order in which automobiles are rented, dolls traded in, and dresses discarded after one-time use. It is the mainstream marriage pattern of tomorrow.
In one sense, serial marriage is already the best-kept family secret of the techno-
75 societies. According to Professor Jessie Bernard, a world-prominent family sociologist, 'Plural marriage is more extensive in our society today than it is in societies that permit polygamy—the chief difference being that we have institu-tionalized plural marriage serially or sequentially rather than contemporaneously.' Remarriage is already so prevalent a practice that nearly one out of every four
80 bridegrooms in America has been to the altar before. It is so prevalent that one IBM personnel man reports a poignant incident involving a divorced woman, who, in filling out a job application, paused when she came to the question of marital status. She put her pencil in her mouth, pondered for a moment, then wrote: 'Unremarried'.

85   Transience necessarily affects the durational expectancies with which persons approach new situations. While they may yearn for a permanent relationship, something inside whispers to them that it is an increasingly improbable luxury.

    Even young people who most passionately seek commitment, profound involvement with people and causes, recognize the power of the thrust towards
90 transience. Listen, for example, to a young black American, a civil-rights worker, as she describes her attitude towards time and marriage:

    'In the white world, marriage is always billed as "the end"—like in a Hollywood movie. I don't go for that. I can't imagine myself promising my whole lifetime away. I might want to get married now, but how about next year? That's
95 not disrespect for the institution [of marriage], but the deepest respect. In The [civil rights] Movement, you need to have a feeling for the temporary—of making something as good as you can, while it lasts. In conventional relationships, time is a prison.'

    Such attitudes will not be confined to the young, the few, or the politically
100 active. They will whip across nations as novelty floods into the society and catch fire as the level of transience rises still higher. And along with them will come a sharp increase in the number of temporary—then serial—marriages. . . .

Extract from *Future Shock* by Alvin Toffler. (1970)

Alvin Toffler

61 The Streamlined Family

Super-industrial man may be forced to experiment with novel family forms. . . .
One simple thing he will do is streamline the family. The typical pre-industrial
family not only had a good many children, but numerous other dependents as
well—grandparents, uncles, aunts, and cousins. Such 'extended' families were well
5 suited for survival in slow-paced agricultural societies. But such families are hard
to transport or transplant. They are immobile.

Industrialism demanded masses of workers ready and able to move off the land
in pursuit of jobs, and to move again whenever necessary. Thus the so-called
'nuclear' family emerged—a stripped-down, portable family unit consisting only
10 of parents and a small set of children. This new-style family, far more mobile
than the traditional extended family, became the standard model in all the industrial countries.

Super-industrialism, however, the next stage of eco-technological development, requires even higher mobility. Thus we may expect many among the
15 people of the future to carry the streamlining process a step further by remaining
childless, cutting the family down to its most elemental components, a man and a
woman. Two people, perhaps with matched careers, will prove more efficient at
navigating through education and social shoals, through job changes and geo-
graphic relocations, than the ordinary child-cluttered family. Indeed, anthro-
20 pologist Margaret Mead has pointed out that we may already be moving towards
a system under which, as she puts it, 'parenthood would be limited to a smaller
number of families whose principal function would be child-rearing', leaving the
rest of the population 'free to function—for the first time in history—as individuals'.

25 A compromise may be the postponement of children, rather than childlessness.
Men and women today are often torn in conflict between a commitment to career
and a commitment to children. In the future, many couples will sidestep this
problem by deferring the entire task of raising children until after retirement.

This may strike people of the present as odd. Yet once child-bearing is broken
30 away from its biological base, nothing more than tradition suggests having
children at an early age. Why not wait, and buy your embryos later, after your
work career is over? Thus childlessness is likely to spread among young and
middle-aged couples; sexagenarians who raise infants may be far more common.
The post-retirement family could become a recognized social institution.

BIO-PARENTS AND PRO-PARENTS

35 If a smaller number of families raise children, however, why do the children have
to be their own? Why not a system under which 'professional parents' take on the
child-rearing function for others?

Raising children, after all, requires skills that are by no means universal. We
don't let 'just anyone' perform brain surgery or, for that matter, sell stocks and

40 bonds. Even the lowest ranking civil servant is required to pass tests proving competence. Yet we allow virtually anyone, almost without regard for mental or moral qualification, to try his or her hand at raising young human beings, so long as these humans are biological offspring. Despite the increasing complexity of the task, parenthood remains the greatest single preserve of the amateur.

45 As the present system cracks and the super-industrial revolution rolls over us, as the armies of juvenile delinquents swell, as hundreds of thousands of youngsters flee their homes, and students rampage at universities in all the techno-societies, we can expect vociferous demands for an end to parental dilettantism.

There are far better ways to cope with the problems of youth, but professional
50 parenthood is certain to be proposed, if only because it fits so perfectly with the society's overall push towards specialization. Moreover, there is a powerful, pent-up demand for this social innovation. Even now millions of parents, given the opportunity, would happily relinquish their parental responsibilities—and not necessarily through irresponsibility or lack of love. Harried, frenzied, up
55 against the wall, they have come to see themselves as inadequate to the tasks. Given affluence and the existence of specially-equipped and licensed professional parents, many of today's biological parents would not only gladly surrender their children to them, but would look upon it as an act of love, rather than rejection.

Parental professionals would not be therapists, but actual family units assigned
60 to, and well paid for, rearing children. Such families might be multi-generational by design, offering children in them an opportunity to observe and learn from a variety of adult models, as was the case in the old farm homestead. With the adults paid to be professional parents, they would be freed of the occupational necessity to relocate repeatedly. Such families would take in new children as old ones
65 'graduate' so that age-segregation would be minimized. ...

ibid.

P. M. *Worsley*

62 Authority and the Young

It seems universally agreed among publicists and guardians of public morality that we are in the midst of a crisis, in which traditional values and institutional controls have been rejected, and that nothing has emerged to replace them. This decay of authority is believed to be most visible among young people, not only
5 in Britain, but in all developed countries, whatever their cultural and ideological differences. T. R. Fyvel, for example, has described the 'Teddy boy international': Soviet stilyagi, Swedish skinnknuttar, French blousons noirs, Australian 'bodgies' and 'widgies', Japanese taiyozoku, West German Halbstarken, and so on—a new generation (of vipers) whose language is jazz, who dress alike, who share the
10 same style of non-work life, and who though not radical ideologically, are detached from official society to the point of constituting a delinquent international sub-culture.

Impressionistic as this may be, it is not without some foundation in reality. Yet we lack adequate studies of inter-war youth against which we might more
15 accurately assess just how different post-1945 youth is in fact. The quite limited literature on contemporary youth, too, by no means supports the thesis that the end of World War II inaugurated an era of social disorganization.

Barbara Wootton, in her study of criminality published in 1959, for example, pointed out that the UK statistics of indictable offences of all kinds (with all their
20 acknowledged limitations) exhibited a remarkable stability: 787,482 in 1938; 753,012 in 1952; and 735,288 in 1955. Taking youthful crime separately, young people were responsible for 36 per cent of all indictable offences in 1938, and in 1955—33 per cent. Subsequently there has been a distinct rise, the significance of which is still being debated. What is of particular interest to us in all this, however,
25 is that when the figures are looked at within the framework of age, rather than globally, they suggest that criminality is a phase in the life-cycle of the individual rather than a phase in the 'life' of the whole society.

Changed attitudes to parental authority go hand in hand with changed attitudes to 'the authorities' in general. But it was the parents themselves who started the
30 rot (if 'rot' it is): they overthrew the old Victorian paterfamilias; they urged youth to be free, experimented with bottle feeding, struggled so that 'the kids' could have better homes, more rewarding (in every sense) jobs, better education than themselves. And now, confusingly, 'the kids' are biting the hands that fed them. The 'scholarship boys', absorbed into middle-class ways, can't even find
35 anything to talk to their parents about. ...

There are very distinctive styles of crime, too. Crime, here, is not a mode of production, or a career: it is more commonly a mode of expression, or a phase during which personality needs are satisfied in precisely the ways held out as desirable by respectable society in other contexts. It is frequently opportunity-
40 crime, or by rationalistic standards, purely destructive. And, classically, it is often oriented towards the acquisition or use of consumption goods, such as clothes

and cars. Its values are the values of a consumption-oriented society, not those generated by basic poverty.

The emergence of a specialized 'youth industry', engaged in selling goods to
45 young people, obviously reflects the fact, as we are always being reminded, that youth can now afford to buy what it wants, or is led to want. Teenagers' real earnings have risen faster than those of adults (though as Mark Abrams has noted, their share of the national wealth is 'very modest ... (and) ... scarcely sustains a picture of an extremely prosperous body of young people'). It becomes profit-
50 able to exploit this market. This is indeed a necessary departure point in analysis, but it does not tell us why these kinds of goods are produced and consumed and not others. Clothes, for example, are important because they make the man: they express a personality, buttress a personality if it needs it, provide an artificial one if a real one is effectively lacking. So young people are interested in what they
55 look like, how they project an image of themselves (for they are not too sure of themselves yet), particularly to the opposite sex they have so marvellously dis- covered. They are so insecure, in exchanging the controlled and hierarchical regularities of school for what is, for so many, visibly a dead-end job at the bot- tom of the ladder, in changing their status within the family (and soon in leaving it
60 altogether), that they cling together and create a new world which quickly be- comes powerfully normative.

Nothing is more striking than the way in which the very revolt of youth is so standardized. 'Deviance', indeed, has its quite prescriptive uniform and regalia, and fashion exercises as authoritative a sway over the beatniks as it does over the
65 readers of *Vogue*. Hence the dictatorship of the 'Top Twenty' reflects and responds to far deeper wants than could ever be artificially induced by the most ingenious or unscrupulous public relations teams. Yet the media do command very con- siderable power, and the values they purvey are importantly internalized: when the young audience says that they'll buy it 'because it'll be a hit', they are at once
70 internalizing commercial values (it will sell), and the social values of identifica- tion and solidarity with the culture of the peer-group: their friends will be playing it, dancing to it, and talking about it.

If youth is 'materialistic', this is precisely the path pioneered for them by their parents, and in particular by those who run the world in which their parents are
75 pretty powerless and confused, too. ...

Extract from *New Society* (1965). This first appeared in *New Society London*, the weekly review of the Social Sciences.

Margaret Mead

63 Culture and Commitment

THE PAST

Postfigurative Cultures and Well-Known Forebears

The distinctions I am making among three different kinds of culture—*postfigurative*, in which children learn primarily from their forebears, *cofigurative*, in which both children and adults learn from their peers, and *prefigurative*, in which adults learn also from their children—are a reflection of the period in which we live.
5 Primitive societies and small religious and ideological enclaves are primarily postfigurative, deriving authority from the past. Great civilizations, which necessarily have developed techniques for incorporating change, characteristically make use of some form of cofigurative learning from peers, playmates, fellow students, and fellow apprentices. We are now entering a period, new in history, in
10 which the young are taking on new authority in their prefigurative apprehension of the still unknown future.

A postfigurative culture is one in which change is so slow and imperceptible that grandparents, holding newborn grandchildren in their arms, cannot conceive of any other future for the children than their own past lives. The past of the
15 adults is the future of each new generation; their lives provide the ground plan. The children's future is shaped in such a way that what has come after childhood for their forebears is what they, too, will experience after they are grown.

Postfigurative cultures, in which the elders cannot conceive of change and so can only convey to their descendants this sense of unchanging continuity, have
20 been, on the basis of present evidence, characteristic of human societies for millennia or up to the beginning of civilization. ...
It is true that the continuity of all cultures depends on the living presence of at least three generations. The essential characteristic of postfigurative cultures is the assumption, expressed by members of the older generation in their every act,
25 that their way of life (however many changes may, in fact, be embodied in it) is unchanging, eternally the same. In the past, before the present extension of life span, living greatgrandparents were very rare and grandparents were few. Those who embodied the longest stretch of the culture, who were the models for those younger than themselves, in whose slightest tone or gesture acceptance of the
30 whole way of life was contained, were few and hale. Their keen eyesight, sturdy limbs, and tireless industry represented physical as well as cultural survival. For such a culture to be perpetuated, the old were needed, not only to guide the group to seldom-sought refuges in time of famine, but also to provide the complete model of what life was. When the end of life is already known—when the song
35 that will be sung at death, the offerings that will be made, the spot of earth where one's bones will rest are already designated—each person, according to age and sex, intelligence and temperament, embodies the whole culture. ...

The conditions for change are of course always present implicitly, even in the mere repetition of a traditional procedure. As no man steps in the same river
40 twice, so there is always a possibility that some procedure, some custom, some belief, acceded to a thousand times, will rise into consciousness. This chance increases when the people of one postfigurative culture are in close contact with those of another. Their sense of what indeed constitutes their culture is accentuated. ...

45 In the 1940s, in Venezuela, within a few miles of the city of Maracaibo, Indians still hunted with bows and arrows, but cooked their food in aluminum pots stolen from Europeans, with whom they had never communicated in any way. And in the 1960s, living as enclaves within a foreign country, European or American occupying troops and their families looked with equally uncomprehend-
50 ing and unaccepting eyes at the "natives"—Germans, Malays·or Vietnamese— who lived outside their compounds. ...

THE PRESENT

Cofigurative Cultures and Familiar Peers

A cofigurative culture is one in which the prevailing model for members of the society is the behavior of their contemporaries. Although there are records of postfigurative cultures in which the elders provide the model for the behavior of
55 the young and in which there has been as yet no break in the acceptance of the ways of the ancestors, there are few societies in which cofiguration has become the only form of cultural transmission and none is known in which this model alone has been preserved through generations. In a society in which the only model was a cofigurative one, old and young alike would assume that it was
60 "natural" for the behavior of each new generation to differ from that of the preceding generation.

In all cofigurative cultures the elders are still dominant in the sense that they set the style and define the limits within which cofiguration is expressed in the behavior of the young. There are societies in which approbation by the elders is
65 decisive for the acceptance of new behavior; that is, the young look not to their peers, but to their elders, for the final approval of change. But at the same time, where there is a shared expectation that members of a generation will model their behavior on that of their contemporaries, especially their adolescent age mates, and that their behavior will differ from that of their parents and grandparents,
70 each individual, as he successfully embodies a new style, becomes to some extent a model for others of his generation.

Cofiguration has its beginning in a break in the postfigurative system. Such a break may come about in many ways: through a catastrophe in which a whole population, but particularly the old who were essential to leadership, is deci-
75 mated; as a result of the development of new forms of technology in which the old are not expert; following migration to a new land where the elders are, and always will be, regarded as immigrants and strangers; in the aftermath of a conquest in which subject populations are required to learn the language and ways

of the conqueror; as a result of religious conversion, when adult converts try to
80 bring up children to embody new ideals they themselves never experienced as
children and adolescents; or as a purposeful step in a revolution that establishes
itself through the introduction of new and different life styles for the young.

The conditions for change to a cofigurative type of culture became increasingly
prevalent after the development of high civilization as access to greater resources
85 made it possible for the members of one society to annex, subjugate, incorporate,
enslave, or convert members of other societies and to control or direct the behavior of the younger generation. Often, however, cofiguration, as a style, lasts
only for a short period. In situations in which the cultural style of the dominant
group is essentially postfigurative, second-generation members of a subjugated
90 group (whose parents had no certain models except their peers) may be completely
absorbed into a different, but still wholly postfigurative culture like the Israeli-
born children in the kibbutz. ...

THE FUTURE

Prefigurative Cultures and Unknown Children

Our present crisis has been variously attributed to the overwhelming rapidity of
change, the collapse of the family, the decay of capitalism, the triumph of a
95 soulless technology, and, in wholesale repudiation, to the final breakdown of the
Establishment. Behind these attributions there is a more basic conflict between
those for whom the present represents no more than an intensification of our
existing cofigurative culture, in which peers are more than ever replacing parents
as the significant models of behavior, and those who contend that we are in fact
100 entering a totally new phase of cultural evolution.

Most commentators, in spite of their differences in viewpoint, still see the future
essentially as an extension of the past. Teller can still speak of the outcome of a
nuclear war as a state of destruction relatively no more drastic than the ravages
wrought by Genghis Khan. Writing about the present crisis, moralists refer to
105 the decay of religious systems in the past and historians point out that time and
again civilization has survived the crumbling of empires.

Similarly, most commentators treat as no more than an extreme form of adolescent rebellion the repudiation of present and past by the dissident youth of
every persuasion in every kind of society in the world. So Max Lerner can say
110 "Every adolescent must pass through two crucial periods: one when he identifies
with a model—a father, an older brother, a teacher—the second when he disasso-
ciates himself from his model, rebels against him, reasserts his own selfhood". ...

Extracts from *Culture And Commitment* by Margaret Mead. (1970)

Alvin Toffler

64 A Diversity of Life Styles

Seldom has a single nation evinced greater confusion over its sexual values than America has. Yet the same might be said for other kinds of values as well. America is tortured by uncertainty with respect to money, property, law and order, race, religion, God, family and self. Nor is the United States alone in suffering from a kind of value vertigo. All the techno-societies are caught up in the same massive upheaval. This collapse of the values of the past has hardly gone unnoticed. Every priest, politician and parent is reduced to head-shaking anxiety by it. Yet most discussions of value change are barren for they miss two essential points. The first of these is acceleration.

Value turn-over is now faster than ever before in history. While in the past a man growing up in a society could expect that its public value system would remain largely unchanged in his lifetime, no such assumption is warranted today, except perhaps in the most isolated of pre-technological communities.

This implies temporariness in the structure of both public and personal value systems, and it suggests that *whatever* the content of values that arise to replace those of the industrial age, they will be shorter-lived, more ephemeral than the values of the past. There is no evidence whatsoever that the value systems of the techno-societies are likely to return to a 'steady state' condition. For the foreseeable future, we must anticipate still more rapid value change.

Within this context, however, a second powerful trend is unfolding. For the fragmentation of societies brings with it a diversification of values. We are witnessing the crack-up of consensus.

Most previous societies have operated with a broad central core of commonly shared values. This core is now contracting, and there is little reason to anticipate the formation of a new broad consensus within the decades ahead. The pressures are outwards towards diversity, not inwards towards unity.

This accounts for the fantastically discordant propaganda that assails the mind in the techno-societies. Home, school, corporation, church, peer group, mass media—and myriad subcults—all advertise varying sets of values. The result for many is an 'anything goes' attitude—which is, itself, still another value position. We are, declares Newsweek magazine, 'a society that has lost its consensus ... a society that cannot agree on standards of conduct, language and manners, on what can be seen and heard'. ...

As we rush towards super-industrialism, therefore, we find people adopting and discarding life styles at a rate that would have staggered the members of any previous generation. For the life style itself has become a throw-away item.

This is no small or easy matter. It accounts for the much lamented 'loss of commitment' that is so characteristic of our time. As people shift from subcult to subcult, from style to style, they are conditioned to guard themselves against the inevitable pain of disaffiliation. They learn to armour themselves against the sweet sorrow of parting. The extremely devout Catholic who throws over his

religion and plunges into the life of a New Left activist, then throws himself into some other cause or movement or subcult, cannot go on doing so for ever. He becomes, to adapt Graham Greene's term, a 'burnt-out case'. He learns from past
45 disappointment never to lay too much of his old self on the line.

And so, even when he seemingly adopts a subcult or style, he withholds some part of himself. He conforms to the group's demands and revels in the belonging-ness that it gives him. But this belongingness is never the same as it once was, and secretly he remains ready to defect at a moment's notice. What this means is
50 that even when he seems most firmly plugged into his group or tribe, he listens, in the dark of night, to the short-wave signals of competing tribes.

In this sense, his membership in the group is shallow. He remains constantly in a posture of non-commitment, and without strong commitment to the values and styles of some group, he lacks the explicit set of criteria that he needs to pick his
55 way through the burgeoning jungle of overchoice.

Extract from Toffler *Future Shock*.

Stanley Milgram

65 The Perils of Obedience

Obedience is as basic an element in the structure of social life as one can point to. Some system of authority is a requirement of all communal living, and it is only the person dwelling in isolation who is not forced to respond, with defiance or submission, to the commands of others. For many people, obedience is a deeply
5 ingrained behavior tendency, indeed, a potent impulse overriding training in ethics, sympathy, and moral conduct.

The dilemma inherent in submission to authority is ancient, as old as the Biblical story of Abraham, who is commanded by God to sacrifice his son as a test of his faith. And the question of whether one should obey when commands
10 conflict with conscience has been argued by Plato, dramatized in Sophocles' *Antigone*, and treated to philosophic analysis in almost every historical epoch. Conservative philosophers argue that the very fabric of society is threatened by disobedience, while humanists stress the primacy of the individual conscience.

The legal and philosophic aspects of obedience are of enormous import, but
15 they say very little about how most people behave in concrete situations. I set up a simple experiment at Yale University to test how much pain an ordinary citizen would inflict on another person simply because he was ordered to do so by an experimental scientist. Stark authority was pitted against the subjects' strongest moral imperatives against hurting others. With the subjects' ears ringing
20 with the screams of the victims, authority won more often than not. The extreme willingness of adults to go to almost any lengths on the command of an authority constitutes the chief finding of the study and the fact most urgently demanding explanation.

In the basic experimental design, two people come to a psychology laboratory
25 to take part in a study of memory and learning. One of them is designated as a "teacher" and the other a "learner". The experimenter explains that the study is concerned with the effects of punishment on learning. The learner is conducted into a room, seated in a kind of miniature electric chair; his arms are strapped to prevent excessive movement, and an electrode is attached to his wrist. He is told
30 that he will be read lists of simple word pairs, and that he will then be tested on his ability to remember the second word of a pair when he hears the first one again. Whenever he makes an error, he will receive electric shocks of increasing intensity.

The real focus of the experiment, however, is the teacher. After watching the
35 learner being strapped into place, he is seated before an impressive "shock generator." The instrument panel consists of thirty lever switches set in a horizontal line. Each switch is clearly labeled with a voltage designation ranging from 15 to 450 volts, with verbal descriptions ranging from Slight Shock to Moderate Shock, Strong Shock, Very Strong Shock, Intense Shock, Extreme Intensity Shock,
40 and finally Danger: Severe Shock.

Each subject is given a sample 45-volt shock from the generator before his run as teacher, and the jolt strengthens his belief in the authenticity of the machine.

Conscience at Work

The teacher is a genuinely naive subject, who has come to the laboratory for the experiment in response to an advertisement placed in a local newspaper
45 asking for volunteers for a scientific study of memory. The learner, or victim, is actually an actor who receives no shock at all. The point of the experiment is to see how far a person will proceed in a concrete and measurable situation in which he is ordered to inflict increasing pain on a protesting victim.

Conflict arises when the man receiving the shock begins to show that he is
50 experiencing discomfort. At 75 volts, he grunts; at 120 volts, he complains loudly; at 150 volts, he demands to be released from the experiment. As the voltage increases, his protests become more vehement and emotional. At 285 volts, his response can be described only as an agonized scream. Soon thereafter, he makes no sound at all.
55 For the teacher, the situation quickly becomes one of gripping tension. It is not a game for him; conflict is intense and obvious. The manifest suffering of the learner presses him to quit; but each time he hesitates to administer a shock, the experimenter orders him to continue. To extricate himself from this plight, the subject must make a clear break with authority.
60 A number of subjects, but a minority, did make this break and refused to go on with the experiment, as indicated by the following exchange:

> *Learner:* Get me out of here. I told you I had heart trouble. My heart's beginning to bother me now. Get me out of here, please.
> *Teacher:* I think we ought to find out what's wrong in there first.
65 > *Experimenter* (wearing a technician's coat): As I said before, although the shocks may be painful, they are not dangerous.
> *Teacher:* Look, I don't know anything about electricity. But I won't go any further until I find out if the man is OK.
> *Experimenter:* It's absolutely essential that you continue. You have
70 > no other choice.
> *Teacher:* Oh. . . .

Extract from *Obedience to Authority* by Stanley Milgram. (1974)

David Riesman

66 Tootle

A Modern Cautionary Tale

Tootle is a young engine who goes to engine school, where two main lessons are taught: stop at a red flag and "always stay on the track no matter what". Diligence in the lessons will result in the young engine's growing up to be a big streamliner. Tootle is obedient for a while and then one day discovers the delight of going off
5 the tracks and finding flowers in the field. This violation of the rules cannot, however, be kept secret; there are telltale traces in the cowcatcher. Nevertheless, Tootle's play becomes more and more of a craving, and despite warnings he continues to go off the tracks and wander in the field. Finally the engine school-master is desperate. He consults the mayor of the little town of Engineville, in
10 which the school is located; the mayor calls a town meeting, and Tootle's failings are discussed—of course Tootle knows nothing of this. The meeting decides on a course of action, and the next time Tootle goes out for a spin alone and goes off the tracks he runs right into a red flag and halts. He turns in another direction only to encounter another red flag; still another—the result is the same. He turns
15 and twists but can find no spot of grass in which a red flag does not spring up, for all the citizens of the town have cooperated in this lesson.

Chastened and bewildered he looks toward the track, where the inviting green flag of his teacher gives him the signal to return. Confused by conditioned reflexes to stop signs, he is only too glad to use the track and tears happily up and down.
20 He promises that he will never leave the track again, and he returns to the round-house to be rewarded by the cheers of the teachers and the citizenry and the assurance that he will indeed grow up to be a streamliner.

Extract from *The Lonely Crowd* by David Riesman, ed. J.H. Schild. (1967)

67   Planning for the Holocaust

For most people, nuclear war, civil defence and annihilation are things of novels and films; a subject which we all got excited about in the 1960s. We all think that the world is more responsible now; that there are fewer loopholes for the megalomaniac prime minister or president to begin an atomic war.

However, recently Bexley Council decided to spend £77,000 on an underground fallout shelter. It seems that emergency planning is still very much alive. According to the Greater London Council, Bexley is one of five emergency planning centres.

Although this all seems extraordinary and like a science fiction novel, if a nuclear war broke out tomorrow, the first warning would be issued to the people of Britain through the United Kingdom Monitoring Organisation. It consists of the R. A. F.'s early warning system and 10,000 voluntary Royal Observer Corps men who would be stationed in 900 underground shelters located about 14 miles apart throughout the country. Since 1974, Britain's 54 major local authorities have been appointing Home Defence and Emergency Planning Departments to take on this responsibility.

Every council is supposed to have a special wartime headquarters already marked out at its town hall, plus a secondary one, in case the first is blown up. These would hold up to 90 people. The main communication centre for wartime operations is situated deep beneath High Holborn in the centre of London. There, with enough supplies and water for five weeks, all telephone, radio and microwave communications links will be maintained. There is also believed to be a major headquarters on the outskirts of London with room for 200 scientists, civil servants and politicians. If an attack was impending, ministers and selected civil servants would go to their appointed regions, taking shelter until the bombs stopped falling and radiation dropped, and would then emerge to restore effective government. Meanwhile, the rescue work would be carried out by local emergency officers and local councillors. All this depends, of course, on adequate warning of impending nuclear disaster. This, at present, is estimated at a minimum of three weeks, during which the international situation would steadily deteriorate. The immediate pre-attack period is estimated at seventy-two hours, when the media would be saturated with advice on the working of the 18,000 warning sirens and on how to survive. Some experts disagree, suggesting that there might be no warning at all.

There are no plans to provide any shelter-type protection for the population in general, however. Seven deep shelters were constructed during and after the last war, along the path of the Northern Line Underground system. They have room for up to 56,000 people, but they are now liable to flooding. Several hundred shelters under council housing blocks have also been demolished. The Home Office expects the three-week warning period to be long enough for householders to convert one room into a shelter, improving, it claims, the survival factor by ten times.

Amazingly, in a time of peace, current annual spending in Britain on emergency defence services is £12 million. One North London Defence Officer, when recently interviewed, still talked in quotations from a ten-year-old pamphlet on civil defence and advised stocking up with tinned food, filling the bath with water and keeping the children amused with books and games ! The pamphlet, although updated, still contains phrases such as 'the public should take the best available cover from gamma radiation for at least one week. . .' Where such cover is to be found remains still a puzzle.

The central assumption of all government civil defence planning is that any possible level of nuclear attack will still leave many survivors. According to recent computer forecasts, it would be impossible for an enemy to devise a plan which would wipe out the entire population of Britain. Under any possible range of targets, the population remaining after a nuclear attack would be about forty million. That means that fifteen million people would die. Ardent supporters of the Campaign for Nuclear Disarmament say that the figure is more like fifty per cent of the population.

Whichever way one looks at it, one bomb would annihilate London completely. If there ever was a three-week warning, I, for one, would be first on a plane for a remote island in the South Pacific! What would *you* do ?

From the Article in *Current 6/77* Series 10. (1977)   (*unabridged*)

Paul and Anne Ehrlich

68 Thermonuclear Warfare

A final kind of assault on ecosystems must be mentioned. Much has been written, especially by military theoretician Herman Kahn, on the effects of thermonuclear warfare, the possibilities of limited thermonuclear warfare, and so on. Since modern societies seem bent on continuing to prepare for such conflicts, we have little
5 sympathy for those of Kahn's critics who feel that it is immoral to try to analyze the possible results. It would be pleasant (but probably incorrect) to assume that if everyone were aware of the terrible magnitude of the devastation that could result from a nuclear war, the world's stockpiles of fission and fusion weapons would soon be dismantled. This does not mean that Kahn's analysis is sound—
10 quite the contrary. One major flaw in his evaluation of the results of thermonuclear war is one that is common to the analyses of many physical scientists. He grossly underrates the possible environmental consequences of these projected wars. In addition to the instantaneous slaughter of humans and demolition of property, the effects of any reasonably large thermonuclear exchange would
15 inevitably constitute an unbelievable ecological and genetic disaster—especially for a world already on the edge of nutritional and environmental catastrophe.

Consider the effects that even a rather limited nuclear exchange among the United States, Russia, China, and various European powers would have on the world food supply. Suddenly, all international trade would come to a halt, and
20 the developed world would be in no position to supply either food or any technological aid to the underdeveloped. No more high-yield seed, no more fertilizers, no more grain shipments, no more tractors, no more pumps and well-drilling equipment, trucks, or other manufactured products or machines would be delivered. Similarly, the UDCs would not be able to send DCs minerals, petroleum,
25 and their food products. The world could be pitched into chaos and massive famine almost immediately, even if most countries were themselves untouched by the nuclear explosions.

But of course no country would be left unscathed. All over the world radiation levels would rise and would prevent cultivation of crops in many areas. Blast
30 effects and huge fires burning in the Northern Hemisphere would send large amounts of debris into the atmosphere, probably dwarfing the volcanic and pollution effects previously discussed. The entire climate of the Earth would soon be altered. In many areas, where the supply of combustible materials was sufficient, huge fire-storms would be generated, some of them covering hundreds
35 of square miles in heavily forested or metropolitan areas. We know something about such storms from experiences during the Second World War. On the night of July 27, 1943, Lancaster and Halifax heavy bombers of the Royal Air Force dropped 2,417 tons of incendiary and high-explosive bombs on the city of Hamburg. Thousands of individual fires coalesced into a fire-storm about 6 square
40 miles in area. Flames reached 15,000 feet into the atmosphere, and smoke and gases rose to 40,000 feet. Winds, created by huge updrafts and blowing in toward the center of the fire, reached a velocity of more than 150 miles per hour. The

temperature in the fire exceeded 1,450 degrees Fahrenheit, high enough to melt aluminum and lead. Air in underground shelters was heated to the point where, 45 when they were opened and oxygen was admitted, flammable materials and even corpses burst into flame. These shelters had to be permitted to cool *10 days to two weeks* before rescuers could enter.

Anyone interested in further details of what a *small* fire-storm is like is referred to Martin Caiden's excellent book, *The Night Hamburg Died.* From this account 50 one can imagine the ecological results of the generation of numerous fire-storms and the burning off of a large portion of the Northern Hemisphere. In many areas the removal of all vegetation would not be the only effect; the soil might be partly or completely sterilized as well. There would be no plant communities nearby to effect rapid repopulation, and rains would wash away the topsoil. Picture defoli- 55 ated California hills during the winter rains, and then imagine the vast loads of silt and radioactive debris being washed from northern continents into offshore waters, the site of most of the ocean's productivity. Consider the fate of aquatic life, which is especially sensitive to the turbidity of the water, and think of the many offshore oil wells that would be destroyed by blast in the vicinity of large 60 cities and left to pour their loads of crude oil into the ocean with no way of shutting them off. Think of the runoff of solvents, fuels, and other chemicals from ruptured storage tanks and pipelines.

The survivors of any large-scale thermonuclear war would face a severely devastated environment. If a full-scale war were waged, most of the survivors 65 would be in the Southern Hemisphere. They would be culturally depauperate, since much of mankind's technology would be irretrievably lost. If the technolog- ical structure of society is destroyed, man will find it almost impossible to rebuild it because of resource depletion. Most high-grade ores and rich and accessible fossil fuel deposits have long since been used up. Technology itself is necessary 70 for access to what remains. Only if enough scrap metals and stored fuel remained available would there be a hope of reconstruction, and it would have to begin promptly before these rusted, drained away, or were lost in other ways. From what we know of past large disasters, it seems unlikely that survivors, without a source of outside assistance, would psychologically be able to start rapid re- 75 construction.

If there were extensive use of weapons in the Northern Hemisphere, or of chemical or biological weapons were used simultaneously, the survivors would probably consist of scattered, isolated groups. Such groups would face genetic problems, since each would contain only a small part of mankind's genetic varia- 80 bility and would be subject to a further loss of variability through inbreeding. Studies of certain Japanese and Italian populations have shown that inbreeding profoundly affects infant mortality. In addition it appears that prenatal damage increases linearly with the degree of inbreeding. In such a situation it is pro- blematical whether culturally and genetically deprived groups of survivors could 85 persist in the face of much harsher environmental conditions than they had faced previously. In short, it would not be necessary to kill every individual with blast, fire, and radiation in order to force *Homo sapiens* into extinction.

Chapter from *Population, Resources, Environment: Issues In Human Ecology*, 2nd Edn. by Paul R. Ehrlich and Anne H. Ehrlich. (1972)

Tom Galt

69 How We Can End War

The United Nations has been trying to keep peace—whenever possible—by talk. The U.N. has recommended a cease-fire or a new boundary line, and hoped the quarreling nations would accept it. More often the U.N. has sent a committee to listen to both sides and gradually write a treaty that they would accept.

5 The United Nations has attempted to keep peace also by force. This is new. No world organization ever tried it before. When the leaders of a country, defying the U.N., send soldiers with big guns, tanks, and airplanes to make war, the U.N. can reply with soldiers, big guns, tanks, and airplanes supplied by many countries.

For many centuries nations have been slowly learning how to work together.
10 International organization grew all the way from the Telegraph Union in 1865, through the Postal Union and the League of Nations, to the much larger United Nations in only eighty years.

The U.N., too, is changing and growing. It now represents nearly all of us. But this use of force is new. Maybe we are not yet doing it the best way. Couldn't
15 the U.N. send police to arrest only the guilty leaders?

The U.N.'s International Law Commission (twelve experts appointed by the General Assembly) studied the question whether a whole nation should be punished if its leaders start a war. Those experts reported, "Crimes against international law are committed by men." Crimes, such as starting a war, are not
20 committed, they said, by a whole nation. And the U.N. can keep peace "only by punishing individuals who commit such crimes."

In December, 1950, the U.N. General Assembly accepted this idea. The Assembly appointed a committee to plan an international criminal court. This court will try men who start wars or who even plan to begin a war. But no one can
25 be arrested and tried justly except under laws that are just and humane. Therefore, some world authority—a new U.N. perhaps—must first make those laws.

Fifty years previously this idea would have sounded like a beautiful but impossible dream. But times have changed. The delegates of most of the nations in the world, meeting in the U.N. General Assembly, voted for a committee to
30 work on it.

What powers must we add to the U.N. for it to become strong enough to stop war?

In order to stop war the U.N. might take command over all soldiers. Each country would keep merely a police force with which to catch robbers and
35 manage mobs. Only the U.N. would have any army.

The United States Government has' urged that only the U.N. should control atomic energy. The U.N. should see to it that atomic energy is used for electricity and to heat houses, not for bombs.

If the U.N. could regulate world trade, it could help the poor countries to stop
40 becoming poorer. If the U.N. could set minimum-wage standards everywhere, the rich countries would at last be protected against unfair competition by cheap foreign labor.

Many people have said the U.N. should not allow any iron curtain. If the U.N. had power, it should make laws that any book, newspaper, or magazine that tells
45 the truth may go anywhere in the world. Then any person who behaves himself will be allowed to go, too, anywhere in the world and take his money with him.

That is about all that's needed to stop war.

The U.N. must not interfere in local affairs. Every state or town ought to keep its right to make its own laws about robbery, murder, gambling, liquor, divorce,
50 and the censorship of comic books. The people of each country must keep the right to decide for themselves what languages their country will use, what economic system it will encourage, what political methods it will be governed by.

Many of the government leaders in the world agree that that stronger U.N., having real powers, could at last prevent war.
55 The method has been growing for nearly a hundred years. It is becoming stronger as the U.N. gets more power. Do you want it soon to become strong enough?

Surely it ought to have a world bill of rights, enforced by U.N. courts, guaranteeing personal freedoms to everyone everywhere, not only in your own
60 country. But you may have to study, think, and talk and vote many times in order to achieve this world-wide freedom.

When the U.N. has become strong enough we shall no longer have to waste our time, our money, our thought, blood, and suffering on war. War, invented by apes, is stupid. It is boring. The future, with its new tasks, can be far more
65 interesting.

Edited extract from *The Story of Peace and War* by Thomas F. Galt Jr. (1932)

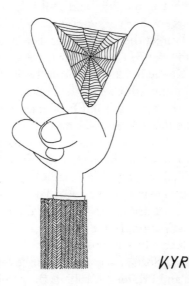

KYR

Roy Hoopes

70 A Monument to JFK

Neither money nor technical assistance, however, can be our only weapon against poverty. In the end the crucial effort is one of purpose, requiring not only the fuel of finance but the torch of idealism. And nothing carries the spirit of American idealism and expresses our hopes better and more effectively to the far corners of the earth than the Peace Corps.

> —President John F. Kennedy in his last
> State of the Union Address, January
> 14, 1963.

It is becoming increasingly obvious, that no American organization, governmental or private, has been received around the world as enthusiastically and affectionately as the organization which grew directly out of the presidential campaign of 1960. As President Kennedy said in his last State of the Union

5 address, "...nothing carries the spirit of American idealism and expresses our hopes better and more effectively to the far corners of the earth than the Peace Corps."

There is no more fitting monument to the late President than the Peace Corps. As a thriving, bustling government agency, the Peace Corps stands as the mani-

10 festation of perhaps the most exciting and powerful idea harnessed by John F. Kennedy and his Administration. As will be seen in the following pages, the basic idea of a Peace Corps had been kicking around for some time before it was mentioned by Senator Kennedy at the University of Michigan during the presidential campaign of 1960. But it was John F. Kennedy who had the instinct and

15 the vision to take an idea which had already captured the imagination of the intellectual and academic communities and pull it into the mainstream of American political action. Sargent Shriver, appointed by his brother-in-law, President Kennedy, to create and direct the Peace Corps, is fond of quoting the remark that "No army can withstand the force of an idea whose time has come." And from

20 the first time Senator Kennedy mentioned the Peace Corps, it was obvious that the Peace Corps was an idea whose time had come.

Four years later, by the time of John F. Kennedy's tragic death in Dallas on November 22, 1963, the Peace Corps was more than an idea: it was 5,937 Volunteers overseas in 46 countries; 1,215 more Volunteers in training for overseas

25 assignments; 76,003 applications from Americans of all ages anxious to serve; and there were unfulfilled requests for Peace Corps Volunteers from 24 underdeveloped nations. And to many people abroad it was Kennedy's Peace Corps.

Shriver said that when he arrived in Israel on the first leg of a journey around the world after the assassination, Prime Minister David Ben Gurion told him that

30 the death of President Kennedy was the occasion of the "first world-wide mourning in the history of man." Shriver also noted that "everywhere, mayors and tribal chiefs, as well as Kings and Presidents, told us they had never seen such a universal outpouring of emotion, of grief and loss, at the death of a foreign leader."

And he could not help but be impressed. "Why was it that Kennedy, by himself,
35 one man, could penetrate into corners of the world more effectively than all our
propaganda apparatus for twenty years?" Shriver asked a *New York Times* correspondent. "We all need to study what it was that he did or said and why our society
was so incapable of perceiving that he was so effective."

Shriver also could not help but see the similarity between the worldwide effect
40 of Kennedy's assassination and the impact of the Peace Corps on the people of
every country in which Peace Corps Volunteers have served. As Shriver saw it,
both impacts rested on the same foundation: John F. Kennedy was a man of
ideas and ideals; the Peace Corps is committed to an ideal. President Kennedy
was a man of peace; the Peace Corps is an instrument of peace. President Kennedy
45 was a man of this generation; Peace Corps Volunteers are primarily men and
women of this generation. President Kennedy, although an extremely wealthy
man, was not content to sit back and idly enjoy the comforts which great affluence
could provide; Peace Corps Volunteers, although citizens of the most affluent
nation on earth, are not content to sit back and idly enjoy that affluence, but have
50 given up opportunities to live in comfort because they find more meaning in
service than in the pursuit of pleasure. President Kennedy cared—for the hungry,
the dispossessed, the hated, and the fearful; the Peace Corps is an organization
which cares, its Volunteers are overseas because they want to help.

It is the pure intention of the Peace Corps that has most impressed the rest of
55 the world. For instance, Peace Corps Volunteers in the Far East were awarded
the Ramón Magsaysay Award, the first time a group of non-Asians had received
the honor. In explaining its selection, the Magsaysay Board said:

> The problem of achieving peace amidst the tensions and dangers of a
> nuclear age occupies the mind of much of the human race, yet few within it
60 > discover a useful way to contribute. In reaffirming the essential community
> of interest of all ordinary people, regardless of creed or nationality, the
> Peace Corps Volunteers belong to that small but growing fraternity who by
> their individual efforts do make a difference.

The Peace Corps has also been awarded the "Silver Medal of Arequipa"—from
65 that second largest city in Peru. In honor of Peace Corps Volunteers in Thailand,
the Chulalongkorn University presentend Sargent Shriver with an honorary
degree. "Many of us who did not know about the United States," said the
Foreign Minister of Thailand in presenting the award, "thought of this great
nation as a wealthy nation, a powerful nation, endowed with great material
70 strength and many powerful weapons. But how many of us knew that in the
United States ideas and ideals are also powerful. This is the secret of your greatness,
of your might, which is not imposing or crushing people, but is filled with hope
of future good will and understanding. It is indeed striking that this important
idea, the most powerful idea in recent times, should come from this mightiest
75 nation on earth—the United States."

Although by 1964 the Peace Corps had become an American institution almost
as sacrosanct as motherhood, there were, of course, still some dissenters. In Illi-

nois the *Rockford Star* called it the "most over-rated, over-publicized and over-
sold travel club in the world," and the *San Diego Union* thought that the "Peace
80 Corps rests on the fundamental error that we are going to advance civilization
and world peace by helping a handful of people on the edge of a sea of human
want." It must be borne in mind that the Peace Corps was created not to eliminate
worldwide poverty, but to provide an outlet for a whole generation of frustrated,
idealistic young Americans who wanted to show that they *cared* about the poverty
85 and lack of opportunity in the emerging nations.

As the stories of the individual Volunteers' experiences and accomplishments
began to filter back to a nation preoccupied with the problems of overabundance,
it was becoming increasingly apparent that maybe the Peace Corps had helped
discover a new American. Sargent Shriver, at least, thinks so: "The Peace Corps
90 Volunteer is a new breed of American. He journeys to a foreign land to work
within that nation's system; to speak a strange language; to live as nationals do
and under their laws. Because of this he has been welcomed where others have
been turned away. And he is admired. Because of this, the world is learning that
Americans have not gone soft and really do care about people living in faraway
95 places."

Another observer agrees. Morris Stein, a New York University psychologist
who tested Peace Corps Volunteers in training for Colombia says, "These kids
represent something many of us thought had disappeared from America—the old
frontier spirit. These kids are skilled, resourceful, nonmaterialistic, and definitely
100 socially oriented. They love working with people and do so without sloppy
sentiment. I think we're leading with our best in Colombia."

Edited extract from *What The President Does All Day* by Roy Hoopes Jr. (1965)

Philip Callow

71 In the Factory

I was fifteen. I remember being intimidated at first by the sprawling, prison-like buildings, the intent look of people going in and the grim faces of the works police. I was taken into the concrete box with slits for windows and told to sit down and wait. Two men were inside, and as there was hardly any space, the
5 sourness was very strong. One of the men glanced up from pouring tea into a chipped cup. I was sitting right against him. My gaze strayed around and I saw the long row of keys over his head, all labelled and hung on brass hooks. The other man had squatted down, jamming his knees under the little table where there was a phone, and my brand-new insurance card was sticking up unnaturally
10 in his beefy hand. He was squinting at it with great concentration, waiting, and then somebody must have answered. He shouted angrily into the mouthpiece that he had a new apprentice with him, pronouncing my surname wrongly. He listened again, scowling, then suddenly slammed the phone down as if disgusted.

I followed him out, feeling ridiculous and pathetic because of the neat bundle I
15 was clutching, which had my new overall and my sandwiches in it. Nothing was worse than being a beginner. We passed between the dismal low sheds stretching ahead endlessly, past holes in the walls, and doorways, entering and leaving the different smells. I caught a glimpse of a square orange fire, deep inside one of the places, and saw some dark burrowing figures. Then a man in a filthy boiler-suit
20 came into the road ahead of us, pushing a barrowful of steel cuttings. The steel ribbons were brown and in rapid spirals, short and long pieces, tangled like snakes. He pushed them across, a high swaying heap, and disappeared.

We went along the side of a pool of stagnant water, about twenty paces square, edged with tubular railings, the surface coloured and veined with oil. Going past,
25 my guide spoke for the first time since we had set out.

'Over this way,' he said, because he had turned sharply and I was not quick enough. Then after a few yards: 'In here.' He lumbered down a short, narrowing passage which ended in a blue door.

Until this moment he had been almost swaggering along, big-chested, aggres-
30 sive, but now he seemed to shrink and become timid. He leaned on the door carefully, opening it with his shoulder. I was filled with foreboding at the sight of his sudden respect. Then he led me into the training centre and I was astonished because it looked so small and orderly, in the flood of bright light.

In the supervisor's office, after I closed the door on the noise, there was a
35 curious numbed silence. I heard a faint drone, as if from something a long way off, and that was all. Through the glass sides I saw lads opening and shutting their mouths, bending over silent machines, banging away noiselessly with hammers. I noticed them while I waited for the supervisor to speak. He looked up from his papers reluctantly and said a few words, moving his bottom jaw sideways like a
40 cow chewing. He had a thick Scottish accent. I started to reply, and with his eyes fixed on my face he lifted one arm and waved it about. This was a signal for one of the charge-hands to come in and attend to me.

I understood things, but it was like living in a cloud. After a few hours the surroundings were sharper, though it took days for them to be real.

45 We were in a corner of one of the main sheds, in a kind of special pen, half wooden and half wire mesh. You stood by the mesh and looked through at men and women, many of them smoking. The machines out there were massive, dwarfing ours. Every so often they gave hideous shrieks and groans. But there was only bluish fog hanging over them, and occasional handfuls of white sparks

50 jumping out from the bottoms of grinding-wheels. Things were dirtier, more casual and realistic, that was the difference. The lofty roof and the space made it seem more heartless. I was glad to be where I was, but the squalor on that side of the fence was more alive and it attracted me.

If a girl saw us squinting through she would wave, and one of the men would

55 notice and shout across to his mate, showing his teeth in a laugh. The white barriers which penned us in were a joke.

Our two charge-hands had been told not to swear in front of us. When the tea came, they sat squashed in their cubby-hole of an office, whispering and glancing out furtively. Their names were Morgan and Stokes. The youngest apprentices

60 said 'sir' to them, as if speaking to schoolteachers.

Mr Morgan fascinated me. He was a tall, fair-headed Welshman with a lumpy, bulging forehead. He took strict, fastidious steps. Nobody trusted him, he was accepted as a deceitful person, yet he was popular. He stuck down his hair with grease and kept a pencil behind his ear. His overall pockets were full of junk.

65 From behind he looked slovenly, his frayed trousers dropping over his heels.

If you happened to be talking and he spotted you he would sidle up and press between you cunningly, making it seem accidental; or he would say: 'All right, lads? No trouble?' Looking into his face you would find it blandly innocent, but with the eyes smirking.

70 I did not like Mr Stokes at all. He had a fat neck, a black thinned-down moustache, and his black hair was cropped short like a wrestler's. He was crude and shambling. He stood with his legs apart and looked across with little cynical eyes, rocking on his heels.

Once I was working on a bench lathe near a boy who had been brought in one

75 Monday morning three weeks earlier, staring hard without comprehension as I must have done, shepherded by the same policeman. Now Mr Stokes stood behind him idly, watching, when suddenly the drill snapped. I heard the small crunching sound myself. Mr Stokes stepped forward and said: 'That another sod gone?'

80 'Yes,' the boy stammered. His hand that had been guiding the drill forward was fluttering about aimlessly.

'You dozy bastard,' Mr Stokes said.

The boy lost control and broke down. Crying hopelessly, he dragged at a white handkerchief, struggling to pull it out of his trouser pocket while he turned his

85 head away, utterly disgraced. Apprentices were nudging each other and pretending to look disgusted. Mr Stokes did not know what to do—it was perhaps the first time this had ever happened to him. The back of his neck reddened like a flame, and he went off to stand with Mr Morgan, at a distance. I raged inwardly at

them all, even at the boy, whose name I did not even know. I felt sickened and
90 lost, dropping into a void where there was only misery.

I overheard someone mention the name of the boy. He was Brian Wiltshire.
Later on that day, when I was forced to speak to him about a blueprint, he swung
round on me like a cornered animal. I had startled him, and I stopped looking
into his face. Recovering almost at once, he made himself brash and jaunty.
95 'How long did you want it for, old boy?' he said, curling his lip.

I was angry with him for treating me as an enemy, lumping me with all the
others indiscriminately. Even though I guessed it was not really him, this manner,
but only a defence, it made no difference. My sympathy had dwindled.

After about a month I was taken off bench work and put in charge of a small
100 shaping machine. A long greased ram on a crank drove the tool forward slowly,
then snatched it back to begin again. It needed dozens of strokes to travel across
the piece of metal clamped in the vice. All I needed to do was turn the handles a
fraction at a time, in the middle of each stroke, and gaze around me. It was simple,
leisurely work.
105 Mr Morgan wandered round from one group to another, looking bored and
glancing at his watch. He sometimes stood by me, pressing up too close, dog-
like, until I thought he was doing it for some reason. But his face gave nothing
away: I was never certain. He jingled the odds and ends in his pockets and made
a pretence of examining my blueprint, hanging his long impudent nose over it.
110 I knew he was not really interested.

Once he asked me, smiling slyly: 'Like it here?'

'Oh yes,' I said in confusion. It was impossible to trust him with the truth.

'Not bad, is it?'

I thought he might be trying to trick me.
115 'No,' I answered.

'Happy?'

'I think so, yes,' I said, and grinned. It was a kind of game.

'Live anywhere round here?' he asked familiarly, smiling away.

I told him.
120 'No—do you? How d'you get here, then—bus it?'

'On my bike,' I said.

'Really?' he exclaimed, and drew the word out in a cultured drawl. Now and
then he affected this. We used to imitate him in the canteen.

'Unless the weather's too bad,' I added.
125 'Rather you than me,' he smirked. He gave me a waggish prod in the ribs with
his elbow. Then he noticed the supervisor beckoning through the glass, so he
disowned me. He sprang over to the door, brisk and bustling, suddenly pompous
with responsibility.

That Easter I came to the end of my three months' probation. I was called into
130 the glass-walled office and told to report the next day to a section in another part
of the factory.

From *Native Ground* in *Story* by David Jackson and Dennis Pepper. (1973)

John H. Goldthorpe

72 Attitudes and Behaviour of Car Assembly Workers

In the literature of industrial sociology since the Second World War studies of workers in car assembly plants have almost certainly outnumbered those of any comparable industrial or occupational group. The essentials of the characterization are by now familiar. The car assembly line is 'the classic symbol of the sub-
5 jection of man to the machine in our industrial age'; the assembler 'approaches the classic model of the self-estranged worker'; he is 'the blue-collar prototype of "the mass men in mass society"' and, often, he is 'the prototype of the militant worker as well'.

In this paper, our first aim is to present results obtained from a study of wor-
10 kers in a British car assembly plant; results which, in certain respects, differ fairly clearly from the pattern which has emerged from previous investigations.

The study on which we report was based chiefly on interviews with workers in six assembly departments of the Luton plant of Vauxhall Motors Ltd. Our sample was a random one of men in these departments who were: (i) Grade I assemblers;
15 (ii) between the ages of 21 and 46; (iii) married; and (iv) resident in the town of Luton itself. The number in the original sample was 127; and of these exactly 100 (79 per cent) agreed to be interviewed at work. In connection with the wider purposes of our research project, 86 of these men were then re-interviewed in their homes and together with their wives. ...

The Assembler and his Job
20 In this respect, our findings were closely comparable with those produced by earlier inquiries.

(1) Assemblers appeared to derive little intrinsic satisfaction from their jobs; rather, in performing their work-tasks they tended to experience various forms of deprivation: Primarily monotony (reported by 69 per cent), and to a lesser degree
25 physical tiredness (48 per cent) and having to work at too fast a pace (30 per cent).

·(2) These deprivations were directly related to characteristic features of assembly-line jobs: the minute sub-division of tasks, repetitiveness, low skill requirements, predetermination of tools and techniques, and mechanically controlled rhythms and speeds of work. Of the men in our sample 63 per cent said
30 that they would prefer some other shop-floor job to their present one; and of these men, 87 per cent said they would have liked to move off the 'track' altogether, chiefly into jobs such as inspection, maintenance, rectification and testing. Moreover, among the reasons given for favouring such a move, those relating to the content of work were paramount. Jobs off the 'track' were seen as offering
35 more opportunity to exercise skill and responsibility, greater variety and challenge, and more freedom and autonomy.

(3) Consequently, the workers we studied were for the most part attached to their present employment chiefly through the extrinsic economic rewards which

it afforded them. Thirty-one per cent stated that the level of pay was the *only*
40 reason why they remained in their present work, and, in all, 74 per cent gave pay
either as the sole reason for this or along with others. The reason next most frequently mentioned was that of 'security' (25 per cent), and this, it was clear, was
thought of far more in relation to long-run income maximization than to the
minimum requirement of having a job of some kind. On the other hand, in con-
45 trast to this emphasis on economic considerations, only 6 per cent of the sample
said that they stayed with their present employer because they liked the actual
work they performed. In other words, then, our assemblers defined their work in
an essentially *instrumental* way; work was for them primarily a means to ends
external to the work situation. More specifically, one could say that work was
50 seen as a generally unsatisfying and stressful expenditure of time and effort which
was necessary in order to achieve a valued standard and style of living in which
work itself had no positive part.

These findings are, we repeat, in all respects markedly similar to those of other
studies of car assembly workers. To this extent, thus, our results tend to confirm
55 the idea that the responses of men to the work-tasks and roles of the car assembly
line are likely to vary little more, from plant to plant, than does the technology
itself.

However, to our last point above—concerning the assembler's instrumental
view of work—we would wish to give an emphasis which differs rather signifi-
60 cantly from that of most previous writers. Generally, the 'devaluation' of work
which is implied here has been taken as perhaps the clearest symptom of the car
assembler's alienated condition. For Blauner, for instance, this concentration on
the purely extrinsic rewards of work is 'the essential meaning of self-estrange-
ment'; and in Chinoy's view, the alienation of the auto worker basically results
65 from the fact that this work has become, in the words of Marx, 'not the satisfaction of a need but only the means to satisfy the needs outside it'. It is not our
aim here to dispute this interpretation. But, at the same time, we would wish to
stress the following point: that, at least in the case of our sample, the predomi-
nantly instrumental orientation to work was not simply or even primarily a *conse-
70 quence* of these men being car assemblers; rather, one could say that most had
become car assemblers *because of* a desire, and an eventual decision, on their part
to give priority to high-level economic returns from work at the expense, if
necessary, of satisfactions of an intrinsic kind. In other words, their instrumental
orientation had led to their present employment, rather than *vice versa*.

75 These data would suggest, then, that the workers we studied had for the most
part been impelled, by their desire for higher incomes, into taking work which
was in fact better paid than most other forms of employment available to them
largely to compensate for its inherent strains and deprivations. If, therefore, these
workers are to be considered as 'alienated', the roots of their alienation must be
80 sought not merely in the technological character of the plants in which they are
now employed but, more fundamentally, in those aspects of the wider society
which generate their tremendous drive for economic advancement and their disregard for the costs of this through the impoverishment of their working lives.

Furthermore, it also follows that in seeking to explain the industrial attitudes
85 and behaviour of these workers generally, one must always be prepared to treat
their essentially instrumental orientation towards their employment as an *independent* variable relative to the work situation, rather than regarding this simply
as a product of this situation.

Extracts from article in *British Journal of Sociology*, Vol. XVII, No. 3. (September 1966)

George Sturt

73 A Wheelwright Describes Part of His Ancient Craft

Of the stock (the nave or hub) I hardly dare speak, such a fine product it was,
and so ignorant about it do I feel.

A lumpish cylinder in shape—eleven or twelve inches in diameter and twelve
or thirteen inches from end to end—a newly turned stock was a lovely thing—to
5 the eyes, I thought, but more truly to sentiment, for the associations it hinted at.
Elm from hedgerow or park, it spoke of open country. Well seasoned, it was a
product of winter labour, of summer care in my own loft under my own hands.
Long quiet afternoons it had lain there, where I could glance from the stocks
across the town to the fields and the wooded hills. I had turned it over and over,
10 had chopped the bark away, had brushed off the mildew while the quiet winter
darkness had stolen through the shed, and at last I had chosen the stock for use,
and put it into Cook's hands.

And now it lay, butter-coloured, smooth, slightly fragant, soon to begin years
of field-work, after much more skill—the skill of ancient England—had been
15 bestowed on it, though already telling of that skill in every curve. Certainly we
did not consciously remember all these matters at the time: rather we concerned
ourselves with the utility this block of elm would have, with its grip for many
years of the oak spokes to be driven into it by and by. But without thinking, we
felt the glamour of the strong associations; and the skilled craftsmen must have
20 felt it more than I, because they lived in that glamour as fishes live in water. They
knew, better than any other may do, the answer of the elm when the keen blade
goes searching between its molecules. This was, this is, for ever out of my reach.
Only, I used to get some fellow-feeling about it, looking at a newly turned stock.
I understood its parts—the shallow hollows at back and front where the black-

25 smith would presently put on the bonds, the sloping 'nose', the clean chisel-cut
of the 'breast stroke'. This last was cut in all round the stock to mark where the
face of the spokes was to be.

So, when I had had my look, the wheel-maker—Cook or another—carried the
stock to his bench, there to mark on it with straddling compasses the place for the
30 first auger-holes, preliminary to mortising it for the spokes. A tricky job, this.
One young man, I remember, marking out his stock, prepared for an odd number
of spokes—eleven or thirteen; though, every felloe (sections of the wheel's rim)
requiring two, the spokes were always in even numbers; which error he did not
detect until he had bored his stock and spoilt it. Too big for the fire, and too cross-
35 grained to be easily split and thrown away, it lay about for months, an eyesore to
the luckless youth who had spoilt it and a plain indication that it is not quite easy
to mark a stock correctly.

Likewise was it not altogether a simple thing, though the skilled man seemed to
find it easy enough, to fix the wobbly stock down for working upon. It was laid
40 across a 'wheel-pit'—a narrow trench with sills, about three feet deep—where
iron clamps, themselves tightly wedged into the sills, held the stock steady back
and front. Then the mortices were started, with auger-holes. How easy it looked!
In my childhood I had heard the keen auger biting into elm, had delighted in the
springy spiral borings taken out; but now I learnt that only a strong and able
45 man could make them.

Extract from *The Wheelwright's Shop* by George Sturt. (1923)   (*unabridged*)

Ray Gosling

74 A Night at the Dogs

When I hear the Leeds Police Choir sing, their massive voices raised in harmony praising the Lord Messiah, I think what a wonderful country we live in for half-hidden pleasures. Who edits the Wayside Pulpit? And think of all the people who win prize cups and medallions for dahlias, darts, or chihuahuas. There are more
5 people about than we think taking part in pleasures that never hit the headlines but are immensely popular, like choir practice, darts and dogs. The second most popular sport in the country is dog-racing. I met this fanatic who said to me: 'Do you know that the greyhound's the only dog mentioned by name in Holy Scripture, in the Book of Solomon, and it's on Egyptian coins—the greyhound is as
10 old as Tutenkhamun.'

Certainly in England since cock-fighting stopped and mill chimneys were built, the working class have bred and kept greyhounds and whippets. Whippets are half-castes, a cross between a pure greyhound and a terrier. They don't have whippets at proper dog-tracks. But miners and others have used them for don-
15 key's years to race and go rabbiting with, and no matter what the law of the land has said, people have held race-meetings with whippets and greyhounds, and someone has kept a book in which people can bet. That's the point of it: at the dogs there is no pomp and camp, no royal patronage—you cannot pretend you're there only to watch the pure joy of an animal racing, its muscles moving. If there
20 wasn't betting there wouldn't be dog-tracks.

Twice as many people in Britain watch dogs race as watch horses: it's a proletarian sport. If you thought it had all died out with Music Hall it hasn't. There are more dog-tracks in England than casinos, and that's just counting official ones.
25 In the summer I went to a New Town just outside Liverpool. The proud local council had laid on an annual show: a gymkhana, an exhibition of prize-winning jam and beetroot, and a fair. Half-way through the day, on one edge of the big school field, a man in a flat cap appeared. Cool, swift and silent, he stretched out some wire a few hundred yards long, to which he attached a flapping handkerchief
30 rag and an apparatus, and rigged it all to a car battery. Then from nowhere, with nothing spoken, ten or twenty folk appear, with muzzles in hands, wire cages to put over a dog's head, and little jackets with numbers on. And then there's a hundred more watching. And men open books. Pound notes and fivers change hands almost in silence, as if performing an ancient religious rite, with no laugh-
35 ter, no advertisement. Some dogs line up and the owners hold them back, but how they yap. The flat-cap man puts a wire to the car battery, and the rag speeds nervously flapping, up the field, the dogs yapping and straining. Their owners let them go. Bawling and shouting from the crowd, from everybody, and one dog wins. In seconds it's over. Money changes hands. And then they do it again, and
40 again: different dogs, same dogs, I couldn't tell. Was a vet present? I doubt it. It lasted for a couple of hours, and then the crowd evaporated, just as if nothing

had happened. It was unbelievable. I watched as the flat-cap man put the battery
into a car boot, and the rag that had done for a hare in his pocket. He wrapped the
wire up, put it into a box, and off he went. I followed him through the Morris
45 dancing as far as the flower-arrangement tent where I lost him among the potted
cacti.

The Chinese bet on two flies crawling up a wall, or don't they do that now?
Some Englishmen still bet on which dog will kill a live hare over a course. But
that's uncertain for the promoter and for the punter. What put the big time into
50 hounds was electricity: a substitute for a hare on electric wire. They did it first at
the back of the Welsh Harp pub in North London in 1876, and it didn't catch on.
Then a man called O. P. Smith got it organized in the United States, and a Cana-
dian, Brigadier Critchley, brought it back to England in 1926, the year of the
General Strike, when he opened a greyhound-racing track at Belle Vue, Manches-
55 ter. Seventeen hundred people went to his first meeting, and a few weeks later the
crowd was more than ten thousand. Between 1927 and 1932 scores of tracks
opened everywhere. It boomed like Ten Pin Bowling has—no, more like Bingo
in our time. Overnight the dogs rivalled soccer, and in some towns there'd be a
bigger crowd at the dog-track than the soccer field. Local newspapers ran weekly
60 Dog Supplements, and a whole legend grew, made up of apocryphal stories of
mythical dogs: 'Feed it on gin to get its spirits up and then it'll win,' 'Feed it on
meat pies to bring its handicap down,' and 'Did you hear the one about the dog
that ran so fast it caught the hare and got electrocuted?' All that legend is un-
recorded. I can't find a short-story writer from the dog-track.

65 The success was because in those days, and up to 1961, there were no betting-
shops. The law of the land said you could only bet at a racecourse. Horse race-
meetings happened only now and then, and generally only in the daytime and in
the country. The bookie's runner was illegal and unreliable, so the dogs provided
a bet for the working classes. In your town, every town, a course for racing dogs
70 at night, in your own free time, two or three times a week, and not Mrs Grundy
or the police could stop you from having your bet. In the beginning the promoters tried to get people like colonels onto the board, aping horse-racing, but
they failed: it was never to be a sport of kings.

They then realized that if you'd got enough ordinary people it didn't matter
75 that you hadn't the patronage of those who supposedly matter. Admission charges
were always kept low, as in the Bingo boom of a quarter of a century later. The
small punter was encouraged. In its heyday, in the thirties, there were 220 tracks
in Britain: today there are only 118. Since the coming of the betting-shop there's
been a rationalization. But still eight million people went to watch the dogs last
80 year: twice the number who go to watch horses race. They went to small flapper
tracks—that's where the rag flaps—in Scottish mining villages, the North-East,
the West Riding, South Wales and the Asian town of Southall. But the big tracks
are in the big cities, and they thrive.

On the swamp behind the gasworks, I went to a matinee meeting at Hackney
85 Wick: clean and professional, almost dull it was. They don't proselytise at the
dogs, and at a big track the owner of a dog doesn't keep it at home, and the dog
isn't even English. Sixty per cent of them are born in Ireland, trained there for the

first 15 months of life and then bought by the stadium who re-sell to an owner, your dentist or publican, a business man, a musician or an independent lady. I
90   wonder if they could do that with football-players? Anyway, the owner of the dog pays the track, the stadium, about £3 a week to feed and groom it. And when it wins, the owner picks up the prize: £10, £15—it's not a lot, surprisingly. The dog never leaves the stadium until, after two and a half years, its racing life is over. No dog can race more than once at any meeting, and no more than three
95   times in a fortnight. There's a vet to see the dog's fit and undoped, and they're stricter about that than they are with horses today. A little tannoy fanfare sounds, and out come six competitors, never more than six to a race, led by kennel lads. At some places they have girls, but at Hackney it's lads. It's a full-time job and nobody who works on the kennel staff can bet. The six are paraded before the
100 spectators: they put their little paws up and take a last pee and the spectators make knowledgeable remarks. The dogs are then led to the traps and their tails wag. They look surprisingly happy: Makokis, Sleeping Judy, Credition Flash, Be Virile. The background music stops. 'Your last chance to place a bet. Your last chance to place a bet.' The bookmakers go mad. There's waving elbows and
105 fingers—it's a tic-tac. The bells are rung and the bookie's bags are shut, shutters on tote windows, and all eyes then turn to the track. A hush fills the stadium. Then the electric whir like a train rushing into a tunnel, and a bright-coloured electric toy hare on a rail rushes past the stand at amazing speed and the dogs are off. Eveyone shouting: 'Come on number six!'
110   It would be very boring to watch dogs go round an oval track, except that it happens so fast. It's over in seconds. More bells are rung. In fact, all that after-noon bells rang and people came and went like it was school or a Scottish bar. The race pattern is repeated eight times at a Hackney matinee, and it's all on the flat—no hurdles. Fifteen minutes between each race, and the bars are open all
115 afternoon. The crowd was quite small because the point of a Hackney matinee is to provide a betting service for the afternoon punter in 75 per cent of Britain's betting-shops. On a cold and frosty afternoon when horse-racing's abandoned, the dogs can save the bookie's bacon—and my God, how fat the bookies have got! Since 1961, 15,000 betting-shops have opened and a hundred dog-tracks closed.
120 Since 1961, attendance at dog meetings has gone down by 4.5 per cent a year, and last year by 10 per cent. But last year was exceptional. It was ironic, because the miners were on strike, so the power was cut: no floodlights, and no electric hare.
       Since the betting-shop has been legalized, attendance at horse race-meetings
125 has also declined. But the horse-race people get compensation through a levy on bets placed in all betting-shops. But the dogs get nothing. They've got no George Wigg. The dogs' heyday was when they were the only place a working man could regularly legally bet. Now they're still the number two sport and more money goes on dogs than football pools. On the actual courses, £100 million is
130 bet a year. But the stadiums are having to advertise themselves and chic them-selves up—cricket is having to, too.
       On the Friday after Christmas, I looked in the London midday paper, still half as much of it devoted to dogs as horses, and I went to Wimbledon. They

advertise themselves as the South London Excitement Centre and they've doubled
135 up so that when the dogs aren't there they've got ... hot-rod cars and speedway.

It was an evening meeting, and where you'd expect it: on the watery side of
town, beside the River Wandle and behind the sewage farm. But inside, Wimbledon is as smart as the Palais, with coloured lights and beer: a fountain plays by a
Christmas tree in the centre of the track, Tom Jones sings muzak, closed-circuit
140 television has replaced the blower, and nearly all the accommodation was under
cover. Working-class, yes, but the working class have money, and the immigrants,
Chinese, Negroes, Sikhs and Jews, are as smart at the cheap end of eight bobs as
at the posh end at 70p. Well-shod folk: I looked at the shirt cuffs and the stocking
heels—not many of them had holes. It's a different world. It was like a commer-
145 cial to prove there's nothing wrong with a little flutter if you can afford it, and
obviously people at Wimbledon could. Air-conditioning took cigar smoke to
heaven. A winner bought a bottle of champagne and a glass for the barmaid—'for
you, my lovely'. The young, and there were lots of them, weren't at all like soccer
spectators. They were quiet and well-behaved, more like Billy Graham con-
150 verts.

It was almost as if the dogs were an incidental break in a night out. A moment
of silence and concentration when the lights are dimmed, then the roar of the
crowd as the flash of the colour is seen behind the plate-glass. Then the lights go
up and it's back to social intercourse. There was a dog disqualified for fighting,
155 Gypsey Myross. Well, I never saw it. There was as much commotion over the
winner of the ladies' lucky number on the programme. Everybody jolly: friends
and regulars, 4,500 of them, enthusing, hobby-type people, carefree—a lot of
laughter and free spending on their thing. Few loners—and the absence of the
poor puzzled me. Where had they gone: the nail-biting, shirt-losing, lonely,
160 marriage-broken men, the dirty-haired and baggy-eyed, cheating the devil. They
weren't at Wimbledon and they weren't at the Hackney matinee meeting. Nor at
that sturdy do in the Liverpool New Town. Have they died? No, I don't think so.
We've hidden them. We've taken them off the tracks by putting a betting-shop
on every council house estate. That's where they are.
165 As horse-racing has become like the theatre, and gets a subsidy, the dogs have
become like cinema—and when was the last greasy mackintosh you saw in yours?
Poverty is out of fashion: pushed into the corner bookie's is the dirt and the debt
and despair. And the dog-tracks? They stand to become cliquey, a bit beery, most
enthusiastic, a little in-grown, but a rather respectable pleasure.

Extract from radio broadcast and from *The Listener*, vol. 89. (1973)   *(slightly abridged)*

William Whyte

75 The Decline of the Protestant Ethic

Let us go back a moment to the turn of the century. If we pick up the Protestant Ethic as it was then expressed we will find it apparently in full flower. We will also find, however, an ethic that already had been strained by reality The country had changed. The ethic had not.

5   Here, in the words of banker Henry Clews as he gave some fatherly advice to Yale students in 1908, is the Protestant Ethic in purest form:

> *Survival of Fittest:* You may start in business, or the professions, with your feet on the bottom rung of the ladder; it rests with you to acquire the strength to climb to the top. You can do so if you have the will and the force to back you.
> 10   There is always plenty of room at the top. ... Success comes to the man who tries to compel success to yield to him. Cassius spoke well to Brutus when he said, "The Fault is not in our stars, dear Brutus, that we are underlings, but in our natures."
>   *Thrift:* Form the habit as soon as you become a money-earner, or money-
> 15   maker, of saving a part of your salary, or profits. Put away one dollar out of every ten you earn. The time will come in your lives when, if you have a little money, you can control circumstances; otherwise circumstances will control you. ...

Note the use of such active words as *climb, force, compel, control.* As stringently
20   as ever before, the Protestant Ethic still counseled struggle against one's environment—the kind of practical, here and now struggle that paid off in material rewards. And spiritually too. The hard-boiled part of the Protestant Ethic was incomplete, of course, without the companion assurance that such success was moral as well as practical. To continue with Mr. Clews:

25   Under this free system of government, whereby individuals are free to get a living or to pursue wealth as each chooses, the usual result is competition. Obviously, then, competition really means industrial freedom. Thus, anyone may choose his own trade or profession, or, if he does not like it, he may change. He is free to work hard or not; he may make his own bargains and set his price
30   upon his labor or his products. He is free to acquire property to any extent, or to part with it. By dint of greater effort or superior skill, or by intelligence, if he can make better wages, he is free to live better, just as his neighbor is free to follow his example and to learn to excel him in turn. If anyone has a genius for making and managing money, he is free to exercise his genius, just as another
35   is free to handle his tools. ... If an individual enjoys his money, gained by energy and successful effort, his neighbors are urged to work the harder, that they and their children may have the same enjoyment.

It was an exuberantly optimistic ethic. If everyone could believe that seeking his self-interest automatically improves the lot of all, then the application of hard

40 work should eventually produce a heaven on earth. Some, like the garrulous Mr. Clews, felt it already had.

Without this ethic capitalism would have been impossible, and without this ideology, society would have been hostile to the entrepreneur. Without the comfort of the Protestant Ethic, he couldn't have gotten away with his acquisi-
45 tions—not merely because other people wouldn't have allowed him, but because his own conscience would not have. But now he was fortified by the assurance that he was pursuing his obligation to God, and before long, what for centuries had been looked on as the meanest greed, a rising middle class would interpret as the earthly manifestation of God's will.

50 But the very industrial revolution which this highly serviceable ethic begot in time began to confound it. The inconsistencies were a long while in making themselves apparent. The nineteenth-century inheritors of the ethic were creating an increasingly collective society but steadfastly they denied the implications of it. In current retrospect the turn of the century seems a golden age of individualism,
55 yet by the 1880s the corporation had already shown the eventual bureaucratic direction it was going to take. As institutions grew in size and became more stratified, they made all too apparent inconsistencies which formerly could be ignored. One of the key assumptions of the Protestant Ethic had been that success was due neither to luck nor to the environment but only to one's natural
60 qualities—if men grew rich it was because they deserved to. But the big organization became a standing taunt to this dream of individual success. Quite obviously to anyone who worked in a big organization, those who survived best were not necessarily the fittest but, in more cases than not, those who by birth and personal connections had the breaks.

65 Reform was everywhere in the air. By the time of the First World War the Protestant Ethic had taken a shellacking from which it would not recover; rugged individualism and hard work had done wonders for the people to whom God in his infinite wisdom, as one put it, had given control of society. But it hadn't done so well for everyone else and now they, as well as the intellectuals, were all too
70 aware of the fact.

The ground, in short, was ready, and though the conservative opinion that drew the fire of the rebels seemed entrenched, the basic temper of the country was so inclined in the other direction that emphasis on the social became the dominant current of U.S. thought. In a great outburst of curiosity, people became
75 fascinated with the discovering of all the environmental pressures on the individual that previous philosophies had denied. As with Freud's discoveries, the findings of such inquiries were deeply disillusioning at first, but with characteristic exuberance Americans found a rainbow. Man might not be perfectible after all, but there was another dream and now at last it seemed practical: the perfecti-
80 bility of *society*.

Adapted extract from *The Organization Man* by William H. Whyte Jr. (1956)

Alvin Toffler

76 The New Nomads

Every Friday afternoon at 4.30, a tall, greying Wall Street executive named Bruce Robe stuffs a mass of papers into his black leather briefcase, takes his coat off the rack outside his office, and departs. The routine has been the same for more than three years. First, he rides the elevator twenty-nine floors down to
5 street level. Next he strides for ten minutes through crowded streets to the Wall Street Heliport. There he boards a helicopter which deposits him, eight minutes later, at John F. Kennedy Airport. Transferring to a Trans-World Airlines jet, he settles down for supper, as the giant craft swings out over the Atlantic, then banks and heads west. One hour and ten minutes later, barring delay, he steps
10 briskly out of the terminal building at the airport in Columbus, Ohio, and enters a waiting automobile. In thirty more minutes he reaches his destination: he is home.

Four nights a week Robe lives at a hotel in Manhattan. The other three he spends with his wife and children in Columbus, 500 miles away. Claiming the
15 best of two worlds, a job in the frenetic financial centre of America and a family life in the comparatively tranquil Midwest countryside, he shuttles back and forth some 50,000 miles a year. . . .

Never in history has distance meant less. Never have man's relationships with place been more numerous, fragile and temporary. Throughout the advanced
20 technological societies, and particularly among those I have characterized as 'the people of the future', commuting, travelling, and regularly relocating one's family have become second nature. Figuratively, we 'use up' places and dispose of them in much the same way that we dispose of Kleenex or beer cans. We are witnessing a historic decline in the significance of place to human life. We are breeding a new
25 race of nomads, and few suspect quite how massive, widespread and significant their migrations are. . . .

This busy movement of men back and forth over the landscape (and sometimes under it) is one of the identifying characteristics of super-industrial society. By contrast, pre-industrial nations seem congealed, frozen, their populations pro-
30 foundly attached to a single place. Transportation expert Wilfred Owen talks about the 'gap between the immobile and the mobile nations'. . . .

[More frequent than the case of Bruce Robe is the relocating of the whole family.] The *Wall Street Journal* refers to 'corporate gypsies' in an article headlined 'How Executive Family Adapts to Incessant Moving About Country'. It describes
35 the life of M. E. Jacobson, an executive with the Montgomery Ward retail chain. He and his wife, both forty-six at the time the story appeared, had moved twenty-eight times in twenty-six years of married life. 'I almost feel like we're just camping,' his wife tells her visitors. While their case is atypical, thousands like them move on the average of once every two years, and their numbers multiply. This
40 is true not merely because corporate needs are constantly shifting, but also

because top management regards frequent relocation of its potential successors as a necessary step in their training.

This moving of executives from house to house as if they were life-size chess-men on a continent-sized board has led one psychologist to propose facetiously a
45 money-saving system called 'The Modular Family'. Under this scheme, the executive not only leaves his house behind, but his family as well. The company then finds him a matching family (personality characteristics carefully selected to duplicate those of the wife and children left behind) at the new site. Some other itinerant executive then 'plugs into' the family left behind. No one appears to have
50 taken the idea seriously—yet.

'The man who leaves home is not the exception in American society but the key to it. Almost by definition, the organization man is a man who left home and, as it was said of the man who went from the Midwest to Harvard, kept on going. There have always been people who left home, and the number of them is not
55 decreasing but increasing—and so greatly that those who stay put in the home town are often as affected by the emigration as those who leave.'*

In seventy major United States cities, for example, including New York, average residence in one place is less than four years. . . .

In short, throughout the nations in transition to super-industrialism, among the
60 people of the future, movement is a way of life, a liberation from the constrictions of the past, a step into the still more affluent future.

Dramatically different attitudes, however, are evinced by the 'immobiles'. It is not only the agricultural villager in India or Iran who remains fixed in one place for most or all of his life. The same is true of millions of blue-collar workers,
65 particularly those in backward industries. As technological change roars through the advanced economies, outmoding whole industries and creating new ones almost overnight, millions of unskilled and semi-skilled workers find themselves compelled to relocate. . . .

For coalminers in Appalachia or textile workers in the French provinces, how-
70 ever, this proves to be excruciatingly painful. Even for big-city workers uprooted by urban renewal and relocated quite near to their former homes, the disruption is often agonizing. . . .

Extracts from Toffler, *Future Shock*.

* This paragraph is from *The Organization Man* by William H. Whyte (1956)

Alvin Toffler

77 How to Lose Friends...

Rising rates of occupational turn-over and the spread of rentalism into employment relationships will further increase the tempo at which human relationships
are formed and forgotten. This speed-up, however, affects different groups in
society in different ways. Thus, in general, working-class individuals tend to live
5 closer to, and depend more on their relatives than do middle- and upper-class
groups. In the words of psychiatrist Leonard Duhl, 'Their ties of kinship mean
more to them, and with less money available distance is more of a handicap.'
Working-class people are generally less adept at the business of coping with
temporary relationships. They take longer to establish ties and are more reluctant
10 to let them go. Not surprisingly, this is reflected in a greater reluctance to move
or change jobs. They go when they have to, but seldom from choice.

In contrast, psychiatrist Duhl points out, 'The professional, academic and
upper-managerial class [in the United States] is bound by interest ties across wide
physical spaces and indeed can be said to have more functional relationships. Mo-
15 bile individuals, easily duplicable relationships, and ties to interest problems
depict this group.'

What is involved in increasing the through-put of people in one's life are the
abilities not only to make ties but to break them, not only to affiliate but to dis-
affiliate. Those who seem most capable of this adaptive skill are also among the
20 most richly rewarded in society. ...

They support the findings of sociologist Lloyd Warner who suggests that 'The
most important component of the personalities of successful corporate managers
and owners is that, their deep emotional identifications with their families of
birth being dissolved, they no longer are closely intermeshed with the past, and,
25 therefore, are capable of relating themselves easily to the present and future. They
are people who have literally and spiritually left home ... They can relate and
disrelate themselves to others easily'. ...

The friends of earlier years must be left, for acquaintances of the lower-status
past are incompatible with the successful present. Often the church of his birth is
30 left, along with the clubs and cliques of his family and of his youth. But most
important of all, and this is the great problem of the man on the move, he must,
to some degree, leave his father, mother, brothers, and sisters, along with the
other human relationships of his past.'

This so, it is not so startling to read in a business magazine a coolly detached
35 guide for the newly promoted executive and his wife. It advises that he break
with old friends and subordinates gradually, in order to minimize resentment.
He is told to 'find logical excuses for not joining the group at coffee breaks or
lunch.' Similary, 'Miss the department bowling or card sessions, occasionally at
first, then more frequently.' Invitations to the home of a subordinate may be
40 accepted, but not reciprocated, except in the form of an invitation to a whole
group of subordinates at once. After a while all such interaction should cease.

Wives are a special problem, we are informed, because they 'don't understand the protocol of office organization'. The successful man is advised to be patient with his wife, who may adhere to old relationships longer than he does. But, as
45 one executive puts it, 'a wife can be downright dangerous if she insists on keeping close friendships with the wives of her husband's subordinates. Her friendships will rub off on him, colour his judgement about the people under him, jeopardize his job.' Moreover, one personnel man points out, 'When parents drift away from former friends, kids go too'. ...
50 Today training for disaffiliation or dis-relating begins early. Indeed, this may well represent one of the major differences between the generations. For schoolchildren today are exposed to extremely high rates of turn-over in their classrooms. According to the Educational Facilities Laboratories, Incorporated, 'It is not unusual for city schools to have a turn-over of more than half their
55 student body in one school year.' This phenomenal rate cannot but have some effect on the children.

William Whyte in *The Organization Man* pointed out that the impact of such mobility 'is as severe on the teachers as on the children themselves, for the teachers are thereby robbed of a good bit of the feeling of achievement they get
60 from watching the children develop.' Today, however, the problem is compounded by the high rate of turn-over among teachers too. This is true not only in the United States but elsewhere as well. Thus a report on England asserts: 'Today it is not uncommon, even in grammar schools, for a child to be taught one subject by two or three different teachers in the course of one year. With teacher loyalty
65 to the school so low, the loyalty of children cannot be summoned either. If a high proportion of teachers are preparing to move on to a better job, a better district, there will be less care, concern and commitment on their part'. ...

There is a definite tendency for the more nomadic children to avoid participation in the voluntary side of school life—clubs, sports, student government and
70 other extra-curricular activities. It is as though they wish, where possible, to avoid new human ties that might only have to be broken again before long. ...

If to this picture of declining durations we add the factor of diversity--the recognition that each new human relationship requires a different pattern of behaviour from us—one thing becomes starkly clear: to be able to make these
75 increasingly numerous and rapid on-off clicks in our interpersonal lives we must be able to operate at a level of adaptability never before asked of human beings.

ibid.

Alvin Toffler

78 The Future-Shocked Society

Today, according to the chief White House adviser on urban affairs the United States 'exhibits the qualities of an individual going through a nervous breakdown'. For the cumulative impact of sensory cognitive or decisional overstimulation, not to mention the physical effects of neural or endocrine overload, creates sickness
5 in our midst.

This sickness is increasingly mirrored in our culture, our philosophy, our attitude towards reality. It is no accident that so many ordinary people refer to the world as a 'madhouse' or that the theme of insanity has recently become a staple in literature, art, drama and film. ...
10 Despite its extraordinary achievements in art, science, intellectual, moral and political life, the United States is a nation in which tens of thousands of young people flee reality by opting for drug-induced lassitude; a nation in which millions of their parents retreat into video-induced stupor or alcoholic haze; a nation in which legions of elderly folk vegetate and die in loneliness; in which
15 the flight from family and occupational responsibility has become an exodus; in which masses tame their raging anxieties with Miltown, or Librium, or Equanil, or a score of other tranquillizers and psychic pacifiers. Such a nation, whether it knows it or not, is suffering from future shock. ...

Millions sense the pathology that pervades the air, but fail to understand its
20 roots. These roots lie not in this or that political doctrine, still less in some mystical core of despair or isolation presumed to inhere in the 'human condition'. Nor do they lie in science, technology, or legitimate demands for social change. They are traceable, instead, to the uncontrolled, non-selective nature of our lunge into the future. They lie in our failure to direct, consciously and imaginatively,
25 the advance towards super-industrialism. ...

Social rationality presupposes individual rationality, and this, in turn, depends not only on certain biological equipment, but on continuity, order and regularity in the environment. It is premised on some correlation between the pace and complexity of change and man's decisional capacities. By blindly stepping up
30 the rate of change, the level of novelty, and the extent of choice, we are thoughtlessly tampering with these environmental preconditions of rationality. We are condemning countless millions to future shock.

ibid.

Alvin Toffler

79 Beyond Bureaucracy

'Bureaucracy,' Warren Bennis says, 'thrives in a highly competitive undifferentiated and stable environment...' But it is now clear that the acceleration of change has reached so rapid a pace that even bureaucracy can no longer keep up. ...

5 What, then, will be the characteristics of the organizations of super-industrial society? 'The key word,' says Bennis, 'will be "temporary"... Problems will be solved by task forces composed of relative strangers who represent a set of diverse professional skills.'

Permanence—the recognition that the link between man and organization
10 would endure through time—brought with it a commitment to the organization. The longer a man stayed within its embrace, the more he saw his past as an investment in the organization, the more he saw his personal future as dependent upon that of the organization. Longevity bred loyalty. In work organizations, this natural tendency was powerfully reinforced by the knowledge that termina-
15 tion of one's links with the organization very often meant a loss of the means of economic survival. In a world wracked by scarcity for the many, a job was precious. The bureaucrat was thus immobile and deeply oriented towards economic security. To keep his job, he willingly subordinated his own interests and convictions to those of the organization. ...

20 Finally, the organization man needed to understand his place in the scheme of things; he occupied a well-defined niche, performed actions that were also well defined by the rules of the organization. Faced by relatively routine problems, he was encouraged to seek routine answers. ...

The old loyalty felt by the organization man appears to be going up in smoke.
25 In its place we are watching the rise of professional loyalty. Thus John Gardner declares: 'The loyalty of the professional man is to his profession and not to the organization that may house him at any given moment. Compare the chemist or electronics engineer in a local plant with the non-professional executives in the same plant. The men the chemist thinks of as his colleagues are not those who
30 occupy neighbouring offices, but his fellow professionals wherever they may be throughout the country, even throughout the world.'

ibid.

THE OBSERVER

80 Spaceship Earth's Greatest Danger

EUROPEAN Conservation Year is over. It must be counted a remarkable success. It burned an awareness of what we are doing to the environment so deeply into
5 men's minds that interest is not now likely to fade. It saw Britain, Germany and France overhaul their administrative machinery for the environment, and several other European countries start
10 to do so. It saw more action, large and small, than is generally realised, from a mass of anti-pollution legislation, co-operative agreements and new industrial pollution policies to an estimated 200,000
15 organised 'environmental events' which alone justify ECY's claim to have been the world's largest cooperative exercise in peacetime.

All this is an encouraging start. Yet
20 there is still a long way to go. Air, water and soil are still being poisoned. Government policies on the environment are largely piecemeal and *ad hoc*: a decision on a brewery here, a new reservoir there.
25 There is nothing in Europe to compare with the World Bank's recent commitment that all development projects must be 'ecologically validated,' or with the power of President Nixon's new Council for Environmental Quality to demand an 30 assessment of the environmental impact of any new technical development.

More serious, no society has yet fully grasped the essential message of conservation: that the earth cannot much 35 longer support an expanding species that tries to get rich by living recklessly off capital resources while excreting its wastes into any convenient hole. Our soaring growth curves and a healthy 40 global environment are totally incompatible; our survival depends on paring our demands and *expectations* to the finite capacities of spaceship earth. To translate this message into political 45 terms without penalising the poor everywhere will be a formidably difficult task – perhaps the greatest challenge of the next decades. There is no choice but to try to meet it. 50

Extract from article in *The Observer* (3rd January 1971)   (*unabridged*)

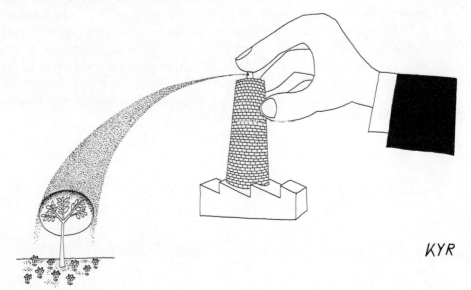

KYR

W. T. Singleton

81 Environmental Systems

Surroundings are important to the person at many different levels. The basic level is that he wishes to survive without damage, and thus excessive heat or cold, noise, vibration and acceleration must be avoided. These problems are not quite as easy to deal with scientifically as they might appear at first sight. The
5 difficulty is that the dimensions found to be simple in physical science terms are not so simple in biological or behavioural terms and vice versa. For example, the electromagnetic spectrum makes for a nice integrating concept of all radiation but it does not provide a method of predicting or measuring effects on people: different parts of the spectrum provide quite different sensations. Conversely the uni-
10 tary human concept of feeling cold for example is affected by a number of physical science variables such as temperature, humidity and windspeed. Thus for each potential environmental stressor a complex index must be devised which incorporates a variety of physical variables. It is then necessary to evaluate several risk levels such as immediate danger, longer term danger, performance decrement and
15 discomfort. All this is complicated enough and the situation could hardly be described as fully sorted out for any of the above variables; certainly we know almost nothing about the combined effects of stressors (Poulton, 1970).

Things get even more complex if we begin to look for mild stress effects. What happens to the learning efficiency of schoolchildren if the class room is slightly
20 too hot or too cold? What happens to travellers subjected to moderate noise and vibration levels? What are the effects on pedestrians of exhaust fumes in city streets? There is some research in this area (Davis, 1970) and progress is fairly rapid, but it is not adequate to supply comprehensive evidence to facilitate decisions where there are obvious cost penalties of proposed improvements.

25 Beyond the mild stress problem we come to the concept of amenity. In this area it is not yet clear whether or not the dialogue should be conducted in cost terms. It can be argued that, to make a reasonable and rapid impact on the planners and other policy makers, it is necessary to translate the problem into financial terms so that comparison with other relevant factors is direct (Waller 1970). It
30 can also be argued that, to take a games analogy, it is always easier to win when playing at home rather than playing away, and that the research worker concerned with higher level human functions and aspirations should refuse to conduct the argument at a mere financial level. On the one hand it does not seem entirely appropriate to assess the value of a cathedral in terms of what people are prepared
35 to pay to preserve it, or to measure the effect of noise from an airport in terms of the reduced market value of houses under the flight path. On the other hand it is hardly legitimate for the environmentalist to campaign that something must be done without specifying who must do it and who must pay for it. The danger in this area of study is that the investigators become men with a mission so that,
40 either deliberately or unconsciously, they generate, select and publicize evidence that supports their own prejudices. Even worse is to utilize the status of science

and technology to support a claim for which the protagonist's opinion is no more and no less important than that of a layman.

45 The remedy is to stick to the evidence and to methods of generating evidence which control individual bias. It must be accepted that this leaves important areas of human decision making, at least temporarily, without the support of systematic inquiry. If there is no way of generating valid evidence then there is nothing to be said by the technologist, however important the problem is in human terms. Many problems of educational methods, of violence in society, of penology and

50 of drugs come in this category. Inevitably the higher the level of the problem the less secure is the evidence and the less systematic are the design procedures. Consider for example an aircraft passenger compartment. There are physical environment problems of air supply, noise and so on. These can be measured, effects predicted and appropriate action taken by the designer. There are func-

55 tional environment problems of mobility, provision of facilities, supply of food and drink and so on. These also can be dealt with in a satisfactory fashion making a reasonable trade-off between the system as a flying machine and the system as a passenger carrier. There are then problems of comfort, pleasure, security, personal space and other high level amenity variables. Here the system designer can

60 only consult with industrial designers and interior decorators who work as artists rather than scientists. Consider the problem of office design; how is a decision to be made about whether to incorporate open offices or closed offices? How can evidence be accumulated relevant to this decision? It is not very much use asking the people who will work there. It has been demonstrated that the opinions of

65 those who have worked in open plan offices are very different from those who have no experience but are asked if they would like to. There are isolated bits of reliable evidence, for example Canter (1968) showed in one experiment that test performance was poorer in larger offices, but how valid is this in relation to the overall objectives of persons working in such offices and of those employing

70 them?

The present state of knowledge in this field is such that research on techniques and principles is needed even more than evidence on particular cases. This is not to deny that the techniques and principles might best be generated by studies of particular cases. Given that the answer to a question is unknown or even currently

75 unknowable the proper strategy is to leave adequate flexibility in the system for modification based on experience. For example, rather than attempt to predict pedestrian flows between a group of buildings, the whole area can be covered in grass, and paved ways can be added later following the paths worn through the grass. This kind of contingency reserve in design is usually obtained by allocating

80 functions to human operators and adding further procedures and hardware later as it proves desirable.

Extract from *Man-Machine Systems* by W.T. Singleton (Penguin Modern Psychology). (1974)   (*unabridged*)

Paul and Anne Ehrlich

82 The Falk Projections

In his superb book *The Endangered Planet*, international lawyer Richard A. Falk of Princeton University gives two fundamental scenarios of the course of politics in a world threatened by ecological catastrophe. ...

The decade of the 1980s will feature *The Politics of Desperation.* Governments
5 will realize their helplessness in the face of human problems, but the elites who run them will turn more and more to repression to maintain their privileges. The suffering people of the world will become increasingly hostile toward the fortunate few living in islands of affluence. UDCs may start to develop nuclear or biological warfare capability in an attempt to force resource redistribution on the
10 DCs. Realignments of power among DCs and token concessions to the UDCs will not halt their drive, and DCs may "recolonize" some in order to enforce "peace" and maintain the world trade system which favors them. The U.S. finds itself powerless to intercede.

The Politics of Catastrophe will take over in the 1990s. In that decade an immense
15 disaster, ecological or thermonuclear, will overtake mankind. The reorganization (if any) of the post-catastrophe world will depend on the exact form of the disaster and who survives. The reorganization would most likely be world-oriented rather than nation-state oriented. If, by chance, the outmoded world-order system is not irremediably damaged in the 1990s, then it certainly will be in the
20 21st century, which Falk labels the *Era of Annihilation.*

Falk's second scenario is more optimistic. It envisions a rapid recognition that the world-system based on sovereign states cannot possibly deal with the problems of the endangered planet. ...

The 1980s would be *The Decade of Mobilization*, in which awareness would be
25 converted into action taking mankind away from the primacy of the sovereign state. A new world political movement, based on transnational thinking, would overwhelm the conservative forces dedicated to maintenance of the status quo.

The 1990s would be *The Decade of Transformation*, in which mankind moves in the direction of stability in both population and economic systems. "A new poli-
30 tical man will emerge from such a climate of opinion and change. The planet will be governed as a system that needs to guard against relapse and reversions, and regards the diversities within itself as a source of vitality and vigor." That decade will lead to the 21st century as *The Era of World Harmony*—based on ecological humanism and men living in harmony with nature.

Summary in Ehrlich, *Population, Resources, Environment* from *This Endangered Planet.* (1971)

Alvin Toffler

83 Break with the Past

It has become a cliché to say that what we are now living through is a 'second industrial revolution'. . . . For what is occurring now is, in all likelihood, bigger, deeper, and more important than the industrial revolution. Indeed, a growing body of reputable opinion asserts that the present moment represents nothing less
5 than the second great divide in human history, comparable in magnitude only with that first break in historic continuity, the shift from barbarism to civilization. . . .

One of the most striking statements of this theme has come from Kenneth Boulding, an eminent economist and imaginative social thinker. In justifying his view that the present moment represents a crucial turning point in human history,
10 Boulding observes that 'as far as many statistical series related to activities of mankind are concerned, the date that divides human history into two equal parts is well within living memory.' In effect, our century represents The Great Median Strip running down the centre of human history. Thus he asserts, 'The world of today . . . is as different from the world in which I was born as that world was
15 from Julius Caesar's. I was born in the middle of human history, to date, roughly. Almost as much has happened since I was born as happened before.'

This startling statement can be illustrated in a number of ways. It has been observed, for example, that if the last 50,000 years of man's existence were divided into lifetimes of approximately sixty-two years each, there have been about 800
20 such lifetimes. Of these 800, fully 650 were spent in caves.

Only during the last seventy lifetimes has it been possible to communicate effectively from one lifetime to another—as writing made it possible to do. Only during the last six lifetimes did masses of men ever see a printed word. Only during the last four has it been possible to measure time with any precision. Only in
25 the last two has anyone anywhere used an electric motor. And the overwhelming majority of all the material goods we use in daily life today have been developed within the present, the 800th, lifetime.

This 800th lifetime marks a sharp break with all past human experience because during this lifetime man's relationship to resources has reversed itself. This is
30 most evident in the field of economic development. Within a single lifetime, agriculture, the original basis of civilization, has lost its dominance in nation after nation. Today in a dozen major countries agriculture employs fewer than 15 per cent of the economically active population. In the United States, whose farms feed 200,000,000 Americans plus the equivalent of another 160,000,000
35 people around the world, this figure is already below 6 per cent and it is still shrinking rapidly.

Moreover, if agriculture is the first stage of economic development and industrialism the second, we can now see that still another stage—the third—has suddenly been reached. In about 1956 the United States became the first major
40 power in which more than 50 per cent of the non-farm labour force ceased to wear the blue collar of factory or manual labour. Blue-collar workers were out-

numbered by those in the so-called white-collar occupations—in retail trade, administration, communications, research, education, and other service cate-gories. Within the same lifetime a society for the first time in human history not
45 only threw off the yoke of agriculture, but managed within a few brief decades to throw off the yoke of manual labour as well. The world's first service economy had been born. ...

Ten thousand years for agriculture. A century or two for industrialism. And now, opening before us—super-industrialism. ...

50 But the final, qualitative difference between this and all previous lifetimes is the one most easily overlooked. For we have not merely extended the scope and scale of change, we have radically altered its pace. We have in our time released a totally new social force—a stream of change so accelerated that it influences our sense of time, revolutionizes the tempo of daily life, and affects the very way we
55 'feel' the world around us. We no longer 'feel' life as men did in the past. And this is the ultimate difference, the distincton that separates the truly contemporary man from all others. For this acceleration lies behind the impermanence—the transience — that penetrates and tinctures our consciousness, radically affecting the way we relate to other people, to things, to the entire universe of ideas, art
60 and values.

To understand what is happening to us as we move into the age of super-industrialism, we must analyse the processes of acceleration and confront the concept of transience . If acceleration is a new social force, transience is its psychological counterpart, and without an understanding of the role it plays in
65 contemporary human behaviour, all our theories of personality, all our psycho-logy, must remain pre-modern. Psychology without the concept of transience cannot take account of precisely those phenomena that are peculiarly con-temporary.

By changing our relationship to the resources that surround us, by violently
70 expanding the scope of change, and, most crucially, by accelerating its pace, we have broken irretrievably with the past. We have cut ourselves off from the old ways of thinking, of feeling, of adapting. We have set the stage for a completely new society and we are now racing towards it. This is the crux of the 800th life-time. And it is this that calls into question man's capacity for adaptation—how
75 will he fare in this new society? Can he adapt to its imperatives? And if not, can he alter these imperatives?

Extract from Toffler, *Future Shock*.

Alvin Toffler

84 Organizations: The Coming Ad-Hocracy

One of the most persistent myths about the future envisions man as a helpless cog in some vast organizational machine. In this nightmarish projection, each man is frozen into a narrow, unchanging niche in a rabbit-warren bureaucracy. The walls of this niche squeeze the individuality out of him, smash his personality,
5 and compel him, in effect, to conform or die. Since organizations appear to be growing larger and more powerful all the time, the future, according to this view, threatens to turn us all into the most contemptible of creatures, spineless and faceless, the organization man.

It is difficult to over-estimate the force with which this pessimistic prophecy
10 grips the popular mind, especially among young people. ... What makes the entire subject so emotional is the fact that organization is an inescapable part of all our lives. ...

If the orthodox social critics are correct in predicting a regimented, super-bureaucratized future, we should already be mounting the barricades, punching
15 random holes in our IBM cards, taking every opportunity to wreck the machinery of organization. If, however, we set our conceptual clichés aside and turn instead to the facts, we discover that bureaucracy, the very system that is supposed to crush us all under its weight, is itself groaning with change.

The kinds of organizations these critics project unthinkingly into the future are
20 precisely those least likely to dominate tomorrow. For we are witnessing not the triumph, but the breakdown of bureaucracy. We are, in fact, witnessing the arrival of a new organizational system that will increasingly challenge, and ultimately supplant bureaucracy. This is the organization of the future. I call it 'Ad-hocracy'.

Man will encounter plenty of difficulty in adapting to this new-style organiza-
25 tion. But instead of being trapped in some unchanging, personality-smashing niche, man will find himself liberated, a stranger in a new free-form world of kinetic organizations. In this alien landscape, his position will be constantly changing, fluid, and varied. And his organizational ties, like his ties with things, places and people, will turn over at a frenetic and ever-accelerating rate. ...

30 So long as a society is relatively stable and unchanging, the problems it presents to men tend to be routine and predictable. Organizations in such an environment can be relatively permanent. But when change is accelerated, more and more novel first-time problems arise, and traditional forms of organization prove inadequate to the new conditions. ...

35 As acceleration continues, organizational redesign becomes a continuing function. ...

THE COLLAPSE OF HIERARCHY

Something else is happening, too: a revolutionary shift in power relationships. Not only are large organizations forced both to change their internal structure

and to create temporary units, but they are also finding it increasingly difficult to
40 maintain their traditional chains-of-command.

It would be pollyannish to suggest that workers in industry or government today truly 'participate' in the management of their enterprises—either in capitalist or, for that matter, in socialist and communist countries. Yet there is evidence that bureaucratic hierarchies, separating those who 'make decisions' from those
45 who merely carry them out, are being altered, side-stepped or broken.

This process is noticeable in industry where, according to Professor William H. Read of the Graduate School of Business at McGill University, 'irresistible pressures' are battering hierarchical arrangements. 'The central, crucial and important business of organizations, ' he declares, 'is increasingly shifting from up and
50 down to "sideways".' What is involved in such a shift is a virtual revolution in organizational structure—and human relations. For people communicating 'sideways'—ie, to others at approximately the same level of organization—behave differently, operate under very different pressures, than those who must communicate up and down a hierarchy. . . .

55 First, the acceleration of the pace of life (and especially the speed-up of production brought about by automation) means that every minute of 'down time' costs more in lost output than ever before. Delay is increasingly costly. Information must flow faster than ever before. At the same time, rapid change, by increasing the number of novel, unexpected problems, increases the amount of
60 information needed. It takes more information to cope with a novel problem than one we have solved a dozen or a hundred times before. It is this combined demand for *more* information at *faster* speeds that is now undermining the great vertical hierarchies so typical of bureaucracy. . . .

This silent but significant deterioration of hierarchy, now occurring in the
65 executive suite as well as at the ground level of the factory floor, is intensified by the arrival on the scene of hordes of experts—specialists in vital fields so narrow that often the men on top have difficulty understanding them. Increasingly, managers have to rely on the judgement of these experts. Solid state physicists, computer programmers, systems designers, operation researchers, engineering
70 specialists—such men are assuming a new decision-making function. At one time, they merely consulted with executives who reserved unto themselves the right to make managerial decisions. Today, the managers are losing their monopoly on decision-making.

More and more, says Professor Read of McGill, the "specialists do not fit
75 neatly together into a chain-of-command system' and 'cannot wait for their expert advice to be approved at a higher level'.

Extract from Toffler, *Future Shock.*

Vance Packard

85 Cornucopia

In Cornucopia City, as I understand it, all the buildings will be made of a special papier-mâché. These houses can be torn down and rebuilt every spring and fall at housecleaning time. The motor-cars of Cornucopia will be made of a light-weight plastic that develops fatigue and begins to melt if driven more than four
5   thousand miles. Owners who turn in their old motorcars at the regular turn-in dates—New Year's, Easter, Independence Day, and Labour Day—will be rewarded with a one-hundred-dollar United States Prosperity-Through-Growth Bond for each motor-car turned in. And a special additional bond will be awarded to those families able to turn in four or more motor-cars at each disposal date.
10   One fourth of the factories of Cornucopia City will be located on the edge of a cliff, and the ends of their assembly lines can be swung to the front or rear doors depending upon the public demand for the product being produced. When demand is slack, the end of the assembly line will be swung to the rear door and the output of refrigerators or other products will drop out of sight and go
15   directly to their graveyard without first overwhelming the consumer market.

Every Monday, the people of Cornucopia City will stage a gala launching of a rocket into outer space at the local Air Force base. This is another of their contri-butions to national prosperity. Components for the rockets will have been made by eighteen sub-contractors and prime contractors in the area. One officially
20   stated objective of the space probing will be to report to the earth people what the back side of Neptune's moon looks like.

Wednesday will be Navy Day. The Navy will send a surplus warship to the city dock. It will be filled with surplus playsuits, cake mix, vacuum cleaners, and trampolines that have been stock-piled at the local United States Department of
25   Commerce complex of warehouses for surplus products. The ship will go thirty miles out to sea, where the crew will sink it from a safe distance.

As we peek in on this Cornucopia City of the future, we learn that the big, heartening news of the week is that the Guild of Appliance Repair Artists has passed a resolution declaring it unpatriotic for any member even to look inside
30   an ailing appliance that is more than two years old.

The heart of Cornucopia City will be occupied by a titanic push-button super mart built to simulate a fairyland. This is where all the people spend many happy hours a week strolling and buying to their heart's content. In this paradise of high-velocity selling, there are no jangling cash registers to disrupt the holiday
35   mood. Instead, the shopping couples—with their five children trailing behind, each pushing his own shopping cart—gaily wave their lifetime electronic credit cards in front of a recording eye. Each child has his own card, which was issued to him at birth.

Conveniently located throughout the mart are receptacles where the people
40   can dispose of the old-fashioned products they bought on a previous shopping trip. In the jewellery section, for example, a playfully designed sign by a receptacle

reads: 'Throw your old watches here!' Cornucopia City's marvellous mart is open around the clock, Sundays included. For the Sunday shoppers who had developed a church-going habit in earlier years, there is a little chapel available for
45 meditation in one of the side alcoves.

Is Cornucopia City to become not a feverish dream, but, instead, an extreme prototype for the City of Tomorrow?

Edited extract from *The Waste Makers* by Vance Packard. (1960)   *(slightly abridged)*

Gerald Leach

86 The Biocrats

INTRODUCTION

The human race is moving towards the future through an endless branching maze of incredible complexity. Every day, at each point in the maze marked 'now', we see a thousand paths spreading out before us, each leading to a slightly different possible future—and another point where a thousand paths diverge.
5 And at each point we have to choose which few paths to take, and which to leave alone. By these choices—some of them trivial in the long run, but some of them very significant—we arrive in one new part of the maze, or another. We choose our own future, for better or for worse.

It is not an easy game, and it is made no easier by science and technology. At an
10 ever-increasing rate, science and technology are gaining far-reaching powers to
shape the world, and ourselves with it. They, and their implications, are also
becoming more difficult to understand. Just as they are complicating the maze by
creating more and more possible paths and creating them more frequently, so it
is becoming harder for most people to help to choose the right ones. As the maze
15 grows more intricate and the decision points rush at us faster, the walls of the
maze are becoming opaque; and we face a growing danger of being led up the
wrong paths by the ignorant or by the forceful but blinkered army of technocrats. . . .

It is no secret that biology and medicine are rapidly discovering the possibility
20 of very radical alterations to the human body, brain and life processes; and that
these new powers closely touch the deepest human and social values. From dealing
with sickness and disability, medicine is being pushed by modern biology into a
control of the human machinery so intimate and pervasive that it has profound
consequences for the basic aspects of life—sex, procreation, birth, the relationship
25 between parents and offspring, the nature of the individual, his role in society
and the nature of society itself. Perhaps more than any other science or technology, biology and medicine threaten to make the changes that will alter men and
societies most. We must therefore learn to steer our way through the biological
maze with all the courage and insight we can muster. If we do not, we may find
30 ourselves in a part of the maze we do not like at all *and* miss the paths that could
have taken us instead to a far better place.

So far we have not managed this well. Time and again society has woken up to
find itself living with a major biomedical trend that it has never agreed to but
which is now very hard to alter. The technocrats of biology and medicine—the
35 biocrats—had taken charge.

The population explosion is the best example: because vastly improved techniques of death-control were used in the developing world before equally effective
techniques of birth-control were available and acceptable, the population explosion was inevitable. But we lacked the social mechanisms for predicting this, for
40 debating it and for applying the necessary correctives in time. It has been much
the same with many other developments, from transplants to artificial organs,
from intensive care for disabled babies to intensive care for the old. And unless
we change our ways it looks as though it will be the same for the more recent,
less well-known trends. . . .

45 Why is this? A short answer is that all the key groups of people who should
be contributing to the debate and decision-making cannot do so effectively
because they are walled off by their own expertise and attitudes, and do not listen
to those outside their narrow confines.

There are the biologists, the generators of the biomedical revolution. They
50 contribute little here because, like other scientists, they have no set of principles
concerned with the social effects of their work. They have many important
ethical attitudes—the most important of which is that they tell each other the truth
about what they are doing—but their attitudes are all concerned with protecting
the profession of science. There is no provision innate in science to ensure that it

55 concerns itself with the needs of society. Indeed, most scientists insist that they must be free to make any discovery they can, whatever its social implications. As far as 'pure' science is concerned—science restricted to experimental results on paper—this does not matter in the narrow view and the short run. As Bertrand Russell once said, 'equations do not explode.' But it does matter overall and in the
60 long run, because it loosely affects what kinds of things scientists set out to discover and it directly affects what ideas scientists produce that *can* be applied. Though there are notable exceptions, it also produces scientists who cannot be bothered to tell the public of the implications of their work—after thinking hard about them (a necessary step that is not always taken).

65 As discoveries *are* applied, as they move from the laboratory into the hospital or surgery, we run into the notorious closed-shop, shut-mouth mystique of medicine. This tradition of silence was crucially important at a time when all the doctor could do to cure the sick was to sit at the bedside, radiate a sense of knowing calm and confidence and let nature take its course. For if it broke down, and
70 the patient was allowed to look in the doctor's black bag, he would find it empty— and faith would be shattered. Today, when the bag is overflowing with therapies that the patient and society may or may not want, it is a dangerous anachronism.

The same applies to the other more important medical attitudes, which we loosely group together under the heading of 'medical ethics'. Traditional medical
75 ethics are mainly concerned with putting the welfare of the individual patient first, to the exclusion—if necessary—of other interests, and with doing all one can to save life. These were and are important principles. But as the escalating power of medical technology produces greater consequences for individuals and society, they are rapidly becoming hopelessly inadequate on their own. Most
80 people, including many doctors, realize that these principles have to be broadened to take into account not only the patient's wishes seen against his home and family background (rather than merely his medical condition), but also the interests of society. While it was once a triumph to be able to save life by putting a patient in an iron lung for twenty years, it is not self-evidently so now. The
85 patient may rather be dead than alive like that; and society might want to spend the money in other ways.

This broadening of principles can create agonizing conflicts of conscience for the doctor and difficult decisions for the patient. But the only way of relieving these pressures is to try to form a social consensus by *talking* about them, so that
90 new principles that most people will accept naturally may emerge. If there are *no* iron lungs because it is agreed that there should not be, then dying because one is totally paralysed becomes easier to bear. In a similar way, taking the life of a foetus is now easier to bear—for doctors, parents and society—because we have begun a debate on abortion that is changing our principles in this field. Yet this is
95 an exception: with most areas of medical practice the medical profession still prevents *informed* public discussion by its determination to hold on to its right to make the decisions.

But assuming that informed public discussion might be possible we face another obstacle, which is that the principles which have traditionally formed the basis of
100 such discussion are crumbling. For this reason our former advisers—theologians,

philosophers, anthropologists, lawyers and do on—are no longer able to provide the foundations on which a discussion of the ethical problems of medicine should be based—even if they were well informed on medical advances.

So we are forced to reconsider beliefs which up to now have been thought of as 105 constants, and decide which we wish to preserve and which to reject. ...

For the moment, the important thing about these problems concerning belief is that, with one crucial proviso, they are not issues which biologists or doctors are either more or less qualified to discuss than any other comparably educated layman. The tension between them and biomedical progress *can* therefore be dis-
110 cussed—and must be discussed if we are to find the best futures in the maze—by everyone who reckons himself a member of the community, backed by whatever help the social thinkers can give him. We must not let the biocrats, whether biologists or doctors, make all the running.

The one proviso is that we all have to be properly informed about the technical
115 side too—the biology and medicine. The fact is that we are not. Most people are unable to enter most areas of the biomedical debate because they are technically ill-informed or misinformed. It is not that they do not know the details or the jargon: they rarely matter. It is that most people have not even the equipment to discriminate between the technical probabilities, improbabilities and impossibilities
120 of the foreseeable future. Neither, very often, can they distinguish between techniques that people will want to take up and those they will want to leave alone. How else can one explain all those earnest television discussions of brain transplants, or articles hinting at the imminent possibility of rearing babies entirely in test-tubes à la *Brave New World?* We might just as well spend our time seriously
125 discussing the ethical implications of an invasion by Martians.

The blame here must fall squarely on the mass media, the source of most people's knowledge for the biomedical debate. Medicine is always news, but how much more newsworthy when one can shout of a new miracle cure (and not cite all the disadvantages) or cry 'scandal' (and not bother to discover the real reasons
130 why the situation is as it is). When this over-dramatization is accompanied by instant predictions of what the biologists are cooking up for the future—visions ranging from the apocalyptic to the euphoric depending on the writer and his mood—no wonder our expectations are totally confused. ...

Extract from *The Biocrats* by Gerald Leach. (1970)

Gerald Leach

87 Life on the Machine

Modern medicine is gaining tremendous powers to postpone death. With a growing armoury of drugs, instruments, surgical skills and machines, doctors are learning how to swop certain doom for precious survival.

Much of the time they make a good job of it. Often they restore us to a full life.
5 But in a growing number of cases their skills are not quite miraculous enough, and they exchange our death only for a kind of half-life that may be full of pain, misery and tragedy for all concerned. When one also remembers that preserving half-lives can be extraordinarily expensive, this combination produces some of the fiercest medico-social dilemmas of our times. . . .

10 In our culture, adults have a commitment to the idea of survival which amounts to a determination to avert death at almost any cost. Many doctors are aware that this cost may sometimes be too high in misery for the individual and his family and in resources for society. They therefore usually do their best to see that the patient understands what his future life will be like. But how can a man, faced
15 with death, believe that *any* kind of life will not be worth living—until he has tried it? Once he has tried it, he and his doctors are committed to the course of keeping him alive and it is far more difficult for them to decide to stop than to decide not to start. This is the central dilemma that biomedical progress, when it only partially saves adult lives, is forcing us to face on quite a new scale.

20 Among all the life-saving techniques of medicine the most spectacularly *partially* successful ones are based on using machines to prop up or entirely take over failed organs. Long ago medicine stumbled on the fact that an enormous number of people are disabled or die when a part of them fails and that they could be saved by man-made spares. In most cases (as Figure 9.1 shows) these spares
25 are simple bits and pieces to replace functionally simple body parts, such as an artery or joint. In other cases they are complex devices that do not save life but alleviate major disability, like an artificial hand. But since they are among the sweetest triumphs of medicine they will not concern us here.

Nor are we concerned here with a third type of mechanical spare part: machines
30 like the artificial respirator that can take over when the brain is so damaged that it cannot keep the lungs breathing, or all the paraphernalia of the cardiac resuscitation unit. Though these produce some of the bitterest triumphs in medicine—consider, for example, the man whose heart is restarted a minute too late so that he survives with irreversible brain damage as an idiot—these are crisis machines
35 and 'resurrection' machines. They are used after a sudden emergency on victims who are in some senses 'dead' and who obviously cannot discuss and understand their treatment. They are also machines that *have* to be used (as long as they are available) because they do give the hope of complete recovery. It is only when recovery is far from complete that they start raising really nasty dilemmas. . . .

40 The artificial kidney and the artificial heart are today's and tomorrow's equivalents of machines like the iron lung that with everyone's prior knowledge

produce 'propped people'—humans who would have died but who now, for better or worse, can live entirely dependent on their machine. As the only alternative to transplants and as a dramatic example of the miraculous powers of
45　medical technology they have been the focus of an enormous amount of ballyhoo. It is time we looked at their true implications.

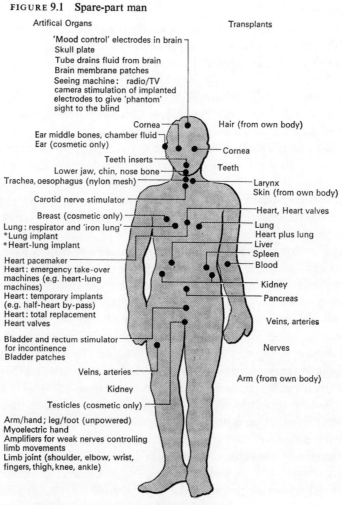

FIGURE 9.1　**Spare-part man**

* = not yet achieved in humans but expected soon
All other items have been achieved and are expected to have a significant clinical impact. Trivial artificial parts such as false teeth are not included; neither are several transplant organs which have been achieved (whole eye) or are often talked about (limbs from other bodies, gonads) because of severe technical and or ethical difficulties.

The kidney machine

Kidneys are blood cleaners. They keep the blood's water and 'salt' content correct and remove waste products of protein metabolism. ... If they do not do so adequately, because the kidneys are damaged by a congenital fault, an accident,
50　or infection, their owner will die the usually slow, agonizing death of terminal uraemia.

A kidney machine can keep such a doomed person alive even if he has no kidneys at all. If his blood is circulated through an artificial kidney, where the natural tubes are replaced by sheets of synthetic membrane surrounded by suitable
55 fluid, it can be cleaned enough to maintain life for a few days, when the process is repeated. This dramatic plug-in technique, called regular dialysis treatment, is now saving thousands who rely on their machines totally for life. It is also a vital aid for kidney transplanting in that it allows patients to wait for spare kidneys to come up, makes them fit for the operation, and saves them if their new kidney
60 fails.

However, despite all the press pictures of smiling groups of patients, their lives saved by the miracle machine, artificial kidneys are not the immortality machines that many people seem to think. . . . They do not 'work' all that well.

One of their major practical drawbacks is that for easy access to his blood the
65 patient has to have plastic tubes permanently joined up to a vein or an artery in an arm or leg. When he is not on the machine these are joined across outside his body by another tube called a shunt. In that way his blood can flow from artery to vein, reducing the risk of clotting. But because the tubes pass through the skin there is always a risk of infection and of the tubes being pulled out. The site must
70 be kept scrupulously clean and dry, which means careful baths and no swimming, while injury is a constant threat, and violent exercise of the limb is frowned on. Despite the shunt, clots do form. If these break loose into the circulation there is a risk of death. If they do not, sooner or later they will clog up the vein or artery close to the tubes and the tubes will have to be moved to a new site.
75 Until recently this had to be done every few months; now it is more likely to happen every year (in the very best units). Quite a few patients have to give up the machine—and so die—because new tube sites cannot be found for them.

Their second big practical drawback is that patients cannot be plugged in continuously. They normally go on a machine twice a week for between ten and
80 fourteen hours at a stretch, usually overnight to disrupt life as little as possible. During this time they can eat, sleep, talk, read, play cards and when they come off in the morning they usually feel fine. But once off they are coasting downhill, accumulating poisons in their blood, and so by the time they are next due they usually feel far from healthy. To help this they have to stick rigidly to a very
85 severe diet, on the principle that what you do not eat you do not have to filter out. Protein is usually cut down to about one ounce a day, salts have to be limited, liquids regulated extremely carefully to avoid dehydration on the one hand or 'water intoxication' on the other. Ungarnished spaghetti is the staple food in one of the most widely used regimes. Many patients find their diet a
90 dreadfully frustrating restriction on life and often break it. This can be fatal.

Obviously, it would also help if patients could go on a machine more frequently, perhaps three or even four times a week. This idea is in fact being pushed hard, but is hardly practical or ethical as long as machines are scarce. But if or when it does become standard practice it will of course make life for the patient in
95 some ways more trying; the strains of dialysis night are hard enough when they come 'only' twice a week. Another thing that would help is to have more efficient machines to allow shorter dialysis time, say six hours rather than ten to fourteen.

Then more frequent dialysis might be less stressful; for instance, it could be done during a long evening rather than overnight away from home. Unfortunately, this might never be technically possible, since it seems that the biggest waste molecules need at least eight hours to diffuse out of the blood cells.

This brings us to the next drawback. Unless dialysis is done very skilfully with just the right dialysis times, fluids etc. for each patient, the patient may get the underdialysis syndrome. This includes chronic loss of appetite, weight loss, skin darkening, uncontrolled high blood pressure, anaemia, gouty arthritis, calcification of the bones and mental changes that can lead to suicide. With a plastic blood shunt in one's arm, suicide (and murder) is all too easy.

With these medical difficulties it is not surprising that kidney machines hardly give a guarantee of an indefinitely prolonged life. Nor is it surprising that mortality rates vary widely, depending on the skills of the doctors and nurses and the standards of their equipment. At the best centres death-rates are in fact remarkably low. As early as mid-1967 the Royal Free Hospital, London, reported that 26 patients had been on machines for 40 patient-years without a death and with all patients returned to 'normal' life. By mid-1969 many experienced units were reporting that, roughly speaking, only 10 per cent of their patients died each year. But if one looks at the pooled results from all types of unit, the results are not so good. ... The commonest causes of death were heart failure from uncontrolled high blood pressure and failure to keep rigidly to the diet.

Is life 'worth' living on the machine? Most patients of course say that it is: when one is alive, however restricted that life is, what else can one say? Most dialysis specialists agree with them—obviously, or they would not be doing what they are. By and large they would agree with the words of Dr Hugh de Wardener (Charing Cross Hospital group): 'With all its limitations life on intermittent dialysis can be pleasant and fruitful. It is certainly a much more normal life than that of a paraplegic, and far less disabling than for many who suffer from rheumatoid arthritis. In spite of the restrictions ... most patients enjoy life and are at work.'

However, some patients offered places on machines do refuse them, while others who have started intermittent dialysis abandon it. All these patients are choosing death rather than life on the machine. Many dialysis specialists insist that by doing so they should not be regarded as suicides, either legally or for insurance purposes. Looking between the lines of what they say, there is an implication that if choosing not to continue is not suicide, then life on the machine is not life in the sense that we usually understand it. With more extraordinary means of prolonging life becoming possible, this question will obviously have to be explored very carefully. When life insurance for a widow may be at stake the question is not a trivial one. ...

ibid.

Alvin Toffler

88 The Pre-Designed Body

Like the geography of the planet, the human body has until now represented a fixed point in human experience, a 'given'. Today we are fast approaching the day when the body can no longer be regarded as fixed. Man will be able, within a reasonably short period, to redesign not merely individual bodies, but the entire
5 human race.

In 1962 Drs J. D. Watson and F. H. C. Crick received the Nobel prize for describing the DNA molecule. Since then advances in genetics have come tripping over one another at a rapid pace. Molecular biology is now about to explode from the laboratories. New genetic knowledge will permit us to tinker with human
10 heredity and manipulate the genes to create altogether new versions of man.

One of the more fantastic possibilities is that man will be able to make biological carbon copies of himself. Through a process known as 'cloning' it will be possible to grow from the nucleus of an adult cell a new organism that has the same genetic characteristics of the person contributing the cell nucleus. The
15 resultant human 'copy' would start life with a genetic endowment identical to that of the donor, although cultural differences might thereafter alter the personality or physical development of the clone. ...

Whole libraries of philosophical speculation could by a single stroke, be rendered irrelevant. An answer to this question would open the way for speedy,
20 qualitative advances in psychology, moral philosophy and a dozen other fields.

But cloning could also create undreamed of complications for the race. There is a certain charm to the idea of Albert Einstein bequeathing copies of himself to posterity. But what of Adolf Hitler? Should there be laws to regulate cloning? Nobel Laureate Joshua Lederberg, a scientist who takes his social responsibility
25 very seriously, believes it conceivable that those most likely to replicate themselves will be those who are most narcissistic, and that the clones they produce will also be narcissists. ...

It is important for laymen to understand that Lederberg is by no means a lone worrier in the scientific community. His fears about the biological revolution are
30 shared by many of his colleagues. The ethical, moral and political questions raised by the new biology simply boggle the mind. Who shall live and who shall die? What is man? Who shall control research into these fields? How shall new findings be applied? Might we not unleash horrors for which man is totally unprepared? In the opinion of many of the world's leading scientists the clock is ticking for a
35 'biological Hiroshima'. ...

Dr. E. S. E. Hafez, an internationally respected biologist, said recently that soon it might be possible for a woman to buy a tiny frozen embryo, take it to her doctor, have it implanted in her uterus, carry it for nine months, and then give birth to it as though it had been conceived in her own body. The embryo would,
40 in effect, be sold with a guarantee that the resultant baby would be free of genetic defect. The purchaser would also be told in advance the colour of the baby's eyes and hair, its sex, its probable size at maturity and its probable IQ.

Indeed, it will be possible at some point to do away with the female uterus altogether. Babies will be conceived, nurtured and raised to maturity outside the
45 human body. It is clearly only a matter of years before [it will be] possible for women to have babies without the discomfort of pregnancy.

The potential applications of such discoveries raise memories of *Brave New World* and *Astounding Science Fiction*. Thus Dr Hafez, in a sweep of his imagination, suggests that fertilized human eggs might be useful in the colonization of the
50 planets. Instead of shipping adults to Mars, we could ship a shoebox full of such cells and grow them into an entire city-size population of humans. 'When you consider how much it costs in fuel to lift every pound off the launch pad,' Dr Hafez observes, 'why send full-grown men and women aboard space ships? Instead, why not ship tiny embryos, in the care of a competent biologist ... We
55 miniaturize other spacecraft components. Why not the passengers?'. ...

A fierce controversy is already raging today among biologists over the problems and ethical issues arising out of eugenics. Should we try to breed a better race? If so, exactly what is 'better'? And who is to decide? Such questions are not entirely new. Yet the techniques soon to be available smash the traditional limits
60 of the argument. We can now imagine re-making the human race not as a farmer slowly and laboriously 'breeds up' his herd, but as an artist might, employing a brilliant range of unfamiliar colours, shapes and forms.

Not far from Route 80, outside the little town of Hazard, Kentucky, is a place picturesquely known as Valley of Troublesome Creek. In this tiny backwoods
65 community lives a family whose members, for generations, have been marked by a strange anomaly: blue skin. According to Dr Madison Cawein of the University of Kentucky College of Medicine, who tracked the family down and traced its story, the blue-skinned people seem perfectly normal in other respects. Their unusual colour is caused by a rare enzyme deficiency that has been passed from
70 one generation to the next.

Given our new, fast-accumulating knowledge of genetics, we shall be able to breed whole new races of blue people—or, for that matter, green, purple or orange. In a world still suffering from the moral lesion of racism, this is a thought to be conjured with. Should we strive for a world in which all people share the
75 same skin colour? If we want that, we shall no doubt have the technical means for bringing it about. Or should we, instead, work towards even greater diversity than now exists? What happens to the entire concept of race? To standards of physical beauty? To notions of superiority or inferiority?

We are hurtling towards the time when we will be able to breed both super- and
80 sub-races. As Theodore J. Gordon put it in *The Future*, 'Given the ability to tailor the race, I wonder if we would "create all men equal", or would we choose to manufacture apartheid? Might the races of the future be: a superior group, the DNA controllers; the humble servants; special athletes for the "games"; research scientists with 200 IQ and diminutive bodies ...' We shall have the power to
85 produce races of morons or of mathematical savants. ...

'It seems inevitable to me that there will also be competitive schools of genetic architecture ... the Functionalists will persuade parents to produce babies fitted for the present needs of society; the Futurists will suggest children who will have

a niche in the culture as it will have evolved in twenty years; the Romantics will
90 insist that each child be bred with at least one outstanding talent; and the Natura-
lists will advise the production of individuals so balanced genetically as to be in
almost perfect equilibrium ... Human body styles, like human clothing styles,
will become *outrè*, or *à la mode* as the genetic *couturiers* who designed them come
into and out of vogue'. ...

95 At a meeting of scientists and scholars, Dr Robert Sinsheimer, a Caltech bio-
physicist, put the challenge squarely:

'How will you choose to intervene in the ancient designs of nature for man?
Would you like to control the sex of your offspring? It will be as you wish. Would
you like your son to be six feet tall—seven feet? Eight feet? What troubles you?—
100 allergy, obesity, arthritic pain? These will be easily handled. For cancer, diabetes,
phenylketonuria there will be genetic therapy. The appropriate DNA will be
provided in the appropriate dose. Viral and microbial disease will be easily met.
Even the timeless patterns of growth and maturity and ageing will be subject to
our design. We know of no intrinsic limits to the life span. How long would you
105 like to live?'

Lest his audience mistake him, Sinsheimer asked: 'Do these projections sound
like LSD fantasies, or the view in a distorted mirror? None transcends the
potential of what we now know. They may not be developed in the way one
might now anticipate, but they *are* feasible, they *can* be brought to reality, and
110 sooner rather than later.'

Not only *can* such wonders be brought to reality, but the odds are they *will*.
Despite profound ethical questions about whether they *should*, the fact remains
that scientific curiosity is, itself, one of the most powerful driving forces in our
society. In the words of Dr Rollin D. Hotchkiss of the Rockefeller Institute: 'Many
115 of us feel instinctive revulsion at the hazards of meddling with the finely balanced
and far-reaching systems that make an indivudual what he is. Yet I believe it will
surely be done or attempted. The pathway will be built from a combination of
altruism, private profit and ignorance.' To this list, worse yet, he might have added political conflict and bland unconcern. Thus Dr A. Neyfakh, chief of the re-
120 search laboratory of the Institute of Development Biology of the Soviet Academy
of Sciences, predicts with a frightening lack of anxiety that the world will soon
witness a genetic equivalent of the arms race. He bases his argument on the notion
that the capitalist powers are engaged in a 'struggle for brains'. To make up for
the brain-drain, one or another of the 'reactionary governments' will be 'com-
125 pelled' to employ genetic engineering to increase its output of geniuses and gifted
individuals. Since this will occur 'regardless of their intention', an international
genetics race is inevitable. ...

In short, it is safe to say that, unless specific counter-measures are taken, if something *can* be done, someone, somewhere *will* do it. The nature of what can and
130 will be done exceeds anything that man is as yet psychologically or morally
prepared to live with.

Extract from Toffler, *Future Shock*.

Paul and Anne Ehrlich

89 Numbers of People

"Prudent men should judge of future events
by what has taken place in the past,
and what is taking place in the present."

Miguel de Cervantes (1547–1616)
Persiles and Sigismunda

Assuming that the first "man" appeared between one and two million years ago, we can estimate that between 60 and 100 billion representatives of *Homo sapiens* have lived on the planet Earth. Today some 3.7 billion people inhabit the Earth, roughly 4—5 percent of all those who have ever lived.

5 We do not have substantial historical data on which to base estimates of population before 1650; such estimates must be based on circumstantial evidence. For instance, we believe that agriculture was unknown before about 8000 B.C.; prior to that date all human groups made their living by hunting and gathering. No more than 20 million square miles of the Earth's total land area of some 58 million
10 square miles could have been successfully utilized in this way by our early ancestors. From the population densities of the hunting and gathering tribes of today, we can estimate that the total human population of 8000 B.C. was about 5 million people.

Population sizes at various times, from the onset of the agricultural revolution
15 until census data first were kept in the seventeenth century, have also been estimated. This was done by projection from census figures that exist for agricultural societies, and by examination of archaeological remains. Such data as number of rooms in excavated ancient villages prove especially useful for calculating village

TABLE 2-1
Doubling Times

Date	Estimated world population	Time for population to double
8000 B.C.	5 million	
		1,500 years
1650 A.D.	500 million	
		200 years
1850 A.D.	1,000 million (1 billion)	
		80 years
1930 A.D.	2,000 million (2 billion)	
		45 years
1975 A.D.	4,000 million (4 billion) Computed doubling time around 1972	35 years

populations. It is thought that the total human population at the time of Christ
20   was around 200 to 300 million people, and that it had increased to about 500
million (½ billion) by 1650. It then doubled to 1,000 million (1 billion) around
1850, and doubled again to 2 billion by 1930. The course of human population
growth can be seen in Figure 2-1. Note that the size of the population has, with
minor irregularities, increased continuously, and that *the rate of increase has also*
25   *increased.*

Perhaps the best way to describe the growth rate is in terms of "doubling
time"—the time required for the population to double in size. To go from 5
million in 8000 B.C. to 500 million in 1650 meant that the population increased
100-fold. This required between 6 and 7 doublings:

30   5 million → 10 → 20 → 40 → 80 → 160 → 320 → 640 million

in a period of 9,000 to 10,000 years. Thus, on the average, the population doubled
about once every 1,500 years during that period. The next doubling, from 500
million to a billion, took 200 years, and the doubling from a billion to 2 billion
took only 80 years. Barring a catastrophic increase in the death rate, the population
35   will reach 4 billion around 1975, having doubled in 45 years. The rate of growth
around 1972 would, if continued, double the population in about 35 years. Table
2-1 summarizes our population history in these terms. To take a slightly different
perspective, it took 1 or 2 million years to achieve a population size of 1 billion
around 1850. The next billion was added in 80 years (1850—1930). The third
40   billion came along in only 30 years (1931—1960), and the next will have taken
only about 15 years (1960—1975), when the population size reaches 4 billion. If
this trend continues, the United Nations forecasts that the fifth billion will be
added in just slightly more than a decade.

Extract from Ehrlich, *Population, Resourses, Environment.* (1972)   (*unabridged*)

Paul and Anne Ehrlich

90 Outer Space

Many Americans, who see science fiction dramas on television and movie screens, in addition to being tax-paying participants in the real-life performances of our astronauts, think it entirely reasonable to regard space as the next frontier. Actually, the obstacles to interstellar or even interplanetary migration are stupen-
5 dous and far beyond present or foreseeable technological capabilities. Even if the technology should become available, in the end we would be defeated by the very source of our present difficulties: numbers. Since this chapter deals with the limits of the Earth, it is necessary to demonstrate clearly that we are, in fact, confined to our own small planet. To make this clear, let us examine for a moment the possi-
10 bilities for shipping surplus people to other planets. For the sake of this discussion, let us ignore the virtual certainty that the other planets of the solar system are uninhabitable. Consider some interesting calculations that have been made on how much time we could gain if we insisted on postponing direct action against the population explosion by occupying the planets of our solar system. For
15 instance, at any given time, and at current population growth rates, it would take only about 50 years before Venus, Mercury, Mars, our moon, and the moons of Jupiter and Saturn all had the same population density as Earth.

What if the fantastic problems of reaching and colonizing the larger and more distant planets of the solar system, such as Jupiter, Uranus, and Pluto, could be

20 solved? It would take only about 200 years of time to fill them "Earth-full." So
we could perhaps gain 250 years for population growth in the solar system after
reaching an absolute limit on Earth. Then, of course, we would still have the
problem, but in greater dimensions.

A fundamental aspect of such a migration scheme would be the cost of the
25 venture. Let us make some optimistic assumptions. Suppose that a small modern
spaceship like Apollo, instead of carrying three men to the moon, could transport
100 people to one of the planets for the same cost. In order to hold the present
population of the Earth constant, we would have to export about 70 million
people per year (assuming no change in the growth rate). To do so would require
30 the launching of very nearly 2,000 spaceships each day, year in and year out. The
cost, not counting the expense of recruiting and training migrants, would exceed
$300 billion daily. Three days' launches would equal the present annual gross
national product of the U.S.

On the optimistic grounds that anything is possible, though, let us suppose
35 that the immense problems of reaching and colonizing the planets of our own
solar system are somehow solved. What then? The optimists would have us next
expand to occupy the planets of *other* stars. Interstellar transport for surplus
people presents an amusing prospect. Since the ships would take generations to
reach most stars, the only people who *could* be transported would be those willing
40 to exercise strict birth control. Population explosions on spaceships could not be
tolerated.

We could continue to outline other speculations and fantasies, but hopefully
you are now convinced that the extremely remote possibility of expanding into
outer space offers no escape from the laws of population growth. The population
45 will have to stop growing sooner or later.

ibid.

Aldous Huxley

91 Overpopulation

On the first Christmas Day the population of our planet was about two hundred and fifty millions—less than half the population of modern China. Sixteen centuries later, when the Pilgrim Fathers landed at Plymouth Rock, human numbers had climbed to a little more than five hundred millions. By the time of the signing
5 of the Declaration of Independence, world population had passed the seven hundred million mark. In 1931, when I was writing *Brave New World*, it stood at just under two billions. Today, only twenty-seven years later, there are two thousand eight hundred million of us. And tomorrow—what? Penicillin, DDT and clean water are cheap commodities, whose effects on public health are out of
10 all proportion to their cost. Even the poorest government is rich enough to provide its subjects with a substantial measure of death control. Birth control is a very different matter. Death control is something which can be provided for a whole people by a few technicians working in the pay of a benevolent government. Birth control depends on the co-operation of an entire people. It must be
15 practised by countless individuals, from whom it demands more intelligence and will power than most of the world's teeming illiterates possess, and (where chemical or mechanical methods of contraception are used) an expenditure of more money than most of these millions can now afford. Moreover, there are nowhere any religious traditions in favour of unrestricted death, whereas reli-
20 gious and social traditions in favour of unrestricted reproduction are widespread. For all these reasons, death control is achieved very easily, birth control is achieved with great difficulty. Death rates have therefore fallen in recent years with startling suddenness. But birth rates have either remained at their old high level or, if they have fallen, have fallen very little and at a very slow rate. In conse-
25 quence, human numbers are now increasing more rapidly than at any time in the history of the species.

Moreover, the yearly increases are themselves increasing. They increase regularly, according to the rules of compound interest; and they also increase irregularly with every application, by a technologically backward society, of the
30 principles of Public Health. At the present time the annual increase in world population runs to about forty-three millions. This means that every four years mankind adds to its numbers the equivalent of the present population of the United States, every eight and a half years the equivalent of the present population of India. At the rate of increase prevailing between the birth of Christ and the
35 death of Queen Elizabeth I it took sixteen centuries for the population of the earth to double. At the present rate it will double in less than half a century. And this fantastically rapid doubling of our numbers will be taking place on a planet whose most desirable and productive areas are already densely populated, whose soils are being eroded by the frantic efforts of bad farmers to raise more food, and
40 whose easily available mineral capital is being squandered with the reckless extravagance of a drunken sailor getting rid of his accumulated pay.

In the Brave New World of my fable, the problem of human numbers in their relation to natural resources had been effectively solved. An optimum figure for world population had been calculated and numbers were maintained at this figure
45 (a little under two billions, if I remember rightly) generation after generation. In the real contemporary world, the population problem has not been solved. On the contrary it is becoming graver and more formidable with every passing year. It is against this grim biological background that all the political, economic, cultural and psychological dramas of our time are being played out. As the
50 twentieth century wears on, as the new billions are added to the existing billions (there will be more than five and a half billions of us by the time my granddaughter is fifty), this biological background will advance, ever more insistently, ever more menacingly, towards the front and centre of the historical stage. The problem of rapidly increasing numbers in relation to natural resources, to social
55 stability and to the well being of individuals—this is now the central problem of mankind; and it will remain the central problem certainly for another century, and perhaps for several centuries thereafter. A new age is supposed to have begun on October 4th, 1957. But actually, in the present context, all our exuberant post-Sputnik talk is irrelevant and even nonsensical. So far as the masses of mankind
60 are concerned, the coming time will not be the Space Age; it will be the Age of Overpopulation. ... A settlement on the moon may be of some military advantage to the nation that does the settling. But it will do nothing whatever to make life more tolerable, during the fifty years that it will take our present population to double, for the earth's undernourished and proliferating billions. And
65 even if, at some future date, emigration to Mars should become feasible, even if any considerable number of men and women were desperate enough to choose a new life under conditions comparable to those prevailing on a mountain twice as high as Mount Everest, what difference would that make? In the course of the last four centuries quite a number of people sailed from the Old World to the
70 New. But neither their departure nor the returning flow of food and raw materials could solve the problems of the Old World. Similarly the shipping of a few surplus humans to Mars (at a cost, for transportation and development, of several million dollars a head) will do nothing to solve the problem of mounting population pressures on our own planet. Unsolved, that problem will render insoluble all
75 our other problems. Worse still, it will create conditions in which individual freedom and the social decencies of the democratic way of life will become impossible, almost unthinkable.

Not all dictatorships arise in the same way. There are many roads to Brave New World; but perhaps the straightest and the broadest of them is the road we are
80 travelling today, the road that leads through gigantic numbers and accelerating increases. Let us briefly review the reasons for this close correlation between too many people, too rapidly multiplying, and the formulation of authoritarian philosophies, the rise of totalitarian systems of government.

As large and increasing numbers press more heavily upon available resources,
85 the economic position of the society undergoing this ordeal becomes ever more precarious. This is especially true of those underdeveloped regions, where a sudden lowering of the death rate by means of DDT, penicillin and clean water

has not been accompanied by a corresponding fall in the birth rate. In parts of
Asia and in most of Central and South America populations are increasing so fast
90 that they will double themselves in little more than twenty years. If the production
of food and manufactured articles, of houses, schools and teachers, could be increased at a greater rate than human numbers, it would be possible to improve the
wretched lot of those who live in these underdeveloped and overpopulated
countries. But unfortunately these countries lack not merely agricultural machin-
95 ery and an industrial plant capable of turning out this machinery, but also the
capital required to create such a plant. Capital is what is left over after the primary
needs of a population have been satisfied. But the primary needs of most of the
people in underdeveloped countries are never fully satisfied. At the end of each
year almost nothing is left over, and there is therefore almost no capital available
100 for creating the industrial and agricultural plant, by means of which the people's
needs might be satisfied. Moreover, there is, in all these underdeveloped countries,
a serious shortage of the trained manpower without which a modern industrial
and agricultural plant cannot be operated. The present educational facilities are
inadequate; so are the resources, financial and cultural, for improving the existing
105 facilities as fast as the situation demands. Meanwhile the population of some of
these underdeveloped countries is increasing at the rate of three per cent per
annum.

Their tragic situation is discussed in an important book, published in 1957—
The Next Hundred Years, by Professors Harrison Brown, James Bonner and John
110 Weir of the California Institute of Technology. How is mankind coping with the
problem of rapidly increasing numbers? Not very successfully. "The evidence
suggests rather strongly that in most underdeveloped countries the lot of the
average individual has worsened appreciably in the last half-century. People have
become more poorly fed. There are fewer available goods per person. And practi-
115 cally every attempt to improve the situation has been nullified by the relentless
pressure of continued population growth."

Whenever the economic life of a nation becomes precarious, the central government is forced to assume additional responsibilities for the general welfare. It
must work out elaborate plans for dealing with a critical situation; it must
120 impose ever greater restrictions upon the activities of its subjects; and if, as is
very likely, worsening economic conditions result in political unrest, or open
rebellion, the central government must intervene to preserve public order and its
own authority. More and more power is thus concentrated in the hands of the
executives and their bureaucratic managers. But the nature of power is such that
125 even those who have not sought it, but have had it forced upon them, tend to
acquire a taste for more. "Lead us not into temptation," we pray—and with good
reason; for when human beings are tempted too enticingly or too long, they
generally yield. A democratic constitution is a device for preventing the local
rulers from yielding to those particularly dangerous temptations that arise when
130 too much power is concentrated in too few hands. Such a constitution works
pretty well where, as in Britain or the United States, there is a traditional respect
for constitutional procedures. Where the republican or limited monarchical
tradition is weak, the best of constitutions will not prevent ambitious politicians

from succumbing with glee and gusto to the temptations of power. And in any
135 country where numbers have begun to press heavily upon available resources,
these temptations cannot fail to arise. Overpopulation leads to economic insecurity
and social unrest. Unrest and insecurity lead to more control by central governments and an increase of their power. In the absence of a constitutional tradition,
this increased power will probably be exercised in a dictatorial fashion. Even if
140 Communism had never been invented, this would be likely to happen. But
Communism has been invented. Given this fact, the probability of overpopulation leading through unrest to dictatorship becomes a virtual certainty. It is a
pretty safe bet that, twenty years from now, all the world's overpopulated and
underdeveloped countries will be under some form of totalitarian rule—probably
145 by the Communist Party.

How will this development affect the overpopulated, but highly industrialized
and still democratic countries of Europe? If the newly formed dictatorships were
hostile to them, and if the normal flow of raw materials from the underdeveloped
countries were deliberately interrupted, the nations of the West would find them-
150 selves in a very bad way indeed. Their industrial system would break down, and
the highly developed technology, which up till now has permitted them to sustain
a population much greater than that which could be supported by locally available
resources, would no longer protect them against the consequences of having too
many people in too small a territory. If this should happen, the enormous powers
155 forced by unfavourable conditions upon central governments may come to be
used in the spirit of totalitarian dictatorship.

The United States is not at present an overpopulated country. If, however, the
population continues to increase at the present rate (which is higher than that of
India's increase, though happily a good deal lower than the rate now current in
160 Mexico or Guatemala), the problem of numbers in relation to available resources
might well become troublesome by the beginning of the twenty-first century.
For the moment overpopulation is not a direct threat to the personal freedom of
Americans. It remains, however, an indirect threat, a menace at one remove. If
overpopulation should drive the underdeveloped countries into totalitarianism,
165 and if these new dictatorships should ally themselves with Russia, then the military position of the United States would become less secure and the preparations
for defence and retaliation would have to be intensified. But liberty, as we all
know, cannot flourish in a country that is permanently on a war footing, or even
a near-war footing. Permanent crisis justifies permanent control of everybody and
170 everything by the agencies of the central government. And permanent crisis is
what we have to expect in a world in which overpopulation is producing a state
of things in which dictatorship under Communist auspices becomes almost
inevitable.

Extract from 'Overpopulation' in *Brave New World Revisited* by Aldous Huxley. (1958)   *(slightly abridged)*

Paul and Anne Ehrlich

92 Science and Technology

For many people, science and technology are in effect taking on the aspect of a new religion. How often one hears statements beginning, "any society that can send a man to the moon can . . . " and ending with some problem, usually immensely more complex and difficult than space travel, that science and technology are
5 expected to solve. The population-food imbalance is a common candidate; others are various types of pollution or ecological problems. Two things are generally wrong with these statements. First, science and technology have not yet reached the point relative to those problems that they had relative to the man-on-the-moon project by 1955. The general outlines of a solution are not clear to all
10 competent scientists in the pertinent disciplines. Second, and equally important, there is no sign of a societal commitment to promote a crash program to solve these non-space problems.

The public, indeed, has developed a touching but misplaced faith in the ability of science and technology to pull humankind's chestnuts out of the fire. There is
15 not the slightest question that with clever and cautious use of our scientific and technological resources, a great deal of good could be accomplished. But can we find the required amount of cleverness and caution? In spite of enormous scientific advances during the past thirty years, it is perfectly clear that the *absolute amount* of human misery has increased (because of the enormous growth in the numbers
20 of poverty-stricken human beings), while the chances of civilization persisting have decreased. There has been an abundance of science and technology, but they have been unbalanced and out of control.

Medicine has attacked the death rate with vigor but largely ignored the birth rate, in the process threatening mankind with unprecedented catastrophe. Physics
25 has given us nuclear and thermonuclear weapons, a legacy so weighty on the minus side of the balance that it is difficult to think of any serious plusses with which to balance it. (It is conceivable that the great impatience of many physicists to introduce the use of fission power stemmed from guilt over their participation in building the first A-bombs. Many of the most prominent promoters of
30 nuclear power were involved in the Manhattan project. It is a double tragedy that in an effort to exculpate themselves they may deal humankind yet another blow.) Biology has provided biological warfare weapons and has seen many millions of dollars poured into molecular genetics, a field offering no immediate improvement in human welfare, but with great future potential for curing or preventing
35 inborn defects, curing cancer, etc. Meanwhile, support for environmental studies has been relatively insignificant, in spite of repeated warnings over a quarter of a century by ecologists that man was threatening to destroy the life-support systems of the planet. The behavioral sciences have also languished, despite their potential value in helping to solve human problems.
40 Most of the great "advances" in technology from DDT and x-rays to automobiles and jet aircraft have caused serious problems for humanity. Some of

these problems would have been difficult to anticipate, but most were foreseen, were warned against, and could have been avoided or ameliorated with sensible societal planning. The question now is, how can such planning be done in the 45 future so as to minimize future unfortunate consequences of technological advances?

It is clear from the records of organizations such as the AMA and AEC and from recent statements by technological optimists and scientific politicians that scientists (like other groups in our population) cannot be relied upon to police 50 themselves. Some way must be found to foster greater participation of other segments of society in the major decision-making processes affecting science and technology. This is essential, of course, to the survival of society, but it is also important as protection for scientists themselves. Burdens of guilt such as those borne by the physicists involved in developing atomic weapons must be avoided 55 wherever possible, or at least more broadly shared.

We are not in a position here to propose a detailed structure for controlling science and technology, but some general directions can be suggested. Governmental agencies such as the National Science Foundation and National Institute of Health regularly employ *ad hoc* committees and panels of scientists to evaluate 60 research programs and individual research projects. Universities also on occasion use such groups of scientists to evaluate programs or departments. *Ad hoc* panels of non-scientists might be integrated into these systems, drawing perhaps on citizens with non-scientific expertise serving their "sabbaticals". Such panels could both advise agencies directly and also report to a paragovernmental central 65 body (perhaps elected) empowered to intervene whenever it was felt that the public interest was endangered. This power would extend to research under *any* auspices: government, military, university, or industry. The central body could also be charged with continually informing both government and the public of pertinent trends in science and technology.

70 Increased awareness and scrutiny of science and technology will not, in themselves, suffice. Although laymen can become very knowledgeable about science and technology, as the performance of several congressmen involved in appropriations for science and technical projects has demonstrated, it is often very difficult or impossible for individual laymen (or even scientists) to foresee the 75 consequences of certain trends. A second element is thus required in the control system: an apparatus, possibly in the form of research institutes, concerned solely with such assessment and reporting to the central body described above. Perhaps a set percentage of all funds used in governmental, university, and industrial research should be assessed for the support of these organizations, which should 80 be kept strictly independent of each of those interests.

Some of the work which might be done by such institutes would be an extension of the sort of programs now being run by systems ecologist K. E. F. Watt's group at the University of California at Davis, and by systems analysts Jay W. Forrester and Dennis L. Meadows of the Massachusetts Institute of Technology. 85 Watt, for instance, has forecast the dismal consequences of continuing various prevailing strategies of resource management and social policies. The MIT group has shown, most convincingly, that many of the results of various proposed

courses of action are "counter-intuitive." Their studies indicated, for example,
that a program of reducing demands on resources (by finding substitutes, recy-
90 cling, etc.), without controlling other influences on the world system such as pollution and population growth, could produce worse results than a future in which
resources were exhausted. To quote Forrester's description of the results of his
computer simulation model in which resource consumption is substantially
curbed, "population and capital investment are allowed to rise until a pollution
95 crisis is created. Pollution then acts directly to reduce birth rate, increase death
rate, and to depress food production. Population, which, according to this sample
model, peaks at the year 2030, has fallen to one-sixth of the peak population
within an interval of 20 years—a world-wide catastrophe of a magnitude never
before experienced." Forrester's and Meadow's analysis projects the collective
100 results of various trends in this way, in each case controlling or altering different
interacting factors. Their study indicates that different forms of disaster lie ahead
unless *all* the factors are controlled: population growth, pollution, resource consumption, and the rate of capital investment (industrialization).

In addition to broad-scope evaluations such as those just described, some re-
105 search institutes must be involved in much more detailed questions. For example, is
medical research being done with adequate attention to the needs of all segments
of the population and to birth control as well as death control? Are the benefits
and risks of the breeder reactor being studied in proper depth? What are the
possible dangerous consequences of further investigating the properties of a
110 given virus or biocidal compound?

Of course, even the most sophisticated assessment apparatus will not avoid all
mistakes, but if it is backed by a growing feeling of social responsibility among
scientists, we should be able to improve our record greatly. The remainder of the
solution of learning to live with science and technology is to leave plenty of
115 margin for error. For safety, we must learn to live somewhat below our means—
not to stress ourselves and the Earth's ecosystems to the absolute limit.

Extract from Ehrlich, *Population, Resourses, Environment.* (1972)   *(unabridged)*

Kurt Vonnegut Jr.

93 Confections

It has been said many times that man's knowledge of himself has been left far behind by his understanding of technology, and that we can have peace and plenty and justice only when man's knowledge of himself catches up. This is not true. We don't need more information. We don't need bigger brains. All that is
5 required is that we become less selfish than we are.

We already have plenty of sound suggestions as to how we are to act if things are to become better on earth. For instance: Do unto others as you would have them do unto you. About seven hundred years ago, Thomas Aquinas had some other recommendations as to what people might do with their lives, and I do not
10 find these made ridiculous by computers and trips to the moon and television sets. He praises the Seven Spiritual Works of Mercy, which are these:

To teach the ignorant, to counsel the doubtful, to console the sad, to reprove the sinner, to forgive the offender, to bear with the oppressive and troublesome, and to pray for us all.

15 He also admires the Seven Corporal Works of Mercy, which are these:

To feed the hungry, to give drink to the thirsty, to clothe the naked, to shelter the homeless, to visit the sick and prisoners, to ransom captives, and to bury the dead.

A great swindle of our time is the assumption that science has made religion
20 obsolete. All science has damaged is the story of Adam and Eve and the story of Jonah and the Whale. Everything else holds up pretty well, particularly the lessons about fairness and gentleness. People who find those lessons irrelevant in the twentieth century are simply using science as an excuse for greed and harshness.

Extract from *Wampeters, Foma and Granfalloon* by Kurt Vonnegut Jr. (1974)   *(unabridged)*

94 Violence and Vandalism in American Schools

The fact is simple but stark: vandalism and violence have become one of the foremost problems of the nation's schools. It is a problem that is elusive; a costly problem that can strike without warning; a problem that involves fear of physical harm and emotional public demands for safer schools, and worst of all a problem that so far defies solution.

Certainly vandalism and violence, to some degree, have been problems in schools at least since the uprisings in the nation's colleges and universities in the mid-1960s, but widespread awareness of their vast extent and pervasiveness in elementary and secondary schools began to dawn with the coming of the 1970s.

In some big city areas school administrators attest to extreme concern due to three factors: gang activity, the prevalence of drugs, and the number of weapons finding their way onto school campuses, many times "carried for protection".

A senator from Indiana reported that in his state a ring was found operating in a junior high school which extorted money from children, A committee of the New York State Legislature revealed that in some New York City high schools students ran narcotics, firearms, and prostitution rings. In explaining the impact of violence and vandalism on education, the senator said that the primary concern in many modern American schools is no longer education but preservation.

City	Number of Students	Number of Schools	Losses due to Vandalism	Cost for Security	Total	Cost per Pupil
New York	1,100,000	1,045	$4,092,000	$8,954,000	$13,046,000	$12
Los Angeles	610,000	627	$3,484,000	$4,500,000	$ 7,984,000	$14
Chicago	540,000	670	$3,515,000	$6,500,000	$10,015,000	$18,50

Vandalism: What, When?

As shown by the Special Report survey, almost everything in, on, near, part of, or belonging to a school, its staff or its students may be vandalized. The building itself is the most frequent target, particularly the windows. In fact, some districts reported that window breakage accounted for 100% of vandalism costs. ...

In Menomonee Falls, Wis., two 18-year-olds broke $3,500 worth of windows in one spree, resulting in a felony conviction for them and an inflated vandalism figure for the district.

The second most frequent act of vandalism cited by school districts, after glass breakage is theft or burglary – before, during or after school hours. What's stolen? Almost anything, judging by the items listed by school districts: typewriters, calculators and other office equipment; musical instruments; industrial arts equipment; tools; furniture; first aid kits and fire extinguishers (a popular item taken from school buses); tape recorders, microphones, film projectors and cameras, amplifiers and other audiovisual equipment; maintenance equipment; television sets, radios and phonographs; balance beam scales; stop watches; cafeteria food and equipment.

Property destruction to buildings, grounds and equipment can also be a major expense item. Here again, almost anything seems to serve as a target, including the playground, signs, walls, trees, turf, shrubbery, furniture, light fixtures, toilet fixtures, lockers and thermostats. Two districts reported having flag pole ropes cut; another reported extensive damage to a large computer; a fourth said its gutters and drainspouts had been stolen, at a cost of $1,850.

Arson: The Single Most Expensive Crime

Arson is the most expensive single school crime reported by school districts, with the cost ranging from several hundred dollars per incident to $1 million. Two rural districts reported "almost complete devastation" when new buildings were burned. One suffered $800,000 damages and the other, $600,000. Harry Wilson, administrative assistant in the Bellevue (Wash.) Public Schools, reports that vandalism to school buildings in the form of arson is a recent, and major, problem for his district. The district serves Bellevue, an affluent community of 65,000 adjacent to Seattle, plus several nearby towns.

Why?

There is no simple, all inclusive answer to the perplexing question, "Why are schools experiencing such an upswing in vandalism and violence?" Instead, the answer seems to depend on one's perspective. Big-city school administrators, for example, generally picture the school as a small part or subsystem of the city with all its problems. Sometimes, they add, the schools experience problems more intensely than the city itself. This can be explained partially by statistics showing half of all arrests are of teenagers and young adults, with 15 the peak age for violent crimes.

Times have changed also, with one of the biggest changes purported to be that of attitude – the attitude of teachers, parents and society in general – toward crime, family life, rights and responsibilities, and toward schooling and what it is expected to provide. Educators say many of the problems that start at home or in the community are acted out in school and that the school is expected to cope without the support of home or community.

Educators say students rights have been extended liberally but that the corresponding responsibilities have not been assumed by youth or demanded by society. Some critics charge that the attitude of parents, teachers and administrators is leaning toward more permissiveness and, at the same time, toward less responsibility for what used to be considered the duties of parent, teacher or administrator.

Student attitude also is said to have undergone a tremendous change. Many students view school as someplace they have to go, rather than someplace they want to go, for whatever reason. Once schools were as neutral territory as churches. Today neither can attest to the same degree of safety or the absence of contemptuous acts as in days past.

The Big Cities: Causes of School Crime

Among big-city administrators, the most frequently cited causes of escalating school crimes are the deteriorating living conditions in many big cities accompanied by the movement of the white population to the fringes or suburban areas; rising costs for services, including schools, accompanied by near empty coffers; overcrowding; separate racial zones often resulting in poverty alongside affluence; increasing youth hostility and alienation in the midst of economically deprived and often educationally starved homes and schools; and frequently, little or no supervision from parents.

A juvenile court judge in Los Angeles County, Joseph Sorrentino, singles out city slums as the worst areas as far as crime is concerned. Sorrentino says four out of five crimes take place in the slums. Part of the reason, he says, is the density of population, which is 30 times that of suburban communities. Leonard M. Friedman, associate justice in the U.S. Third District Court of Appeals, adds that "the festering slums of America's cities generate a never ending supply of recruits to crime."

Gangs and Drugs: Acute Problems

Big-city administrators zero in on two particularly exasperating youthful phenomena: gangs and the prevalence of drugs. Yet, as the chancellor of the New York City Schools told the Senate subcommittee, hard data on the effects of drugs and gangs on the school environment remains elusive. The best estimates place at 350 the number of gangs in New York and 140 in Los Angeles. Gangs are believed to be responsible for much of the fear and violent crimes in some big-city schools. One Los Angeles gang leader, age 19, was arrested 11 times on charges that included assault on a police officer, simple assault, strongarmed robbery and possession of a carbine. The story of the gang leader, known as "Bartender", concurs with various accounts of the activities of violent urban youth gangs. Bartender's account includes a rival gang fight in a school cafeteria, a weapon brought on campus, the killing of 10 members of the rival gangs, easy availability and extensive use of drugs and weapons, particularly guns.

Harmless adolescent frustrations are "given teeth by the availability of dangerous weapons". This conclusion by the *New York Times* is shared by juvenile judge Sorrentino, along with many police, judical officials and educators. All are adamant about the role that guns play in increased school crime, particularly in acts of violence. Sorrentino says the number of guns in the United States has increased 50% since 1963 and that "some 100 million guns are floating around."

In a sketch of life in Chicago, a *Wall Street Journal* reporter described the seriousness of the situation in one school which serves chronic truants and school discipline problems from the city's mostly black South and West sides. Each morning, he wrote, students are frisked for weapons and the school has requested funds from the board of education for a metal detector.

Are the Schools Themselves at Fault?

The schools themselves must be faulted for the current problems of vandalism and violence, according to former NEA President James Harris. Harris told the Senate subcommittee that the causes – even more complex than they were 10 or even 5 years ago – include depersonalization, alienation, outmoded discipline practices, racial hostility and the increased use of violence in the society and in the world as a means of solving problems.

Harris noted further that schools have been in a state of flux during the past several years as a by-product of efforts to eliminate discrimination and segregation from American public education

"The increasing dependency on short-range measures, such as corporal punishment, suspension or expulsion, police in the schools, and detention/isolation, is particularly depressing," he said. The fact is, Harris added, many traditional methods of school discipline are no longer appropriate. "Schools which rely on them in isolation are traveling on a different path than young people today, and the gap between the institution and the students is widening because communication in such situations has become virtually impossible," he charged.

Harris' testimony was in sharp contrast to that offered by rival union leader Albert Shanker. While Shanker agreed that some of the blame belongs with the schools themselves, he was much less prone to support more rights for students. In fact, he told the subcommittee that today's problems are partially due to "the years of literature portraying students as a kind of oppressed colonial minority."

Another educator, Don Richardson of the Los Angeles City Schools, faults the schools, but for different reasons. He says schools often do not offer an option for the kids who cannot operate in the massiveness of a large-body-count, little-attention-to-personal-needs kind of cam-

50 pus. In addition, Richardson remarks, the schools are generally too slow in providing needed programs early enough; for example, for the six-year-old who is already showing signs of being with-
55 drawn or who is not relating to his or her peers. The problem, the educator maintains, is that it is much harder to get political support for preventive programs than it is for those that simply "put out the fire". 60

Youth Misbehavior: It Starts in the Home

The root causes of a student's misbehavior in such acts as extortion, burglary, "strong-arming," and assaults on other students and teachers "can be
5 traced directly to problems stemming from the home situation." This was the conclusion of several police officers who were interviewed for this Special Report. In the case of the child from a lower
10 socioeconomic background, they say, the cause is often child neglect or child abuse. But the most prevalent factor among middle-class youthful offenders, says Joseph Barnes of the Sacramento
15 (Calif.) Police Dept., is the permissiveness of parents. "The kids have lots of time on their hands and their parents supply them the use of a car and plenty of money." Another influential factor among all youth, he noted, is that "they 20 do not think of the consequences of their acts." They will do something on spurring from their friends "and with little thought given to what can happen as a result of their acts." Another officer 25 viewed the kind of peer pressure that can lead to disdainful acts as particularly strong "among those youngsters who don't yet have the confidence to stand on their own." 30

Extract from 'Vandalism in American Schools' from *Violence and Vandalism*. Printed in *Education U.S.A.* (National School Public Relations Association). (1975)

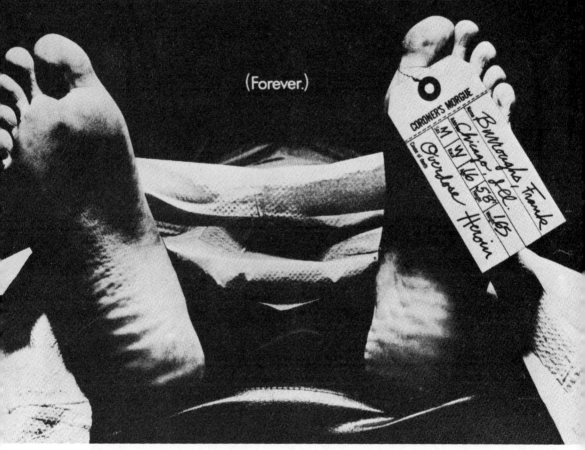

James Patrick

95 A Glasgow Gang Observed

Why do so many adolescent boys in Glasgow choose the violent gang as their form of adaptation to such social and environmental adversities? Why do they become street fighters rather than drug addicts or political activists? Why do they not retreat into social despair or fatalistic acceptance of the status quo? I
5 would speculate that there are two answers to such crucial questions. . . .

Firstly, there is a strong subcultural emphasis on self-assertion and on rebellious independence against authority as the means of attaining masculinity. Glasgow's long history of industrial militancy, culminating in the 1971 'work-in' at Upper Clyde Shipbuilders, is evidence of an active, even aggressive response in
10 times of crisis.

Secondly, economic hardship, suffered by generations of Glaswegians, has narrowed down the possibilities of action. A sense of desperation is created amongst boys who find some forms of action (work, apprenticeships, all forms of higher education) closed to them, while other forms (apathy, hard-line drugs)
15 are excluded by the subculture as being the very antithesis of manliness. The only alternative, and one hallowed in the traditions of Glasgow slum life, is to respond with violence. The large urban centres in England with histories of violence have prospered since the war in ways which leave Glasgow a grey, depressed area in comparison.

20 The Glasgow gang boy feels that he is being pushed around, that he has no control over the social conditions which predetermine his future and yet he is expected to act like a man who is in charge of the situation. Some dramatic reas-surance that he can still make things happen is necessary. That reassurance, I suggest, is likely to take the form of gang fighting, because over the last hundred
25 years in Glasgow acts of extreme and unpredictable violence have become invested with an aura which transcends mere brutality. The leading exponent of such violence, the gang leader, is accorded the title of King, no less. It is only in this social context that the most disturbed personality can come to the fore; through his prowess in explosive acts of violence he is able to capture the leadership of
30 the gang.

Only a radical new policy of regional redevelopment can hope to combat this deeply ingrained malaise of social and economic problems in west central Scot-land. Government intervention is needed urgently to provide jobs, capital invest-ment, housing, and additional educational and medical facilities. Nothing less
35 than a really comprehensive policy of social action on a regional basis is called for; and yet the tragedy lies in the indifference of successive governments who, decade after decade, leave desperate situations to fester. The lesson of Ulster has not yet been learned.

Extract from *A Glasgow Gang Observed* by James Patrick. (1973)

Edward Bond

96 Lear: Author's Preface

I write about violence as naturally as Jane Austen wrote about manners. Violence shapes and obsesses our society, and if we do not stop being violent we have no future. People who do not want writers to write about violence want to stop them writing about us and our time. It would be immoral not to write about
5 violence.

Many animals are able to be violent, but in non-human species the violence is finally controlled so that it does not threaten the species' existence. Then why is the existence of our species threatened by its violence?

I must begin with an important distinction. The predator hunting its prey is
10 violent but not aggressive in the human way. It wants to eat, not destroy, and its violence is dangerous to the prey but not to the predator. Animals only become aggressive – that is destructive in the human sense – when their lives, territory or status in their group are threatened, or when they mate or are preparing to mate. Even then the aggression is controlled. Fighting is usually ritualized, and the
15 weaker or badly-placed animal will be left alone when it runs away or formally submits. Men use much of their energy and skill to make more efficient weapons to destroy each other, but animals have often evolved in ways to ensure they *can't* destroy each other.

A lot has been written on this subject and it is not my job to repeat the evi-
20 dence; but is shows clearly, I think, that in normal surroundings and conditions members of the same species are not dangerous to one another, but that when they are kept in adverse conditions, and forced to behave unnaturally, their behaviour deteriorates. This has been seen in zoos and laboratories. Then they become destructive and neurotic and make bad parents. They begin to behave
25 like us.

That is all there is to our 'innate' aggession, or our 'original' sin as it was first called. There is no evidence of an aggressive *need*, as there is of sexual and feeding *needs*. We respond aggressively when we are constantly deprived of our physical and emotional needs, or when we are threatened with this; and if we are constantly
30 deprived and threatened in this way – as human beings now are – we live in a constant state of aggression. It does not matter how much a man doing routine work in, say, a factory or office is paid: he will still be deprived in this sense. Because he is behaving in a way for which he is not designed, he is alienated from his natural self, and this will have physical and emotional consequences for him.
35 He becomes nervous and tense and he begins to look for threats everywhere. This makes him belligerent and provocative; he becomes a threat to other people, and so his situation rapidly deteriorates.

This is all the facts justify us in concluding: aggression is an ability but not a necessity. The facts are often *interpreted* more pessimistically, but that is another
40 matter.

If we *were* innately aggressive, in the sense that it was *necessary* for us to act aggressively from time to time, we would be condemned to live with an incurable

259

disease; and as the suffering caused by aggression in a technological culture is so terrible, the question would arise: does the human race have any moral
45 justification for its existence? . . .

Why do we behave worse to one another than other animals? We live in ways for which we are not designed and so our daily existence interferes with our natural functioning, and this activates our natural response to threat: aggression. How has this happened? Why, in the first place, do we live in urban, crowded,
50 regimented groups, working like machines (mostly for the benefit of other men) and with no real control of our lives? Probably this situation could not have been avoided. Men did not suddenly become possessors of human minds and then use them to solve the problems of existence. These problems were constantly posed and solved within an inherited organization or social structure, and this structure
55 was redeveloped to deal with new problems as they arose. So there was probably never much chance for new thinking. As men's minds clarified they were already living in herds or groups, and these would have evolved into tribes and societies. Like waking sleepers they would not know dream from reality.

What problems did these half-awake, superstitious men have to face? They
60 were biologically so successful that they probably became too numerous for their environments and they could not go on living as loose bands of scavengers and hunters. And the environment itself changed, sometimes suddenly and some-times gradually but inevitably. And perhaps the relationship between earlier in-stincts and human awareness produced its own problems. All these changes
65 required adaptations in social organization and created new opportunities for leadership. Habits and techniques of control would be strengthened. In critical times any non-conformity would be a danger to the group. People who are controlled by others in this way soon lose the ability to act for themselves, even if their leaders do not make it dangerous for them to do so. And then, as I shall
70 explain, the natural feelings of opposition become moralized and work to per-petuate the very organization they basically oppose – it is an organization held together by the aggression it creates. Aggression has become moralized, and morality has become a form of violence. I shall describe how this happens.

Once the social structure exists it tends to be perpetuated. The organizing
75 groups, the leaders, receive privileges. Some of these were perhaps necessary in the critical situations that created the need for leadership. But the justification for them becomes less when they are inherited by their children. At the same time they become more extensive and entrenched. They become an injustice. But the organizing group becomes self-justifying, because although its position is unjust
80 it is the administrator of justice. At first opposition to it will not be revolutionary or even political; it will be 'meaningless' and involve personal discontents and frustrations. When personal problems become public problems, as they must for the people involved in them, they are distorted, and then people seem to be acting in arbitrary, self-regarding ways. This can always be shown to be socially dis-
85 ruptive, of course. In this way an unjust society causes and defines crime; and an aggressive social structure which is unjust and must create aggressive social disruption, receives the moral sanction of being 'law and order'. Law and order is one of the steps taken to maintain injustice.

People with unjust social privileges have an obvious emotional interest in
social morality. It allows them to maintain their privileges and justifies them in
taking steps to do so. It reflects their fear of an opposition that would often take
everything they have, even their lives. This is one way in which social morality
becomes angry and aggressive.

But there is another way. Social morality is also a safe form of obedience for
many of the victims of the unjust organization. It gives them a form of innocence
founded on fear – but it is never a peaceful innocence. It is a sort of character
easily developed in childhood, when power relations are at their starkest. Then
it is dangerous to have aggressive ideas against those in power because they can
easily punish you, they are stronger and cleverer, and if you destroyed them how
could you live? (In adults this becomes: We can't have a revolution because the
buses wouldn't run and I'd be late for work. Or: Hitler made the trains run on
time.) Our society has the structure of a pyramid of aggression and as the child is
the weakest member it is at the bottom. We still *think* we treat children with
special kindness and make special allowances for them, as indeed most animals
do. But do we? Don't most people believe they have a right, even a duty, to use
crude force against children as part of their education? Almost all organizations
dealing with children are obsessed with discipline. Whenever possible we put
them into uniforms and examine their minds like warders frisking prisoners.
We force them to live by the clock before they can read it, though this makes no
biological sense. We build homes without proper places for them. They interfere
with the getting of money so mothers leave them and go to work – and some of
them are no longer even physically able to feed their own children. Parents are
worn out by daily competitive striving so they can't tolerate the child's natural
noise and mess. They don't know why it cries, they don't know *any* of its inarti-
culate language. The child's first word isn't 'mummy' or 'daddy', it is 'me'. It has
been learning to say it through millions of years of evolution, and it has a biological right to its egocentricity because that is the only way our species can continue.

The point is this: every child is born with certain biological expectations, or
if you like species' assumptions – that its unpreparedness will be cared for, that
it will be given not only food but emotional reassurance, that its vulnerability
will be shielded, that it will be born into a world waiting to receive it, and that
knows *how* to receive it. But the weight of aggression in our society is so heavy
that the unthinkable happens: we batter it. And when the violence is not so crude
it is still there, spread thinly over years; the final effect is the same and so the
dramatic metaphor I used to describe it was the stoning of a baby in its pram.
This is not done by thugs but by people who like plays condemning thugs.

One way or the other the child soon learns that it is born into a strange world
and not the world it evolved for: we are no longer born free. So the small, infin-
itely vulnerable child panics – as any animal must. It does not get the reassurance
it needs, and in its fear it identifies with the people who have power over it. That
is, it accepts their view of the situation, their judgement of who is right and
wrong – their *morality*. . . .

Not all children grow up in this way, of course. Some solve the problem by
135 becoming cynical and indifferent, others hide in a listless, passive conformity,
others become criminal and openly destructive. Whatever happens, most of them
will grow up to act in ways that are ugly, deceitful and violent; and the con-
forming, socially moralized, good citizens will be the most violent of all, because
their aggression is expressed through all the technology and power of massed
140 society. The institutions of morality and order are always more destructive than
crime. This century has made that very clear.

Even if a child escapes undamaged it will still face the same problems as a man.
We treat men as children. They have no real political or economic control of their
lives, and this makes them afraid of society and their own impotence in it. Marx
145 has described adult alienation very well, but we can now understand more about
it. We can see that most men are spending their lives doing things for which they
are not biologically designed. We are not designed for our production lines,
housing blocks, even cars; and these things are not designed for us. They are
designed, basically, to make profit. And because we do not even need most of the
150 things we waste our lives in producing, we have to be surrounded by commercial
propaganda to make us buy them. This life is so unnatural for us that, for straight-
forward biological reasons, we become tense, nervous and aggressive, and these
characteristics are fed back into our young. Tension and aggression are even
becoming the markings of our species. Many people's faces are set in patterns of
155 alarm, coldness or threat; and they move jerkily and awkwardly, not with the
simplicity of free animals. These expressions are signs of moral disease, but we
are taught to admire them. They are used in commercial propaganda and in
iconographic pictures of politicians and leaders, even writers; and of course they
are taken as signs of good manners in the young.
160 It is for these reasons I say that society is held together by the aggression it
creates, and men are not dangerously aggressive but our sort of society is. It
creates aggression in these ways: first, it is basically unjust, and second it makes
people live unnatural lives – both things which create a natural, biological aggressive response in the members of society. Society's formal answer to this is social-
165 ized morality; but this, as I have explained, is only another form of violence, and
so it must itself provoke more aggression. There is no way out for our sort of
society, an unjust society must be violent. Any organization which denies the
basic need for biological justice must become aggressive, even though it claims
to be moral. This is true of most religions, which say that justice can only be ob-
170 tained in another world, and not in this. It is also true of many movements for
political reform. . . .

Our situation has been made much worse, at least for the time being, by our
technological success. The problem can now be described in this brief, schematic
way.
175 We evolved in a biosphere but we live in what is more and more becoming a
technosphere. We do not fit into it very well and so it activates our biological
defences, one of which is aggression. Our environment is changing so rapidly that
we cannot wait for biological solutions to evolve. Se we should either change our
technosphere or use technology to change human nature. But change in our

180 society is really decided on urgent commercial imperatives, so nothing is done to solve our main problem. But a species living in an unfavourable environment dies out. For us the end will probably be quicker because the aggression we generate will be massively expressed through our technology.

This is very over-simplified and our fate is far from being so certain. But the
185 combination of technology and sozialized morality is very ugly, and it could lead to disaster. Alternatively, governments could begin to use technology to enforce socialized morality. That is, by using drugs, selection, conditioning, genetics and so on, they could manufacture people who would fit into society. This would be just as disastrous. So if we do not want either of these things we
190 must do something else. There are signs, in the search for counter-cultures and alternative politics, that we are beginning to do so.

What ought we to do? Live justly. But what is justice? Justice is allowing people to live in the way for which they evolved. Human beings have an emotional and physical need to do so, it is their biological expectation. They *can* only live
195 in this way, or all the time struggle consciously or unconsciously to do so. That is the essential thing I want to say. . . .

We can express this basic need in many ways: aesthetic, intellectual, the need to love, create, protect and enjoy. These are not higher things that can be added when more basic needs are met. *They* are basic. They must be the way in which
200 we express all our existence, and if they do not control our daily life then we cannot function as human beings at all. . . .

I have not answered many of the questions I have raised, but I have tried to explain things that often go unnoticed but which must be put right if anything is to work for us. They are difficult to put right because reforms easily become
205 socially moralized. It is so easy to subordinate justice to power, but when this happens power takes on the dynamics and dialectics of aggression, and then nothing is really changed. Marx did not know about this problem and Lenin discovered it when it was too late. It is important that understanding of this problem becomes part of contemporary socialism. Unless it does, change will
210 become slower and more difficult. . . .

Finally, I have not tried to say what the future should be like, because that is a mistake. If your plan of the future is too rigid you start to coerce people to fit into it. We do not need a plan of the future, we need a method of change.

Extract from author's preface in *Lear* by Edward Bond. (1972)   (*slightly abridged*)

Pete Hamill

97 Two Minutes to Midnight: The Very Last Hurrah

Pete Hamill, who has been a columnist for the *New York Post* and a contributing
editor to *New York* magazine, describes himself as "a free man, a New Yorker, a
Democrat, and an American—in that order. And I would gladly give up the last
three descriptions to retain the first." His reportage of the Vietnam War in 1966
5 grasped the tragedy this country did not feel until several years later. He is the
author of *Irrational Ravings* and most recently a novel, *The Gift*.

Los Angeles—It was, of course, two minutes to midnight and the Embassy
Room of the Ambassador Hotel was rowdy with triumph. Red and blue balloons
drifted up through three golden chandeliers to bump against a gilded ceiling.
10 Young girls with plastic Kennedy boaters chanted like some lost reedy chorus
from an old Ray Charles record. The crowd was squashed against the bandstand,
a smear of black faces and Mexican-American faces and bearded faces and Beverly
Hills faces crowned with purple hair. Eleven tv cameras were turning, their
bright blue arclights changing the crowd into a sweaty stew. Up on the band-
15 stand, with his wife standing just behind him, was Robert Kennedy.
    "I'd like to express my high regard for Don Drysdale," Kennedy said. Drysdale
had just won his sixth straight shutout. "I hope we have his support in this
campaign." There was a loud cheer. He thanked Rafer Johnson and Rosey Grier
(cheers) and Jesse Unruh (timid cheer) and Cesar Chavez (very loud cheers), and
20 he thanked the staff and the volunteers and the voters, and the crowd hollered
after every sentence. It was the sort of scene that Kennedys have gone through a
hundred times and more; on this night, at least, it did not appear that there
would be a last hurrah. Kennedy had not scored a knockout over Eugene
McCarthy; but a points decision at least would keep his campaign going.
25   "I thank all of you," Kennedy was saying. "Mayor Yorty has just sent a message that we have been here too long already" (laughter). "So my thanks to all of
you, and now it's on to Chicago. ..."
    I was at the rear of the stand, next to George Plimpton. Kennedy put his
thumb up to the audience, brushed his hair, made a small V with his right hand,
30 and turned to leave. The crowd started shouting: "We want Bobby! We want
Bobby!" Plimpton and I went down three steps, and turned left through a gaunt-
let of Kennedy volunteers and private cops in brown uniforms.
    We found ourselves in a long grubby area called the pantry. It was the sort of
place where Puerto Ricans, blacks and Mexican Americans usually work to fill
35 white stomachs. There were high bluish fluorescent lights strung across the ceiling, a floor of raw sandy-colored concrete, pale dirty walls. On the right were a
rusty ice machine and shelves filled with dirty glasses. On the left, an archway led
into the main kitchen and under the arch a crowd of Mexican American cooks
and busboys waited to see Kennedy. Against the left wall, three table-sized serving

40 carts stood end to end, and at the far end were two doors leading to the press
room where Kennedy was going to talk to reporters.

Kennedy moved slowly into the area, shaking hands, smiling, heading a platoon
of reporters, photographers, staffers, the curious tv men. I was in front of him,
walking backward. I saw him turn to his left and shake the hand of a small
45 Mexican cook. We could still hear the chants of "We want Bobby!" from the
Embassy Room. The cook was smiling and pleased.

Then a pimply messenger arrived from the secret filthy heart of America. He
was curly haired, wearing a pale blue sweatshirt and bluejeans, and he was planted
with his right foot forward and his right arm straight out and he was firing a
50 gun.

The scene assumed a kind of insane fury, all jump cuts, screams, noise, hurtling
bodies, blood. The shots went pap-pap, pap-pap-pap, small sharp noises like a
distant firefight or the sound of firecrackers in a back-yard. Rosey Grier of the
Los Angeles Rams came from nowhere and slammed his great bulk into the
55 gunman, crunching him against a serving table. George Plimpton grabbed for the
guy's arm and Rafer Johnson moved to him, right behind Bill Barry, Kennedy's
friend and security chief, and they were all making deep animal sounds and still
the bullets came.

"Get the gun, get the gun."
60 "Rafer, get the gun!"
"Get the fucking gun!"

"No," someone said. And you could hear the stunned horror in the voice, the
replay of old scenes, the muffle of drums. "No, No. Noooooooooooo!"

We knew then that America had struck again. In this slimy little indoor alley
65 in the back of a gaudy ballroom, in this shabby reality behind the glittering facade,
Americans were doing what they do best: killing and dying, and cursing because
hope doesn't last very long among us.

I saw Kennedy lurch against the ice machine, and then sag, and then fall forward slowly, to be grabbed by someone, and I knew then that he was dead. He
70 might linger a few hours, or a few days; but his face reminded me somehow of
Benny Paret the night Emile Griffith hammered him into unconsciousness.
Kennedy's face had a kind of sweet acceptance to it, the eyes understanding that
it had come to him, the way it had come to so many others before him. The price
of the attempt at excellence was death. You saw a flicker of that understanding
75 on his face, as his life seeped out of a hole in the back of his skull to spread like a
spilled wine across the scummy concrete floor.

It was as if all of us there went simultaneously insane: a cook was screaming,
"Kill him, kill him now, kill him, kill him!" I tried to get past Grier, Johnson,
Plimpton, and Barry to get at the gunman. The Jack Ruby in me was rising up
80 white, bright, with a high singing sound in the ears, and I wanted to damage that
insane little bastard they were holding. I wanted to break his face, to rip away
flesh, to hear bone break as I pumped punches into that pimpled skin. Budd
Schulberg was next to me; I suppose he was trying to do the same. Just one punch.
Just one for Dallas. Just one for Medgar Evers, just one for Martin Luther King.
85 Just one punch. Just one. One.

Kennedy was lying on the floor, with black rosary beads in his hand, and blood on his fingers. His eyes were still open, and as his wife Ethel reached him, to kneel in an orange-and-white dress, his lips were moving. We heard nothing. Ethel smoothed his face, running ice cubes along his cheeks. There was a lot of
90 shouting, and a strange chorus of high screaming. My notes showed that Kennedy was shot at 12.10, and was taken out of that grubby hole at 12.32. It seemed terribly longer.

I don't remember how it fits into the sequence, but I do have one picture of Rosey Grier holding the gunman by the neck, choking the life out of him.
95 "Rosey, Rosey, don't kill him. We want him alive. Don't kill him, Rosey, don't kill him."

"Kill the bastard, kill that sum of a bitch bastard," a Mexican busboy yelled.

"Don't kill him, Rosey."

"Where's the doctor? Where in Christ's name is the doctor?"
100 Grier decided not to kill the gunman. They had him up on a serving table at the far end of the pantry, as far as they could get him from Kennedy. Jimmy Breslin and I were standing up on the table, peering into the gunman's face. His eyes were rolling around, and then stopping, and then rolling around again. The eyes contained pain, flight, entrapment, and a strange kind of bitter endurance. I didn't
105 want to hit him anymore.

"Where the fuck is the doctor? Can't they get a fucking doctor?"

"Move back."

"Here comes a doctor, here's a doctor."

"MOVE BACK!"
110 Kennedy was very still now. There was a thin film of blood on his brow. They had his shoes off and his shirt open. The stretcher finally arrived, and he trembled as they lifted him, his lips moved, and the flashbulbs blinked off one final salvo and he was gone.

The rest was rote: I ran out into the lobby and picked up my brother Brian and
115 we rushed to the front entrance. A huge black man, sick with grief and anger and bitterness, was throwing chairs around. Most landed in the pool. The young Kennedy girls were crying and wailing, knowing, I suppose, what the guys my age discovered in Dallas: youth was over. "Sick," one girl kept saying. "Sick. Sick. What kind of country is this? Sick. Sick." Outside, there were cops every-
120 where, and sirens. The cops were trying to get one of the wounded into a taxi. The cabbie didn't want to take him, afraid, I suppose, that blood would sully his nice plastic upholstery.

When we got through the police barricades, we drove without talk to the Hospital of the Good Samaritan, listening to the news on the radio. The unspoken
125 thought was loudest: the country's gone. Medgar Evers was dead, Malcolm Y was dead, Martin Luther King was dead, Jack Kennedy was dead, and now Robert Kennedy was dying. The hell with it. The hatred was now general. I hated that pimpled kid in that squalid cellar enough to want to kill him. He hated Kennedy the same way. That kid and the bitter Kennedy haters were the same. All those
130 people in New York who hated Kennedy's guts, who said "eccch" when his name was mentioned, the ones who creamed over Murray Kempton's vicious

diatribes these past few months: they were the same. When Evers died, when King died, when Jack Kennedy died, all the bland pundits said that some good would come of it in some way, that the nation would go through a catharsis, that
135 somehow the bitterness, the hatred, the bigotry, the evil of racism, the glib violence would be erased. That was bullshit. We will have our four-day televised orgy of remorse about Robert Kennedy and then it will be business as usual.

You could feel that as we drove through the empty L. A. streets, listening to the sirens screaming in the night. Nothing would change. Kennedy's death would
140 mean nothing. It was just another digit in the great historical pageant that includes the slaughter of Indians, the plundering of Mexico, the enslavement of black people, the humiliation of Puerto Ricans. Just another digit. Nothing would come of it. While Kennedy's life was ebbing out of him, Americans were dropping bombs and flaming jelly on Orientals. While the cops fingerprinted the gunmen,
145 Senator Eastland's Negro subjects were starving. While the cops made chalk marks on the floor of the pantry, the brave members of the National Rifle Association were already explaining that people commit crimes, guns don't (as if Willie Mays could hit a home run without a bat). These cowardly bums claim Constitutional rights to kill fierce deer in the forests, and besides, suppose the
150 niggers come to the house and we don't have anything to shoot them with? Suppose we have to fight a nigger man-to-man?

America the Beautiful: with crumby little mini-John Waynes carrying guns to the woods like surrogate penises. Yes: the kid I saw shoot Kennedy was from Jordan, was diseased with some fierce hatred for Jews. Sam Yorty, who hated
155 Kennedy, now calls Kennedy a great American and blames the Communists. Hey Sam: you killed him too. The gun that kid carried was American. The city where he shot down a good man was run by Sam Yorty. How about keeping your fat pigstink mouth shut.

At the approach to the Good Samaritan Hospital the cops had strung red flares
160 across the gutter, and were stopping everyone. A crowd of about 75 people were on the corner when we arrived, about a third of them black. I went in, past those black people who must have felt that there was no white man at all with whom they could talk. A mob of reporters was assembled at the hospital entrance. The cops were polite, almost gentle, as if they sensed that something really bad had
165 happened, and that many of these reporters were friends of the dying man.

Most of the hospital windows were dark, and somewhere up there Robert Kennedy was lying on a table while strangers stuck things into his brain looking for a killer's bullet. We were friends, and I didn't want him to die but if he were to be a vegetable, I didn't want him to live either.
170 We drove home, through the wastelands around L.A. and the canyons through the mountains to the south. When I got home, my wife was asleep, the tv still playing out its record of the death watch. Frank Reynolds of ABC, a fine reporter and a compassionate man, was so upset he could barely control his anger. I called some friends and poured a drink. Later I talked to my old man, who came to
175 this country from Ireland in flight from the Protestant bigots of Belfast 40 years ago. I suppose he loved John Kennedy even more than I did and he has never really been the same since Dallas. Now it had happened again.

"If you see Teddy," he said, "tell him to get out of politics. The Kennedys are too good for this country."

180   I remembered the night in 1964, in that bitter winter after John Kennedy's murder, when Robert Kennedy appeared at a St. Patrick's Day dinner in Scranton, Pennsylvania. He talked about the Irish, and the long journey that started on the quays of Wexford and ended in Parkland Hospital. He reminded them of the days when there were signs that said "No Irish Need Apply" (and it was always

185   to his greatest dismay that so many sons of Irishmen he came across in New York were bigots and haters). Bob told them about Owen O'Neill, an Irish patriot whose ideals had survived his martyrdom. Men were crying as he read the old Irish ballad:

> *Oh, why did you leave us, Owen?*
190 > *Why did you die? . . .*
> *We're sheep without a shepherd,*
> *When the snow shuts out the sky.*
> *Oh, why did you leave us, Owen?*
> *Why did you die?*

195   I didn't know. There was some sort of answer for John Kennedy, and another for Robert Kennedy. But I had learned that I knew nothing finally, that when my two young daughters present the bill to me in another 10 years, I won't have much to say. I sat there drinking rum until I was drunk enough to forget that pimpled face cracking off the rounds into the body of a man who was a friend of

200   mine. Finally, easily, with the sun up, I fell asleep on the couch. I didn't have any tears left for America, but I suppose not many other Americans did either.

Extract from article in *The Village Voice*. (1968)   *(unabridged)*

98

A Passage on Drugs From

is DoPE KiLLiNGOUR MUSICiANS?

By Cab Calloway

For years now the public has been aware that many jazz musicians smoke marijuana. There were times when the extent of this was exaggerated by lurid articles and the columnists who thrive on sordid sensationalism. There are still numberless Americans who equate music with marijuana, who feel that every jazzman is automatically a reefer smoker. This kind of publicity has been very harmful to us musicians. It has deprived us of many opportunities for good bookings, and has hurt the average musician who, I know, lives cleanly, works hard and is a law-abiding citizen.

People have often asked me why reefer-smoking is so prevalent among musicians. That is no easy question to answer since it involves an examination of the musician's environment and the economic insecurity from which he suffers so much. The band business is a hectic one, which seldom permits a man to live a fairly stable life. Musicians are constantly on the move, their hours are abnormally irregular and the general pressure of work creates physical fatigue that is sometimes unbearable. Many musicians seek an escape through indulgence in drugs as an antidote to the serious frustration which besets so many musicians. . . .

The so-called experts vary greatly in their opinions on how serious marijuana smoking is to the system. United States Public Health Service experiments revealed:

• Although marijuana lessens inhibitions, it does not incite normally law-abiding people to crime It releases the user's inhibitions in a manner similar to alcohol.

• It does not improve a person's musical ability, though the average smoker is convinced this is so.

Over the years I have known many a superlative musician who occasionally "lights up." One jazz critic . . . claims he knows some top jazzmen whose playing improves when they are very high.

I disagree violently with this statement. My observations have proved to me that marijuana, or any other drug, weakens a player's performance because it slows down his reactions, muddies his thinking, and distorts his tone. There is no acceptable substitute for sobriety while playing. Intoxication, far from releasing talent, creates confusion.

Cab Calloway
"Is Dope Killing Our Musicians?"
Ebony

This last finding is by far the most significant for musicians. I have long known that marijuana injures rather than aids musicianship. Under its influence any mediocre musician feels he is great. I have watched musicians playing while high and noticed that their musical standards drop sharply although they suffer from the tragic delusion that they are playing more brilliantly than when they are sober.

Too often, a couple of reefers serve to bolster a poor musician's opinion of himself. He may have only a slight knowledge of the basic chords and scales but after smoking his quota of "gage," he rapidly becomes in his own estimation a genius somewhere between a Heifetz and a Horowitz. Some persons find enjoyment watching the antics of these poor deluded men playing horribly bad music under the impression they are creating deathless solos. I have always found it a tragic thing to see and to hear.

A person using marihuana finds it harder to make decisions that require clear thinking. And he finds himself more easily open to other people's suggestions.

"Marihuana" Some Questions and Answers

A Passage on Drugs From

MANCHILD IN THE PROMISED LAND

BY CLAUDE BROWN

I never got too involved with drugs, but it gave me a pretty painful moment. I was walking down Eighth Avenue, and I saw somebody across the street. It was a familiar shape and a familiar walk. My heart lit up.

The person looked like something was wrong with her, even though she was walking all right and still had her nice shape. It was Sugar. She was walking in the middle of the street.

I ran across the street and snatched her by the arm. I was happy. I knew she'd be happy to see me, because I hadn't seen her in a long time. I said, "Sugar, hey, baby, what you doin'? You tryin' to commit suicide or somethin'? Why don't you just go and take some sleeping pills? I think it would be less painful, and it would be easier on the street cleaners."

I expected her to grab me and hug me and be just as glad to see me, but she just looked around and said, "Oh, hi." Her face looked bad. She looked old, like somebody who'd been crying a long time because they had lost somebody, like a member of the family had died.

I said, "What's wrong, baby? What's the matter?"

She looked at me and said, "You don't know?"

"Uh-uh, uh-uh."

I looked at her, and she said, "Yeah, baby, that's the way it is. I've got a jones," and she dropped her head.

I was so hurt and stunned I just didn't know what to do. I said, "Come on, Sugar, let me take you someplace where I know you can get some help. Look, there's a man in East Harlem. His name is Reverend Eddie, and he's been doing a lot of good work with young drug addicts, and I think he could help you. He could get you into Metropolitan Hospital or Manhattan General, one of the places where they've started treating drug addicts. Come on, you got to get a cure, baby. This life is not for you."

I pulled on her, and she said, "Claude, Claude, I'm sick. There's only one thing you can do for me if you really want to help me. There's only one thing anybody can do for me right now, and that's loan me five dollars to get me some stuff, because I feel like I'm dyin'. Oh, Lord, I feel so bad."

I looked at her, and she was a part of my childhood. I just couldn't stand to see her suffer. I only had one five-dollar bill and some change. I said, "Look, baby, why don't you get off this thing? Because it's gonna be the same story tomorrow. You'll just be delaying it until another day."

"Look, Claude, I'll go anyplace with you, but I can't go now. In a little while, I'm gon be laying down in the street there holdin' my stomach and hopin' a car runs over me before the pains get any worse."

. . . "Come on with me. I'm not gon give you another five dollars to go and give it to somebody and get bit again. Come on with me. . . . I'll get you some drugs and take care of that. Then we're gon see about doin' something for you." . . .

Ruby brought in the works; she had a make-shift syringe with a spike on the end of it. She was holding it upside down. I'd given her the five dollars when I first came in. She handed the spike to Sugar, and Sugar paid it no mind. She just rolled down her stocking and pinched her thigh. I saw the needle marks on her thigh.

I watched the syringe as the blood came up into the drugs that seemed like dirty water. It just filled up with blood, and as the blood and the drugs started its way down into the needle, I thought, This is our childhood. Our childhood had been covered with blood, as the drugs had been. Covered with blood and gone down into somewhere. I wondered where.

I wanted to say, "Sugar, I'm sorry. I'm sorry for the time I didn't kiss you at the bus. I'm sorry for not telling people that you were my girl friend. I'm sorry for never telling you that I loved you and for never asking you to be my girl friend." I wanted to say, 'I'm sorry for everything. . . .'"

I got up, went over to where Sugar was sitting, bent over, and kissed her. She smiled and went into another nod.

That was the last time I saw her, nodding and climbing up on the duji cloud.

Claude Brown
Manchild in the Promised Land

For every day of the year, at least one junkie dies in New York, a suicide, accident or homicide, due to either an overdose or a scarcity of heroin. They are almost all young people, these junkies dying before their time . . .

Alvin Moscow
Merchants of Heroin

T. C. McLuhan (ed.)

100 Proclamation:
To the Great White Father and All His People

We, the native Americans, re-claim the land known as Alcatraz Island in the name of all American Indians by right of discovery.

We wish to be fair and honorable in our dealings with the Caucasian inhabitants of this land, and hereby offer the following treaty:

5   We will purchase said Alcatraz Island for twenty-four dollars ($24) in glass beads and red cloth, a precedent set by the white man's purchase of a similar island about 300 years ago. We know that $24 in trade goods for these 16 acres is more than was paid when Manhatten Island was sold, but we know that land values have risen over the years. Our offer of $1.24 per acre is greater than the

10   47¢ per acre that the white men are now paying the California Indians for their land. We will give to the inhabitants of this island a portion of that land for their own, to be held in trust by the American Indian Affairs and by the bureau of Caucasian Affairs to hold in perpetuity—for as long as the sun shall rise and the rivers go down to the sea. We will further guide the inhabitants in the proper way

15   of living. We will offer them our religion, our education, our life ways, in order to help them achieve our level of civilization and thus raise them and all their white brothers up from their savage and unhappy state. We offer this treaty in good faith and wish to be fair and honorable in our dealings with all white men. . . .

We feel that this so-called Alcatraz Island is more than suitable for an Indian

20   Reservation, as determined by the white man's own standards. By this we mean that this place resembles most Indian reservations in that:

1. It is isolated from modern facilities, and without adequate means of transportation.
2. It has no fresh running water.
25 3. It has inadequate sanitation facilities.
4. There are no oil or mineral rights.
5. There is no industry and so unemployment is very great.
6. There are no health care facilities.
7. The soil is rocky and non-productive; and the land does not support game.
30 8. There are no educational facilities.
9. The population has always exceeded the land base.
10. The population has always been held as prisoners and kept dependent upon others.

Further, it would be fitting and symbolic that ships from all over the world,

35   entering the Golden Gate, would first see Indian land and thus be reminded of the true history of this nation. This tiny island would be a symbol of the great lands once ruled by free and noble Indians.

Edited extract from *Touch the Earth: A Self-Portrait of Indian Existence* compiled by T.C. McLuhan. (1971)

Mary Danby

101 It Was After Lights Out...

It was after lights-out at the Greengrocer's . . .

'We have always BEAN BERRY GRAPE friends,' said BASIL. 'I think you're a perfect PEACH.'

'I'll always BEETROOT to you,' replied ROSEMARY.

'Then LETTUCE get married,' urged BASIL. 'I'll buy you a 22-CARROT gold nng.'

'Yes, I will MARROW you. Will you ORANGE the wedding? We must fix a DATE and I must buy some pretty CLOVES.'

'Mind you get to the church on THYME.'

They were married last week and are now living in a semi-detached crate. There isn't MUSHROOM and the crate LEEKS, but they're a happy PEAR.

It was after lights-out at the Grocer's . . .

'Enough of your SAUCE OLIVE,' said T. BAG. 'You're ill-BREAD. If you don't POLISH your manners, you'll find you DETER GENTlemen like me. SOAP please do EGGS-actly as I say.

'You're CRACKERS!' re-plied OLIVE with SPIRIT. 'HAM a lot BUTTER than you so mind your TONGUE. OIL be surprised if you CAN ever KETCHUP with me. All this STUFF-ING yourself with SAU-SAGES making you FAT HONEY. SALAMI to do as I please, at YEAST.'

T BAG shrugged. 'SUET yourself.'

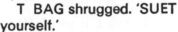

It was after lights-out at the Butcher's . . .

'Hello, SIR LOIN! How do you VEAL?'

'Just OFFAL. Not to MINCE matters, Mrs. BRISKET brought her CHOPping basket and was just about to FILLET when she SAW DUST at the bottom. Imagine!'

'Take HEART, SIR LOIN. I took a cloth to RABBIT clean.'

'But it gave me such a sHOCK, you know.'

'What a silly GOOSE you are. GAMMON, let'S TEAK a trip to VENISON MEAT STEWart and see what's cooking.'

It was a load of TRIPE!

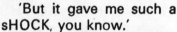

It was after lights-out at the Fishmonger's . . .

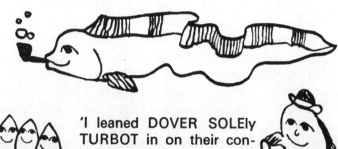

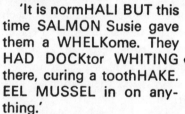

'I leaned DOVER SOLEly TURBOT in on their conversation.'

'Was it in the market PLAICE?'

'It is normHALI BUT this time SALMON Susie gave them a WHELKome. They HAD DOCKtor WHITING there, curing a toothHAKE. EEL MUSSEL in on anything.'

'Well, ROEs, I COD listen all day, but I CONGER on or I'll misS KATE. I said I'd KIPPER look out for her. TARTAR for now.'

(FIN)

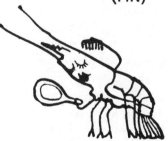

Mary Danby for extracts from 'It Was After Lights Out' from *The Armada Book of Fun*, published by Wm. Collins Sons & Co. Ltd, © 1970.

(unabridged)

J. L. Styan

102 Dramatic Dialogue Is More Than Conversation

Any artificial picture of life must start from the detail of actuality. An audience must be able to recognize it; however changed, we want to check it against experience. Death, for example, is something we cannot know. In *Everyman* it is represented as a man embodying some of our feelings about it. So Death is partly
5 humanized, enough, anyway, for us to be able to explore what the dramatist thinks about it.

So it is with dramatic speech. A snatch of phrase caught in everyday conversation may mean little. Used by an actor on a stage, it can assume general and typical qualities. The context into which it is put can make it pull more than its conver-
10 sational weight, no matter how simple the words. Consider Othello's bare repetition: 'Put out the light, and then put out the light.' In its context the repetition prefigures precisely the comparison Shakespeare is about to make between the lamp Othello is holding and Desdemona's life and being. Its heavy rhythm suggests the strained tone and obsessed mood of the man, and an almost priest-
15 like attitude behind the twin motions. We begin to see the murder of Desdemona in the larger general terms of a ritualistic sacrifice. ... Dramatic speech, with its basis in ordinary conversation, is speech that has had a specific pressure put on it.

Why do words begin to assume general qualities, and why do they become dramatic? Here are two problems on either side of the same coin. The words in
20 both cases depend upon the kind of attention we give them. The artists using them, whether author or actor, force them upon us, and in a variety of ways try to fix the quality of our attention. ...

'Whatever you think, I'm going to tell him what you said' is a remark which in its context can shed light on the speaker, the person spoken to and the person
25 spoken about. For a fourth person listening, as a spectator witnesses a play, there may also be an element of irony, in that he recognizes attitudes and a relationship between the two who are talking that mean something only to himself as observer.

In the play the difference lies first in an insistence that the words go somewhere,
30 move towards a predetermined end. It lies in a charge of meaning that will advance the action. This is argued in a statement in Strindberg's manifesto for the naturalistic theatre. He says of his characters that he has 'permitted the minds to work irregularly as they do in reality, where, during conversation, the cogs of one mind seem more or less haphazardly to engage those of another one, where
35 no topic is fully exhausted'. But he adds that, while the dialogue seems to stray a good deal in the opening scenes, 'it acquires a material that later on is worked over, picked up again, repeated, expounded, and built up like the theme in a musical composition'.

It is a question of economy. The desultory and clumsy talk of real life, with its
40 interruptions, overlappings, indecisions and repetitions, talk without direction, wastes our interest—unless it hides relevance in irrelevances.

When the actor examines the text to prepare his part, he *looks* for what makes the words different from conversation.... . The clues sought by the actor hidden beneath the surface of the dialogue are the playgoer's guides too.

45 The actor and producer Stanislavsky has called these clues the 'subtext' of a play:

'The subtext is a web of innumerable, varied inner patterns inside a play and a part, woven from "magic ifs", given circumstances, all sorts of figments of the imagination, inner movements, objects of attention, smaller and greater truths
50 and a belief in them, adaptations, adjustments and other similar elements. It is the subtext that makes us say the words we do in a play.'

And in another place he says that 'the whole text of the play will be accompanied by a subtextual stream of images, like a moving picture constantly thrown on the screen of our inner vision, to guide us as we speak and act on the stage'.

55 Once we admit that the words must propose and substantiate the play's meaning, we shall find in them more and more of the author's wishes. For dramatic dialogue has other work to do before it provides a table of words to be spoken. In the absence of the author it must provide a set of unwritten working directives to the actor on how to speak its speeches.

50 Some tell the producer how to arrange the figures on the stage. Others tell him what he should hear as the pattern of sound echoing and contradicting, changing tone, rising and falling. These are directives strongly compelling him to hear the key in which a scene should be played, and the tone and tempo of the melody. Others oblige him to start particular rhythmic movements of emotion flowing
65 between the stage and the audience. He is then left to marry the colour and shape of the stage picture with the music he finds recorded in the text.

Good dialogue works like this and throws out a 'subtextual stream of images'. Even if the limits within which these effects work are narrow, even if the effect lies in the barest or the simplest of speeches, we may expect to hear the text
70 humming the tune as it cannot in real life. Dialogue should be read and heard as a dramatic score.

Extract from *The Elements of Drama* by J.L. Styan. (1960)

S.I. Hayakawa

103 Abstraction Ladder

Start reading from the bottom UP

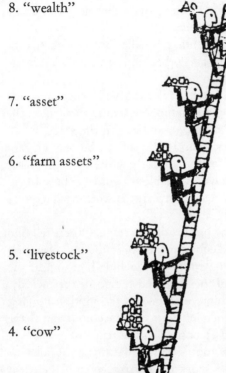

8. "wealth"

8. The word "wealth" is at an extremely high level of abstraction, omitting *almost* all reference to the characteristics of Bessie. 5

7. "asset"

7. When Bessie is referred to as an "asset," still more of her characteristics are left out.

6. "farm assets"

6. When Bessie is included among "farm assets," reference is made 10 only to what she has in common with all other salable items on the farm.

5. "livestock"

5. When Bessie is referred to as "livestock," only those characteristics she 15 has in common with pigs, chickens, goats, etc., are referred to.

4. "cow"

4. The word "cow" stands for the characteristics we have abstracted as common to cow_1, cow_2, cow_3 ... cow_n. Characteristics peculiar to specific cows are left out. 20

3. "Bessie"

3. The word "Bessie" (cow_1) is the *name* we give to the object of perception of level 2. The name *is not* the object; it merely *stands for* the object and omits reference to many of the 25 characteristics of the object.

2.

2. The cow we perceive is not the word, but the object of experience, that which our nervous system abstracts (selects) from the totality that constitutes the process-cow. Many of the char- 30 acteristics of the process-cow are left out.

1. The cow known to science ultimately consists of atoms, electrons, etc., according to present-day scientific inference. Characteristics (represented by circles) are infinite at this level and ever-changing. This is the *process level*. 35

We are grateful to George Allen & Unwin (Publishers) Ltd for permission to reproduce 'Abstraction Ladder' from *Language in Thought and Action* by S.I. Hayakawa © 1974.

Biographies

ALBEE, Edward (1928–), was born in Washington, D. C. and was adopted as a baby by the millionaire Reed Albee. He had a spoilt and troubled adolescence and in 1948 he quarrelled with the strong-minded Mrs Albee and left home for good. During the ten years that followed he was everything from an office boy to a Western Union messenger. His career as a successful playwright began with *The Zoo Story* (1959). *The Sandbox* (1960) is a Beckett-like sketch for *The American Dream* (1961), the most "absurd" of Albee's plays, a savage satire on the materialism, conformism, spiritual emptiness and hypocrisy of the American public, with its desire "to be entertained rather than disturbed". Albee takes the view that it is the playwright's duty "to comment boldly and relentlessly on his time". His plays deal with such subjects as complacency about human suffering, the destructive urge to dominate, loneliness, and the difficulties of communication. His most famous play is *Who's Afraid of Virginia Woolf?* (1962), even better-known in its film version.

AUDEN, Wystan Hugh (1907–1973), was born in York and educated at Oxford. He was a schoolmaster for a time after leaving Oxford, but soon became the most prominent figure in a new group of Left Wing writers of the 1930s. In 1939 he went to America, later becoming a U. S. citizen. In 1956 he was elected Professor of Poetry at Oxford. In addition to poems he wrote opera libretti for Stravinsky, Britten and Hans Werner Henze. Much of Auden's poetry is difficult. The need for social commitment is one of his most important themes, and his verse is full of topical references.

BECKETT, Samuel (1906–), was born into the Protestant middle class in Dublin. As a young man he taught English in Paris and French at Trinity College, Dublin. In 1937 he settled in Paris. His first novel was published the following year. Much of his work has been written in French and then translated by the author into English: writing in a foreign language makes it easier for Beckett to write without style. His play *Waiting for Godot* (1953) won him an international reputation. It is a tragic farce about two tramps, who, like most of Beckett's characters, give the impression of being the very last living beings in a society that has collapsed. *Waiting for Godot* is one of the corner-stones of the Theatre of the Absurd, of which *Come and Go* (1967) is a more extreme example. Beckett was awarded the Nobel Prize for Literature in 1969.

BETJEMAN, Sir John (1906–), who was educated at Oxford, has been Poet Laureate since 1972. His *Collected Poems* (1958) became a best-seller: his preference for simple language and traditional stanza forms, and his nostalgia for the vanishing world of his youth, exactly suited the tastes of the reading public. "I love suburbs and gas-lights and Gothic Revival churches", he has said. His love of Victorian architecture, especially Victorian railway stations, comes out clearly in his works – in prose as well as in verse – and has had considerable influence. Nevertheless what he calls "destructive progress" goes on. In 1960 Betjeman published a verse autobiography, *Summoned by Bells*. He was knighted in 1969.

BLAKE, William (1757–1827), was a great poet who engraved and illustrated his own poems. He was a difficult man who never tried to fit into the world. All his life he was on the side of the common man against authority, at a time when workers, including women and children, were harshly exploited and lived in subhuman conditions. The underlying theme of his *Songs of Innocence* (1789) is the presence of divine love even in trouble and sorrow. The *Songs of Experience* (1794) are gloomier, conveying a sense of the power of evil: in them Blake protests against narrow codes of morality. From 1800 onwards Blake did a large number of watercolours of biblical subjects, and produced designs for illustrations to Dante's *Divina Commedia*.

BRADBURY, Ray (1920–), was born in Waukegan, Illinois. His education went no further than high school. Among his volumes of science fiction short stories are *The Martian Chronicles* (1950), *The Illustrated Man* (1951; including "Marionettes, Inc."), and *The Golden Apples of the Sun* (1953; including "The Pedestrian"). His novel *Fahrenheit 451* (1953), which is full of powerful visual imagery, was filmed by François Truffaut in 1966.

CALMAN, Mel (1931–), was born in London and studied design and illustration at college. He has worked as a cartoonist for various newspapers and magazines (including *The Sunday Times*), for advertising agencies and for television. He has published several books of cartoons and has recently become involved in animated films. It was not until the 1970s that a story of his was published, though he had been writing ever since his schooldays.

CUMMINGS, Edward Estlin (1894–1962), was born in Cambridge, Massachusetts, the son of a professor at Harvard, where he himself read Classics. His experiences in a concentration camp in the First World War are described in his first book, *The Enormous Room* (1922), a prose narrative of poetic sensitivity. His first book of verse was *Tulips and Chimneys* (1923). He was also successful as a painter. His poems are characterized by puzzling eccentricities of typography, punctuation, syntax and diction. Cummings is on the side of human dignity and individuality against the heartless "unman" and the soulless "unworld". In him scrupulous craftsmanship and childlike spontaneity walk hand in hand.

DAHL, Roald (1916–), was born in South Wales, though his parents were Norwegians. In the 1930s he worked for Shell in East Africa. When the Second World War broke out he became a fighter pilot in the R.A.F. and was wounded in the Libyan desert. In 1942, by now Assistant Air Attaché in Washington, he began writing stories on flying themes: these were reprinted in his first book *Over to You* (1945, including "Yesterday was Beautiful"). His best-known book of short stories is probably *Kiss Kiss* (1960), in which he shows a taste for slightly "sick" humour. He has also written a number of screenplays, including *You Only Live Twice* (1967).

ELIOT, Thomas Stearns (1888–1965), was born in St. Louis, Missouri, and educated at Harvard, the Sorbonne and Oxford. He settled in England in 1915 and in 1922 published his best-known poem, *The Waste Land*, which depicts the vacuity, frustration and decadence of modern life. In spite of its obscurity the influence of this poem was enormous. Eliot was also an extremely influential literary critic. In 1927 he became a British subject and a member of the Church of England: works such as the verse drama *Murder in the Cathedral* (1935) testify to his religious faith. In 1948 he was awarded the Nobel Prize for Literature and the Order of Merit.

GREENE, Graham (1904–), is one of the sons of a public school headmaster. He was educated at his father's school (Berkhamsted) and at Oxford. In the 1920s and 1930s he was a journalist and film critic. In 1936 he joined the Roman Catholic Church, whose moral theology is the theme of several of his most impressive novels, including *The Heart of the Matter* (1948). His best novel is perhaps *The Power and the Glory* (1940), which tells of a persecuted "whisky priest" in Mexico. Many of his other novels are equally topical. In spite of a preoccupation with the more squalid, shabby side of life, Greene's books are rich in humour and irony: see especially his short-story collection *May We Borrow Your Husband?* (1967). Graham Greene is also the author of *The Third Man* (1950), one of the classics of the cinema.

HEMINGWAY, Ernest (1898–1961), was born in a suburb of Chicago, the son of a doctor. He was a reporter for a short time, and during the First World War he served in the American Red Cross and in the Italian infantry. He settled in Paris in 1922 and began his literary career: much of his writing is concerned with Americans in Europe. He was a war correspondent in the Spanish Civil War: his novel *For Whom the Bell Tolls* (1940) is based on his experiences in Spain. In 1954 he was awarded the Nobel Prize for Literature; he shot himself in 1961. Hemingway's characters are generally either intelligent people who have turned cynical or simple ones whose courage and honesty contrasts with the brutality of so-called civilization. His style is simple: the content is not. His writings have been compared to an iceberg the greater part of which lies hidden.

HERRICK, Robert (1591–1674), was trained as a goldsmith before going up to Cambridge. He was ordained in 1623 and became vicar of Dean Prior in Devonshire in 1629 (a living from which he was ejected for fifteen years in 1647). He was a great admirer of Ben Jonson. His most important collection of poems is the *Hesperides* (1648): "I sing of brooks, of blossoms, birds, and bowers . . .". "To Daffodils" expresses his love of nature and country life. Herrick has been described as "the most pagan of the English poets", and indeed he seems more at ease in his secular poems, which reveal his delight in the warmth and colour of life, in rich silks and jewels, fruits and flowers, than in his religious ones.

HOPKINS, Gerard Manley (1844–1889), was born at Stratford in Essex and educated at Oxford. In 1866 he became a Roman Catholic and later a Jesuit priest and teacher. As a poet he worked in almost total isolation: his works were not published until many years after his death, but he is now recognized as the first truly modern poet. His revolutionary experiments with rhythm and diction reflect his quest for depth of meaning. Many of his poems are ardent tributes to the beauty of the natural world, which is seen as a manifestation of the glory of God.

HUGHES, Ted (1930–), was born in Yorkshire and began writing poetry at school. After Cambridge University, which he found "a deadly institution", he married the American poet Sylvia Plath (who later killed herself). "The Thought-Fox" comes from his first book of poems, *The Hawk in the Rain* (1957), which won both the New York Poetry Center First Publication Award and the Guiness Award. His work has been accused of morbidity and sadism, but according to him the animals he describes represent not violence but vitality; they are "continually in a state of energy which men only have when they've gone mad. ... Maybe my poems are about the split personality of modern man."

MORGAN, Edwin (1920–), was born and educated in Glasgow. Since 1947 he has been a member of the English Department of Glasgow University, where he is now Reader. He prefers not to be regarded as belonging to any school, though some of his work shows affinities with the international Concrete Poetry movement. "I am interested in a poetry that acknowledges its environment (in my case Glasgow and, beyond that, Scotland), but I am also drawn to . . . a highly imaginative poetry exploring time and space as in science fiction. I have slowly developed my own brand of free verse to enable me to build up effects over paragraphs rather than within single lines. Directness and realism appeal to me strongly." His first book of poems was *The Vision of Cathkin Braes* (1952); his more recent works include *Glasgow Sonnets* (1972), *Instamatic Poems* (1972), *The Whittrick* (1973) and *Essays* (1974).

O'NEILL, Eugene (1888–1953), one of the most famous of American playwrights, was born in New York, the son of a successful actor. His father was temperamental, discontented, and often drunk; his mother was a drug addict; and his brother became an alcoholic. Much of O'Neill's work is autobiographical, reflecting his experiences among outcasts and the oppressed. He worked his way round the world and then tried acting and journalism. His first full-length play was *Beyond the Horizon* (1920), a realistic drama of rural life. Two of his most famous plays are *Mourning Becomes Electra* (1931) and *The Iceman Cometh* (1946). In 1936 he was awarded the Nobel Prize for Literature.

ORWELL, George (Eric Blair, 1903–1950), was born in India and educated at Eton: he then returned to British India as an officer in the imperial police in Burma. On his return to Europe he lived in deliberate poverty in Paris and London, describing his experiences in *Down and Out in Paris and London* (1933). After fighting on the Republican side in the Spanish Civil War he became disillusioned with political parties, though retaining his Left Wing sympathies. His fable *Animal Farm* (1945), a satire on Russian Communism, brought him enormous success. His last novel was *Nineteen Eighty-Four* (1949), a grim picture of life in a totalitarian society. Orwell was a fearless critic of injustice and a rebel at heart.

PATTEN, Brian (1946–), came to prominence in the late 1960s as one of the "Liverpool poets" who planned their poems specifically for reading aloud. But although Patten was labelled a "pop poet" at first, his aim is to write "lyric" poetry. Poetry for him is "a translation into words of a world beyond worlds'. Edward Lucie-Smith wrote of Patten's first book of poems, *Little Johnny's Confessions* (1967), that the author "has been able to get at and describe an entirely new tract of contemporary experience".

POE, Edgar Allan (1809–1849), a son of wandering actors, was born in Boston, orphaned at the age of two and adopted by a tobacco merchant from Virginia. Poe was educated partly in England and Scotland and partly at the University of Virginia, which he left after only one term. Gambling, drinking and debt were his problems, and he had a restless and unlucky life. He published a book of *Poems* in 1831, and also began contributing stories to magazines: *Tales of the Grotesque and Arabesque* (1840) was his first published collection. Some of his stories anticipate the modern detective story: in others the abnormalities of the human psyche are explored by an author-narrator who strikes the reader as a gifted psychopath. "The Black Cat", first published in 1843, belongs to the second category.

SADLER, Barry (1941–), grew up in the American West, left school at 15 and had a period in the Air Force. Then he roamed the West working in orchards during the day and playing drums and guitar in bars at night. He joined the Army and was sent to Vietnam as a member of the Special Forces (Green Berets). The original version of his "Ballad of the Green Berets" was written before he went to Vietnam. For Sadler the burning of draft cards "comes dangerously close to rebellion". His record of the ballad was a best-seller in 1966.

SANDBURG, Carl (1878–1967), was born in Galesburg, Illinois, the son of Swedish immigrants. He was a labourer and a soldier in the Spanish-American War before working his way through college. He then worked in journalism and politics. His fame as a poet began in 1914 when the magazine *Poetry* published a number of his shorter poems, including "Chicago". Sandburg was also a distinguished novelist, biographer, historian and musician, and wrote more than forty books. He twice won the Pulitzer Prize, once for history and once for poetry. Many Americans consider Carl Sandburg as their national poet, though in earlier days his colloquial style and vigorous free verse provoked controversy. He saw beauty in ordinary people and things, and took the crude vitality of everyday America as his subject.

SASSOON, Siegfried (1886–1967), was educated at Cambridge. In the First World War he won the Military Cross, but became a pacifist and published a volume of bitter anti-war poems called *Counter Attack* (1918). These vividly present the horrors and miseries of war, which they contrast with the conventional romantic hypocrisy that attempts to justify them. Sassoon's autobiographical *Memoirs of a Fox-hunting Man* came out in 1928.

284

SHAKESPEARE, William (1564–1616), was born in Stratford-on-Avon. When he was 18 he married a local girl who was pregnant by him. By the late 1590s he had become one of the most successful actors and playwrights in London. The optimism of his earlier plays seems to have changed, around the turn of the century, to gloom and disillusionment such as is expressed in Macbeth's speech about his dead wife; serenity returned to Shakespeare in his last period. *Julius Caesar* dates from 1598–1600, i.e. to the period before gloom set in. Shakespeare's achievement as a poet (not only in the verse of his plays but also in his *Sonnets*) and as a playwright has had no equal for range, depth and variety.

SHAW, Irwin (1913–), was born in New York and educated at Brooklyn College. At one time he was a semi-professional footballer. His first one-act play, *Bury the Dead* (1936), an electrifying semi-Expressionist drama about dead soldiers who leave their graves and go off to speak against war, made him famous overnight. His novels include *The Young Lions* (1948), about American and German soldiers, which was later filmed. He has also written numerous short stories.

SILLITOE, Alan (1928–), was born into a working-class family in Nottingham. His childhood coincided with the great depression, and his father was unemployed until 1939. Sillitoe left school at 14 to work in a bicycle factory. At 18 he joined the R.A.F., trained as a wireless operator and was sent to Malaya. On his return to England he had to spend two years in hospital, and began writing. His first novel, *Saturday Night and Sunday Morning* (1958), which express with unsentimental honesty the post-war mood of the British working classes, was made into a successful film, as was his long short story *The Loneliness of the Long Distance Runner* (1959). It is Sillitoe's belief that "revolution is the only remaining road of spiritual advance". His career as a writer may be seen as associated with the rise of the neo-Marxist "New Left" in Great Britain.

SOUSTER, Raymond (1921–), was born in Toronto and is a bank clerk and poet. The title of the book of poems that includes "The twenty-fifth of December", *The Colour of the Times* (1964), clearly shows his approach to writing – realism without sentimentality. The modern urban world is not always attractive under his scrutinizing eye. "I want", he says, "to make the substance of the poem so immediate, so real, so clear, that the reader feels the same exhilaration – be it fear or joy – that I derived from the experience, object or mood that triggered the poem in the first place."

SPARK, Muriel (1918–), was born and educated in Edinburgh. After some years in South Africa she returned to Britain in 1944. Immediately after the Second World War she entered the world of journalism and then that of miscellaneous literature: her volume of poems *The Fanfarlo* appeared in 1952. The previous year she had won the *Observer* short story competition with a story whose characteristic theme was the effect of a supernatural event on ordinary lives. Her conversion to Roman Catholicism in 1954 coincided with her conversion to prose fiction, which she had previously thought "an inferior way of writing". The first of her novels, *The Comforters*, appeared in 1957. Although it is these novels that form the basis of her lasting literary fame, her short radio plays (or "ear-pieces") show her faultless instinct for dialogue and sharp observation of eccentricity of character.

THURBER, James (1894–1961), America's greatest twentieth-century humorist, was born in Columbus, Ohio. In 1927 he became associated with the *New Yorker*, in which most of his work first appeared. He accompanied his pieces with his own distinctive drawings of the strangely-shaped animals and people of his imagination: resigned dogs, domineering women and weak, docile men. For him humour was "a kind of emotional chaos told about calmy and quietly in retrospect", not without melancholy. It is his achievement to reveal the deeper significance below the surface of modern life.

UPDIKE, John (1932–), was born at Shillington, Pennsylvania, and educated at Harvard and then at the Ruskin School of Drawing and Fine Art, Oxford. For two years from 1955 he was on the staff of the *New Yorker*. He has produced vast numbers of poems and short stories in addition to his novels, of which *Rabbit, Run* (1960) and *Couples* (1968) are among the best-known. For Updike literature is "a kind of concrete homage rendered to the actual world", and his short stories concentrate not on passion, violence or death but on the gradual revelations that everyday experience brings with it.

VONNEGUT, Kurt, Jr. (1922–), was born in Indianapolis, Indiana. During the Second World War he was captured by the Germans and made to work in a factory in Dresden. His best-selling novel *Slaughterhouse Five* (1969), which was made into a film, describes the bombing of Dresden as he himself experienced it. After the war he took a degree in anthropology and worked for a time as a public relations officer with General Electric (satirized in his first novel, *Player Piano*, 1952). The short stories collected in *Welcome to the Monkey House* (1968), which includes "Tomorrow and Tomorrow and Tomorrow", deal with many of his basic themes, notably the dangers of unchecked technology. He has said that he wants his books to be read by the young – the politicians and generals of the future – so that he can "poison their minds with humanity".

WAIN, John (1925–), was born in Stoke-on-Trent, the son of a dentist. He was educated at Oxford, and taught English at Reading University from 1947 until 1955. His first novel, *Hurry On Down* (1953), seemed to place him among the "Angry Young Men", but he has rejected that classification. He also rejects all ideological labels, though he despises the harsh competitive struggle, the hunt for success which even boys and girls at school are exposed to in Western society. Wain is a poet and critic as well as a novelist and short story writer, and in 1973 he was elected Professor of Poetry at Oxford.

WORDSWORTH, William (1770–1850), the great Romantic poet, was born at Cockermouth in the Lake District and educated at Cambridge. His meeting with Samuel Taylor Coleridge in 1795 made him decide to devote himself to poetry. Together they planned the *Lyrical Ballads* (1798), which marked the beginning of a new literary age – that of the English Romantics – and revolutionized poetic values. Wordsworth's preface to the second edition (1800) rejected the rigid rules of taste that had bound English poetry for the past century and a half. Wordsworth said that poetry must use the language of ordinary speech. His own poems are characterized by simplicity, clarity and realism, with a special sense of mystical union with nature.

YEATS, William Butler (1865–1939), a great Irish poet and the leader of the Irish literary renaissance, was born near Dublin. He was the son and brother of well-known painters. In 1883 he became an art student in London, but soon turned his attention to literature. He made friends with many of the leading literary figures of the aesthetic movement, and, by 1895, he had published six books of verse himself. He was interested in the occult, in Eastern mysticism, and in Celtic mythology. He was involved in the founding of the Irish Literary Theatre in Dublin (1899), for which he wrote and produced a number of plays. In 1923 he was awarded the Nobel Prize for Literature.

Acknowledgements

We are grateful to the following for permission to reproduce copyright material:

George Allen & Unwin (Publishers) Ltd for the poems 'Little Johnny's Final Letter' (**14**) and 'Somewhere Between Heaven and Woolworth's' (**15**) from *Little Johnny's Confession* by Brian Patten; Edward Arnold (Publishers) Ltd for poem 'Uncle' (**29**) by Harry Graham from *Most Ruthless Rhymes for Heartless Homes;* Author's agents for story 'The Pedestrian' (**31**) from *Golden Apples Of The Sun* and story 'Marionettes, Inc.' (**30**) from *The Illustrated Man* by Ray Bradbury, published by Hart-Davis MacGibbon Ltd. Reprinted by permission of A.D. Peters & Co. Ltd; Chatto & Windus Ltd and Mrs Laura Huxley for extract from 'Overpopulation' (**91**) in *Brave New World Revisited* by Aldous Huxley; Mel Calman for his story 'The Artist' (**32**) from *Penguin Modern Stories;* Cambridge University Press for extract (**102**) from *The Elements of Drama* by J.L. Styan; and extract (**73**) from *The Wheelwright's Shop* by George Sturt; Jonathan Cape Ltd for 'The Sandbox' (**47**) by Edward Albee from *Zoo Story And Other Plays* and slightly edited extracts (**86**) and (**87**) from *The Biocrats* by Gerald Leach; Author's agents for story 'Yesterday Was Beautiful' (**33**) by Roald Dahl from *Over To You* published by Penguin Books Ltd © 1945 by Roald Dahl; Mary Danby for extracts from 'It Was After Lights Out' (**101**) from *The Armada Book of Fun*, published by Wm. Collins Sons & Co. Ltd, © 1970; André Deutsch for story 'Tomorrow and Tomorrow and So Forth' (**44**) by John Updike from *The Same Door;* Delacorte Press for extracts (**93**) from *Wampeters, Foma and Granfalloon* by Kurt Vonnegut Jr. © 1974 by Kurt Vonnegut Jr. and 'Tomorrow and Tomorrow and Tomorrow' (**45**) excerpted from *Welcome To the Monkey House* by Kurt Vonnegut Jr. © 1954 by Kurt Vonnegut Jr. Originally appeared in *Galaxy* as 'The Big Trip Up Yonder'. Reprinted by permission of Delacorte Press/Seymour Lawrence; Doubleday & Co. Inc. for extracts (**63**) from *Culture And Commitment* by Margaret Mead. Copyright © 1970 by Margaret Mead. Reprinted by permission of the author and Doubleday & Co. Inc.; E.P. Dutton & Co. Inc. for edited extract (**100**) from *Touch the Earth: A Self-Portrait of Indian Existence* compiled by T.C. McLuhan. Copyright © 1971 by T.C. McLuhan. Reprinted by permission of the publishers; Eyre Methuen Ltd for author's preface in *Lear* (**96**) by Edward Bond; Faber & Faber Ltd for poem 'The Unknown Citizen' (**1**) from *Collected Shorter Poems* by W.H. Auden, and poem 'The Cultivation of Christmas Trees' (**8**) from *Collected Poems 1909–1962* by T.S. Eliot and poem 'The Thought-Fox' (**11**) from *The Hawk In The Rain* by Ted Hughes; Food and Drug Administration (U.S.A.) for extract from 'In Only Four Weeks' (**56**) by Margaret Morrison from *HEW*, June 1975 No. 76-4001; W.H. Freeman & Co. for extracts (**68**), (**82**), (**89**), (**90**) and (**92**) from *Population, Resources, Environment: Issues In Human Ecology*, 2nd Edn. by Paul R. Ehrlich and Anne H. Ehrlich, W. H. Freeman & Co. Copyright © 1972; Thomas F. Galt Jr. for edited extract (**69**) from his book *The Story of Peace and War* (1932); Victor Gollancz Ltd for poem 'Superman' (**24**) by John Updike from *Hoping For A Hoopoe;* Author's agents for extract from radio broadcast *A Night At The Dogs* (**74**) by Ray Gosling; Granada Publishing Ltd for poems 'of all the blessings which to man' (**7**) and 'a leaf falls' (**6**) by e e cummings from *Complete Poems* published by MacGibbon & Kee Ltd/ Granada Publishing Ltd; Author's agents for story 'The Destructors' (**34**) by Graham Green from *Collected Stories* published by The Bodley Head and William Heinemann; Hamish Hamilton Ltd for 'The Catbird Seat' (**41**), 'The Owl Who Was God' (**42**) and 'The Unicorn In The Garden' (**43**) from *Vintage Thurber* by James Thurber. The Collection copyright © 1963 Hamish Hamilton Ltd; Harcourt Brace Jovanovich, Inc. for poem 'Chicago' (**17**) from *Chicago Poems* by Carl Sandburg, copyright 1916, by Holt, Rinehart and Winston Inc. Copyright 1944 by Carl Sandburg. Reprinted by permission of publishers; Harper & Row Publishers Inc. for edited extract (**65**) from *Obedience to Authority* by Stanley Milgram. Copyright © 1974 by Stanley Milgram. Reprinted by permission of the publishers; Author's agents for extract from 'What Is Your Opinion, Mr Nader?' (**58**) in *New World Or No World*, edited by F. Herbert, published by Ace Books; Author's agents for edited extract from 'A Monument to JFK' (**70**) by Roy Hoopes Jr. from *What The President Does All Day*, published by John Day Co. Copyright © 1965 by Roy Hoopes Jr. Reprinted by permission of Curtis Brown Ltd; Lister Welch Ltd, Executors for the late Michael Flanders for his poem 'The Giraffe' (**29**) from *The Lion Book of Humorous Verse*, ed. Ruth Petrie; Longman Group Ltd for adapted extract (**59**) from *A Communicative Grammar of English* by G. Leech and J. Svartvik; Mary Glasgow Publications Ltd for extracts from 'What is Luxury?' (**57**) in *Current* 4/76 Series 2 and 'Planning for the Holocaust' (**67**) in *Current* 6/77 Series 10; McGraw-Hill Ryerson Ltd for poem 'The Twenty-Fifth of December' (**23**) from *The Colour of the Times/Ten Elephants on Yonge Street* by Raymond Souster. Reprinted by permission of publishers; Ian·McKelvie (Publisher) for poems 'Chicago May 1971' (**12**) and 'London June 1970' (**13**) from *Instamatic Poems* by Edwin Morgan; Methuen & Co. Ltd for extract from *A Glasgow Gang Observed* (**95**) by James Patrick; Music Music Music Inc., New York, for song 'The Ballad of the Green Berets' (**16**) by Barry Sadler and Robin Moore. Copyright © 1963, 1964 & 1966. Reproduced by kind permission of Francis, Day & Hunter GmbH, Hamburg; National School Public Relations Association for extract (**94**) from 'Vandalism in American Schools' from *Violence and Vandalism* printed in *Education U.S.A.* and reprinted by permission. Copyright 1977 National School Public Relations Assn; The New York Times Company for extract from article 'From the Cradle to the Olympics' (**54**) by Richard Flaste reprinted from *The New York Times* © 1976; John Murray (Publishers) Ltd for poems 'The Liquorice Fields at Pontefract' (**4**), 'Devonshire Street W.1' (**2**) and 'Sun and Fun' (**3**) from *Collected Poems* by John Betjeman; New Science Publications for extract from article 'Authority And The Young' (**62**) by P.M.Worsley in *New Society* 22nd July, 1965. This first appeared in *New Society London*, the weekly review of the Social Sciences; The Observer Ltd for extract from article 'Spaceship Earth's Greatest Danger' (**80**) in *The Observer* 3rd July, 1971; Author's agents for edited extract (**85**) from *The Waste Makers* by Vance Packard; Penguin Books Ltd for extract (**81**) from *Man-Machine Systems* by W.T. Singleton (Penguin Modern Psychology, 1974) pp. 159–162. Copyright © W.T. Singleton 1974; Random House Inc. for 'Before Breakfast' (**49**) from *The Plays Of Eugene O'Neill* by Eugene O'Neill. Copyright 1924 by Boni and Liveright Inc. Reprinted by permission of the publishers; Random House Inc. for adapted extracts (**60**), (**61**), (**64**), (**76**), (**77**), (**78**), (**79**), (**83**), (**84**), (**88**) from *Future Shock* by Alvin Toffler. Adapted by permission of Random House Inc. Copyright © 1970 by Alvin Toffler; Routledge Journals for extracts from article 'Attitudes and Behaviour of Car Assembly Workers' (**72**) by John H. Goldthorpe in *British Journal of Sociology;*

G.T. Sassoon for poems 'They' (21), 'Dreamers' (18), 'Does It Matter?' (19) and 'Progressions' (20) by Siegfried Sassoon from *Selected Poems;* Charles Scribner's Sons for story 'Old Man at the Bridge' (35) reprinted by permission of the publishers from *The Short Stories of Ernest Hemingway* by Ernest Hemingway. Copyright 1938 Ernest Hemingway; Author's agents for story 'The Girls In Their Summer Dresses' (38) by Irwin Shaw © 1952 Irwin Shaw from *Mixed Company* published by Jonathan Cape reprinted by Pan; Author's agents for story 'The Match' (39) from *The Loneliness Of The Long Distance Runner* by Alan Sillitoe; Author's agents for 'The Party Through The Wall' (53) by Muriel Spark from *Voices At Play*, published by J.B. Lippincott Company. Copyright © 1961 by Muriel Spark and 'You Should Have Seen The Mess' (40) by Muriel Spark from *The Go-Away Bird and Other Stories*, published by J.B. Lippicott Co. Copyright © 1958 by Muriel Spark. Reprinted by permission of Harold Ober Assoc. Inc.; Simon & Schuster, Div. of Gulf & Western Corp. for adapted extract (75), (76) from *The Organization Man* by William H. Whyte Jr. Copyright © 1956 William H. Whyte Jr; Syndication International Ltd for extract from article 'You Can't Help Yourself, Can You Madam?' (55) by Alex Valentine © *Mirror Colour Magazine*, Dec. 1969; The Village Voice for extract from 'Two Minutes to Midnight: The Very Last Hurrah' (97) by Pete Hamill. Copyright © The Village Voice Inc. 1968 and reprinted by permission; Author's agents for 'Manhood' (46) by John Wain from *Death of the Hindlegs and Other Stories;* A.P. Watt & Son for poem 'Down by the Salley Gardens' (28) by W.B. Yeats from *The Collected Poems of W.B. Yeats*, by permission of M.B. Yeats, Miss Anne Yeats and Macmillan Co. London & Basingstoke, and poem 'The Termite' (29) by Ogden Nash from *The Lion Book of Humorous Verse* ed. Ruth Petrie, by permission of the Estate of the late Ogden Nash; Yale University Press for extract from 'Tootle, A Modern Cautionary Tale' (66) by David Riesman in *The Lonely Crowd* ed. J.H. Schild, 1967; Whilst every effort has been made, we regret that we have been unable to trace the copyright holders of the following: 'Manchild in the Promised Land' (99) by Claude Brown and 'Is Dope Killing Our Musicians?' (98) by Cab Calloway; poems 'Routine' (29) by Arthur Guiterman and 'The Pessimist' (29) by Ben King; 'In the Factory' (71) by Philip Callow from *Native Ground* in *Story*, Penguin Education, by David Jackson and Dennis Pepper.

We are grateful to the following for permission to reproduce copyright material and photographs:

Wm. Collins Sons and Co Ltd (Armada) from 'The Armada Book of Fun' by Mary Danby for pages 274–77; Crowell-Langenscheidt for the Slang-Chart page 176 bottom; Rex Features Ltd 42556 for page 252 bottom; Syndication International Ltd for 'You Can't Help Yourself, Can You Madam?' page 163; Topix (Longmans print) for page 19 bottom; Mrs Helen Thurber from 'The Thurber Carnival' published by Hamish Hamilton for pages 97 and 99; WGN Continental Broadcasting for 'Drugs' page 257 top; Bilderdienst Süddeutscher Verlag for the photographs on the front and back inside covers and on pages 19 top, 52, 86 bottom, 176 top, 181 bottom, 191 top, 195, 207 bottom, 229 middle, 242 bottom, 252 top, 257 bottom. Our thanks to Mr John Kyriakopoulos for permission to reproduce his drawings on pp. 7, 157, 197 and 220.